Living for Christ in a pagan world

Living for Christ in a pagan world

1 and 2 Peter simply explained

by
Michael Bentley

 EVANGELICAL PRESS

EVANGELICAL PRESS
12 Wooler Street, Darlington, Co. Durham, DL1 1RQ, England.

© Evangelical Press 1990
First published 1990

British Library Cataloguing in Publication Data available.

ISBN 0-85234-279-9

Cover picture Temple of Apollo, Altinkum, Turkey, reproduced by courtesy of Keith Bernstein.

Typeset by Outset Studios, Hartlepool.
Printed in Great Britain at The Bath Press, Avon.

To all members of the congregation of
Great Hollands Free Church
and especially to
JONATHAN and MICHELLE BENTLEY
who wanted to see their names
in this book.

Contents

Preface

The world was thrilled to hear about the greater religious freedoms that came to many countries of Eastern Europe during 1989 and 1990. But in the course of all the excitement there was something which I read that first of all gave me great joy, and then, when I thought more deeply about it, it caused me sadness too. Because people found it much easier to leave Russia, all the members of one Black Sea evangelical church packed up their bags and moved to the United States of America.

We must be pleased when persecuted Christians are given freedom after many years of hardship and restraint, and sympathize with their desire to depart from the land which has given them so many sorrows. Yet if all of the believers have now left the area, who is left in that town to bear witness to the gospel?

To the south of that Russian town, also bordering the Black Sea, lies the country which is now called Turkey. It is there that the ancient districts of Pontus, Galatia, Cappadocia, Asia and Bithynia would have been. It was to the persecuted Christians of this area that Peter wrote his first letter – and probably his second as well.

This book is largely the result of a series of Sunday morning sermons preached at Great Hollands Community Centre from 1 January 1989 to 4 February 1990. As we examined these two letters, we saw how up-to-date and relevant Peter's message is for Christians today. I trust that this book will encourage many to study 1 and 2 Peter and, as a result, be blessed and strengthened in their faith as we were.

Many people have helped me in the preparation of this

book, not least those members of our own congregation whose experiences reflect some of the problems and challenges which faced the first-century believers.

Michael Bentley
Bracknell
October 1990

1 Peter

1.
The writer of the letter

Please read 1 Peter 1:1

We sometimes think how wonderful it would be if we could meet personally one of the twelve special disciples who accompanied Jesus constantly during the last few years of his life on earth, and learn from him some of the many details omitted in the accounts given in the four Gospels.

However, when we examine the letters of Peter, who was one of the Lord's closest companions during his earthly ministry, we find that in fact he does not give us any additional information to satisfy our curiosity about all that Jesus did during the thirty years or so of his life on earth.

But can we really be sure that it was the apostle Peter who wrote this letter? Liberal scholars try to ignore the plain statement in the opening verse and say that this letter was actually written some years after Peter's death. These scholars seem to set out to prove that the Bible is a book written by men rather than the inerrant Word of God. Some of them say that Peter could not have written this letter because a rugged Galilean fisherman would not have used such beautiful Greek. Furthermore, they argue that Acts 4:13 tells us that Peter and John were 'unschooled, ordinary men'.

In answer to this it can be said that a tradesman living in Galilee would have come across many Greek-speaking people. In the same way that the inhabitants of some parts of Wales speak English as fluently as their native Welsh, it is likely that Peter could have had as good a working knowledge of Greek as of his own native language. Besides the statement in Acts 4 gives us the view of Peter and John as they were seen

by 'the rulers and elders of the people' and was not necessarily
an accurate assessment of the real situation.[1]

All we need to know

The Lord is not interested in merely satisfying our curiosity
about the life of Jesus. Do we want to know more so that we
can adore the Lord more fervently, worship him in a richer
way and follow Jesus more closely? I doubt it. The reason why
Peter does not give us any additional information about the
events of Jesus' life on earth is because we do not need to
know any more than is recorded in the Gospels. Everything
that we need to know for our salvation, and in order to live a
full Christian life, has already been supplied.

At the end of John's Gospel (chapter 21) when Peter and
the others were fishing on the Sea of Galilee we read how the
disciples had been working all night long and had caught
nothing. Then, early in the morning, a man on the sea-shore
told them to throw their nets into the sea on the right-hand
side of their boat. When they did so they caught a large
number of fish. The man who spoke to them was the risen
Christ himself and he invited them all to have breakfast with
him. After the meal Jesus asked Peter, 'Do you love me?'
Three times he asked this question and three times Peter
answered, 'Yes, Lord, you know I love you.' After each of
Peter's replies Jesus told him to 'Feed my lambs' (v. 15),
'Take care of my sheep' (v. 17) and 'Feed my sheep' (v. 17).

So when Peter writes his two letters he is doing exactly what
Jesus had commanded him to do on that morning. Here, in 1
Peter, we have apostolic instruction and encouragement on
how we should live the Christian life. This epistle speaks
particularly of preparations for suffering. When he wrote
it, Peter had probably already seen the beginnings of ill-
treatment of Christians.

Scholars believe that Peter wrote this letter some time
before Nero's persecution in the early 60s. According to tradition Peter was crucified outside Rome during the last few
years of Nero's reign (Nero committed suicide in A.D. 68)
and certainly the 'positive view of civil government which
Peter gives in 1 Peter 2:13-17 could not have been written

without further qualification if the persecution under Nero had already begun in Rome'.[2] Furthermore Peter gives no hint that this letter is addressed to second-generation Christians, so a date in the early 60s seems likely.

Now what about us? How will we fare in the suffering which is bound to come upon the people of God? We all know many stories of individual Christians and even whole churches who are being treated very badly, not because of anything they have done wrong, but simply because they are following their Lord and the authorities who are set over them do not like this. Here in Britain we have been relatively free from such persecution for the last 100 years or so, but we do not know what the future holds in store for us. We do know that Satan and all his evil host are seeking to disrupt the work of the gospel wherever it is making headway. We should therefore be actively prepared for the onslaughts of those who oppose the things of God. Let us ask ourselves, 'How will I behave if there is, in my lifetime, a great turning against Christianity and all the followers of Christ?' Will we give way under the pressures and deny that we are Christians or will we follow Jesus more closely? One of the ways in which we can be ready for suffering is to learn more about the Christian faith. This is why Peter wrote this letter. He wanted to encourage Christians to be prepared for whatever the future held.

The opening words

Peter's first words are: **'Peter, an apostle of Jesus Christ'**. This is all that he says about himself at this stage. He knew Jesus. He had witnessed many of the wonderful miracles the Lord had performed, and he had listened to much of the great teaching he had given. Yet he speaks very humbly.

Peter could have reminded us that he was the first one to confess Jesus as the Christ (that is, God's chosen and anointed one). We can read the story of that confession at Cæsarea Philippi in Matthew 16:13-20. There Jesus commends Peter and calls him 'blessed'.

Jesus then goes on to say, 'You are Peter, and on this rock I will build my church.' So why does Peter not say here in this letter, 'The church is going to be built upon me. I'm the most important one'? He does not say it because it is not true. When Jesus said, 'On this rock I will build my church,' he did not mean that the church would be built on Peter. He meant that the church would be built on the kind of faith that Peter had just expressed. If Peter himself was as holy as that why did Jesus call him 'Satan' only a few verses later? (Matthew 16:23). We should also remember that Paul tells us that the church is 'built on the foundation of the apostles and prophets, with Christ Jesus himself as the chief cornerstone' (Ephesians 2:20). So Peter is not the most important one; he is just one among the twelve apostles.

What does the word 'apostle' mean? It refers to a representative. An apostle was a messenger. The twelve disciples, plus Paul, are called apostles. Also there was a much larger group of representatives of the Lord, like Barnabas, who were called apostles too (see Acts 14:14) — perhaps they were apostles with a small 'a'. However, Jesus is the supreme apostle. He was the one sent from heaven (Hebrews 3:1-3). He is 'the one from whom all other apostleships flow'.[3] But does this mean that we can have apostles today? Certainly not. I find it very difficult to understand how certain groups claim to have apostolic oversight in this twentieth century when the apostles (and their doctrine) were foundational to the faith (Ephesians 2:20; 3:4-5), and it is clearly stated that each apostle had seen the Lord with his own eyes (Acts 1:21-22).[4] In addition to the twelve we must remember that Paul also saw the risen Lord (1 Corinthians 9:1).

Peter had been called to be a messenger of Jesus Christ. I find great comfort in this. Think about the life of Peter. He was so impetuous. He so often put his foot in it. He so often spoke out of turn and, in the hour of Jesus' greatest need, Peter denied that he ever knew him. 'While Peter was below in the courtyard, one of the servant girls of the high priest came by. When she saw Peter warming himself, she looked closely at him. "You also were with that Nazarene, Jesus," she said. But he denied it. "I don't know or understand what you're talking about," he said, and went out into the entrance. When the servant girl saw him there, she said again to those standing around, "This fellow is one of them." Again he denied it. After a little while, those standing near said to Peter, "Surely you are one of them, for you are a Galilean."

He began to call down curses on himself, and he swore to them, "I don't know this man you're talking about"" (Mark 14:66-71).

How could Peter ever live with himself, let alone stand up and speak as an apostle, after such a disgraceful act? Yet he could, and he went on to teach many people the things concerning Christ. What does Mark's account of the resurrection tell us? When the women entered the empty tomb they saw an angel who said, 'He has risen ... go, tell his disciples *and Peter*' (Mark 16:7, italics mine). The Lord wanted Peter to be specially included in this message. It was as though Jesus were saying, 'I've forgiven you, Peter, and I want you back as one of my chief messengers.'

Some thirty years later Peter gives us this helpful letter. Because he had been forgiven and restored to his place of authority in the work of the gospel, he was able to be an important leader in the early church and to commit to writing words which are so precious, words which are the very Word of God.

2.
The people addressed in the letter

Please read 1 Peter 1:1-2

We do not know when or how the end of this gospel age will come, but we have seen so many dreadful things happening in the world that we cannot help thinking that God has something of a very solemn nature to say to us. Some say that these awful things that are occurring are all a matter of chance and we should not worry, but I believe that we should take notice and be on our guard. It was for the same kind of reason that Peter wrote his first epistle.

In the previous chapter we took a brief look at the author of this letter; now I want us to see the way Peter describes the recipients of his epistle.

They are God's elect

In other words, Peter is saying that they are God's chosen people. That is another way of referring to the Jewish nation. They were God's special people. He had chosen them for himself. Deuteronomy 7:7-8 tells us that he did not choose them because they were more numerous than other nations; in fact they were the fewest of all peoples. God chose them because he loved them and kept his oath which he swore to their forefathers when he brought them out of slavery in Egypt.

So were these Jews that Peter was addressing? There may well have been Jews among them, but I cannot believe they were all Jews, because of the way Peter writes about them. He says that they had been redeemed from 'the empty way of life *handed down to you from your forefathers*' (1:18). Peter would never have described Jews like that. The forefathers of the Jews would have been God-fearing people, not those who lived an empty way of life. Then in 4:3 he says, 'You have spent enough time in the past doing what pagans choose to do — living in debauchery, lust, drunkenness, orgies, carousing and detestable idolatry.' That is not the way one Jew would describe another, talking about paganism and idolatry. This must surely have meant that there were a great number of non-Jews (called Gentiles by the Jews) among these Christians to whom Peter wrote his letter.

Why, then, does Peter call these Christians 'God's elect', if they were not Jews? He calls them that because all true Christians have been **'chosen according to the foreknowledge of God the Father'** (1:2). Peter, the proud Jew, had had to learn a very hard lesson. When he went to Cornelius' house in Joppa he had a vision bidding him eat all kinds of food which were not 'kosher'. (Kosher is the term used to describe food which is fit to be eaten by Jews — the foods described in Leviticus 11.) That day God taught him that in Christ all the blessings of God's people have been granted to *everyone* who comes to God through faith in the Lord Jesus Christ as Saviour. All who repent of their sins and believe in the Lord Jesus Christ are saved and are part of God's elect.

When we are born again we discover that God has '[chosen] us in him before the creation of the world' (Ephesians 1:4). For many who are brought up in circles where the emphasis is all on man's decision it seems difficult to accept that God has actually chosen each of his people to salvation *before time began*. But those who prayerfully read and study the Scriptures discover that this truth is referred to over and over again. Man's pride fights against accepting this fact, but it is clearly taught in the Bible.

God does not allow things to happen by chance: we worship a God who is sovereign. Just as Christ was 'chosen before the creation of the world' to be a sacrifice for our redemption (1:20), so we too have been chosen according to the foreknowledge of God the Father to be part of his purpose. God does not do things in a 'hit and miss' way. It is not that God knows in advance that we will choose to follow Christ. He actually ordains our salvation. One of our congregation who, at the time of writing, has just come into a full assurance of faith, started to attend our services again after an absence of some eight years. She 'just happened to meet' one of our members on a bus, right at the time when she was feeling very forsaken. But this did not come about by chance; the Lord ordained it. Each Christian can look back on his or her life and see that God has been at work in leading him or her each step of the way.

However, we must remember that we are not robots. We do have a responsibility to do the right thing. We cannot say, when we do something stupid, 'The devil made me do it.' God calls us to salvation, but we have to respond and believe on the Lord Jesus Christ for salvation. An old hymn says,

'Tis done! the great transaction's done!
I am my Lord's and he is mine;
He drew me *and I followed on*,
Charmed to confess the voice divine.[1]

When Peter speaks of the foreknowledge of God he does not merely mean that God knew beforehand which people would choose to follow him. He is talking about a mighty sovereign act of God in which the Lord knew beforehand whom he would choose to salvation. Foreknowledge and pre-destination have similar meanings (Ephesians 1:4-5).

They are strangers in the world

These Christians do not belong in the world. They have homes and they are settled. They are going about their businesses. They are bringing up their children to the best of their abilities and they are preparing for the future as all sensible people do. But Peter tells them that they are strangers in this world. This is not their real home. It is not here that they will spend eternity.

Our own experience tells us that no one lives for ever on this earth. A person's life is 'threescore years and ten' (Psalm 90:10, AV). Some carry on beyond that time — on borrowed time as it were, but some never reach anywhere near that length of life. Christians can say, 'There is another home awaiting us.'

This world can be very beautiful but, through man's disfigurement and greed, it can be very ugly in parts. However, this actual earth will, one day, 'be destroyed by fire' (2 Peter 3:10). The writer of the Hebrews tells us that all true Christians do not belong here: 'For we do not have an enduring city, but we are looking for one that is to come' (Hebrews 13:14).

Christians should be living as pilgrims on this earth. 'Peter is writing a travellers' guide for Christian pilgrims. He reminds them that their hope is anchored in their homeland. They are called to endure alienation as strangers, but they have a heavenly citizenship and destiny.'[2] Because we are temporary residents on this earth, the things of the world should not be held too tightly. There is nothing wrong in enjoying ourselves. But if we behave as though that was our chief concern, then something is the matter somewhere.

John wrote some very solemn words: 'Do not love the world or anything in the world. If anyone loves the world, the love of the Father is not in him' (1 John 2:15). This is not a verse reserved for monks and nuns. It is for all of God's blood-bought people. Temporary residents do not get too involved in the pleasures of this life. They do not give the impression that having a good time is all that matters. They are careful not to get too tangled up with the enjoyments of this wicked worldly system. They live their earthly life in the light of the heavenly one which is to come and they always remember that they are only **'strangers in the world'**.

They are scattered

Peter is not writing to a church in a specific town or city, but to Christians living in a large area of Asia (what we now call Turkey). However, a province eastwards from Ephesus was also called Asia. Another thing to notice is that the area of Galatia was divided in two by a mountain range. Paul wrote his epistle to the church which was in southern Galatia. Peter writes to Christians in northern Galatia.

People from Pontus, Galatia, Cappadocia, Asia and Bithynia came to Jerusalem on the Day of Pentecost (Acts

2:9). Almost certainly some people from these districts, which all lie north of the Taurus mountains, became Christians and went back and established churches in their own areas. We know very little about them. It was these people whom Paul wanted to visit but the Spirit of Jesus forbade him to do so (Acts 16:7-8). God had other directions for Paul to travel: he took the good news to Europe, where few, if any, had heard the gospel. But here, some ten years or so later, Peter is found writing to these scattered Christians in order to encourage them in their faith and witness.

The Holy Spirit has much missionary work for his people to do. It grieves me when I hear of great efforts being put into establishing a new gospel witness in the same area as an existing evangelical church. It seems so sad that this happens when there are many towns and villages which have no gospel witness at all. What a pity it is that believers today do not copy the example of these two apostles! Peter concentrated on northern Turkey and Paul worked extensively in the southern area of that large country.

Salvation is a work of the Trinity

Peter includes the whole Trinity when he speaks of salvation. We have seen that Christians have been chosen according to the foreknowledge of God the Father. Peter goes on to say that this is **'through the sanctifying work of the Spirit'** and it is **'for obedience to Jesus Christ and sprinkling by his blood'**. The Christians, who have been scattered throughout the Roman province of Asia Minor, have been brought by God into a relationship with each person of the Trinity. 'The Father has chosen them and set them apart by the Spirit that they might live a life of obedience to Jesus Christ, being cleansed for such a walk by the sprinkling with his blood.'[3] Paul uses a similar framework in Ephesians 1 to show how each of the three persons in the Trinity co-operates in our salvation. God the Father planned our salvation 'before the creation of the world' (vv. 3-5); God the Son carried out our redemption 'through his blood' (vv. 6-10) and God the Holy Spirit applied the gospel to us. Paul says, '... when you heard the word of truth' (vv. 13-14).

The Father has chosen each of his believing people. This has happened 'through the sanctifying work of the Spirit'. It is the Holy Spirit who sets us apart. That is the meaning of the word 'sanctification'. It means that we are meant to be holy; we are to be different from ordinary people. A temple was a building, but it was different from ordinary buildings because it was set apart for God's special use; it was made holy. An animal was sacrificed, but it was different from ordinary animals because it was set apart for God's special acceptance; it was made holy. God's people today are required to be different from unconverted people; we are called to be set apart for God's special service.

A man in his thirties started attending our church. He told the leaders of our enquirers' group that he 'went forward' at an evangelistic campaign. When they asked him if he had been followed up by anyone he said, 'Yes. A young fellow visited me and said, "Let's go out to the pub for a few pints and we'll talk about this."' Our seeking friend said that he found this comment very off-putting as he was trying to give up that way of life.

We are not different from others because we are better than non-Christians. We are different because God has separated us from the world through the sanctifying work of the Spirit. We have become saints. Saints are not special Christians who have performed a certain number of miracles and have been canonized. Saints are the ordinary Christian people who go to make up the membership of any church. This is why so many letters in the New Testament are addressed to 'the saints that are at ...'

When we are sanctified through the work of the Spirit we are not only separated *from the world*, we are separated *to God*. His honour should be the aim and object of our lives. Our goal should be to love him and glorify him for ever.

We have been sanctified 'for obedience to Jesus Christ'. Our Christian lives start when we turn to Jesus Christ in obedience; when we repent of our sins and turn to him in faith. In other words, we become Christians when we obey the gospel. It is God's choice of his people which leads them to obey Jesus Christ.

In speaking about 'sprinkling by his blood' Peter is directing his readers to the cross. It is there that our Saviour shed his

blood to cleanse us from our sin. Peter is also taking us back
to that scene at the foot of Mount Sinai after the exodus from
Egypt. Moses set up twelve pillars on that spot. 'Then he sent
young Israelite men, and they offered burnt offerings and sacrificed young bulls as fellowship offerings to the Lord. Moses
took half of the blood and put it in bowls, and the other half
he sprinkled on the altar. Then he took the Book of the
Covenant and read it to the people. They responded, "We
will do everything the Lord has said; we will obey." Moses
then took the blood, sprinkled it on the people and said, "This
is the blood of the covenant that the Lord has made with you
in accordance with all these words"' (Exodus 24:5-8).

Dr Clowney says, 'At Sinai Israel was made the people
of God; they were joined to him in his covenant. Now Peter
speaks of Gentiles becoming obedient to Christ through the
new covenant in his blood. We are sprinkled, not with the
blood of oxen, but with the blood of Christ.'[4]

In sending greetings to his readers Peter again reinforces
the fact that the New Covenant has fulfilled the Old Covenant
and transferred all the blessings of Israel to the new Israel of
God. Later he says, 'Once you were not a people, but now
you are the people of God' (2:10). Here, in verse 2 Peter says,
'Grace and peace be yours in abundance.' Peace was a characteristic of the Old Covenant; it spoke of well-being. Grace is
the watch-word of the New Covenant; it speaks of the free
unmerited favour of God. (Or, as Charles Swindoll says,
'Grace is God Reaching Across to Christians Everywhere'.)

Just as these things were true for the people of northern
Turkey nearly 2,000 years ago, so they are vital for believers
today. We live in a world which is just as opposed to the truth
of God as was the first century. Those who trust in the Lord
Jesus Christ alone for their salvation need to live their lives in
the light of the teachings contained in this ancient, but still
highly relevant letter.

3.
Count your blessings

Please read 1 Peter 1:3-5

When I was a boy in Sunday School one of the favourite choruses that was often chosen was:

When upon life's billows you are tempest-tossed,
When you are discouraged, thinking all is lost,
Count your blessings, name them one by one,
And it will surprise you what the Lord hath done.

It is good to stop and look around us and consider all the wonderful blessings which are ours today. We can think of the peace and tranquillity of the countryside (if we are privileged to live in such surroundings). We can consider the gift of health and the blessings that come with it. We can thank God that we can see, hear, speak, taste and feel. We can rejoice that we are able to walk and talk, and that we have warmth, food and shelter to strengthen us. And when we think of those who are less fortunate than ourselves, we realize that we have bountiful supplies of God's goodness, so that we want to thank and praise him for all his blessings to us.

Praise to God

The Jews always started a letter with praise to God. We can see that when we look at the way many of the Psalms begin. We can turn to them and make them ours as we try to enter into the thanksgiving which they express so beautifully.

It is so good to stop and thank God for all his goodness to us. It helps us through life when we consider that it is only by God's mercies that we receive so much blessing. It makes us realize that we do not praise the Lord enough for all his kindness to us. Those who are mothers (or single-parent fathers) know what it is to spend a great deal of time and energy planning a meal, and then putting effort and skill into its cooking, only to receive an ungrateful, 'Oh Mum (or Dad) have I got to eat this?' We treat God in a similar way when we take his goodness to us for granted. We seldom stop really to praise him for who he is and what he has done.

Paul's letters often start with praise to God. Near the beginning of 2 Corinthians we read, 'Praise be to the God and Father of our Lord Jesus Christ' (1:3). Likewise Ephesians 1:3 says, 'Praise be to the God and Father of our Lord Jesus Christ, who has blessed us in the heavenly realms with every spiritual blessing in Christ.'

The blessing of a new birth

Paul and Peter have added spiritual blessings 'in Christ' to their opening greeting. God, as a Father, blesses his children. He has caused them to be born again. Peter says, God has given us 'new birth'. This is different from our original birth. Those of us who are fathers and who have been present at the birth of any of our children know what a beautiful thing the moment of birth is; mothers, despite the pain, have always known this wonderful experience. However, everyone born into this world is contaminated by Adam's disobedience to God. But the new birth is something completely different.

John says that all true Christians have been born in a supernatural way. He says, 'To all who received [Jesus], to those who believed in his name, he gave the right to become children of God.' These, he says, are 'children born not of natural descent, nor of human decision or a husband's will, but born of God' (John 1:12-13).

Jesus himself, speaking to that religious man Nicodemus, told him about the need to be born again. He said, 'I tell you the truth, no one can see the kingdom of God unless he is born again' (John 3:3). Jesus said this new birth is essential. It is vital because our old life is tainted by sin. We need a brand new life if we are going to be able to serve God effectively. By our natural birth we have been born in sin and shapen in iniquity. No one, in his or her old nature, can truly experience the presence and power of God. That sinful life needs to be taken away. Everyone needs a new life in Christ before they can fully experience God's spiritual blessings.

People who are not real Christians (who have never been born again) can never understand this; they find it very difficult to accept. This is because they are still living in their unregenerate life; they are still in their sin. They think that all they have to do to please God is to try harder. They think that if only they engage in more religious ritual and thought, then they will be on their way to heaven. But Jesus himself says that it all comes down to this fact: 'You must be born again. He means by this that there has to be a complete change around in the whole of a person's being. He or she has to have a totally different attitude to everything. Neither we ourselves nor any other person can bring this about by our own efforts. Nothing but a thorough washing away of a person's sinfulness can open up the way to God for him or her. A completely new birth is called for if he or she is to become one of God's children. And here in his first letter Peter says, **'In his great mercy [God] *has* given us new birth.'**

If we are true Christians then we have been born again and our new birth has been by God's great mercy. It is not something anyone can earn. We may try to buy our way into God's presence. Some people try to do good because they think they will attract God's attention and then he will think well of them and save them. Others try to engage in religious duties in the hope that God will overlook their failings and shortcomings. Many try to pretend that everything is all right with them, and think God will not notice anything sinful about their words, deeds or thoughts. But no one can ever succeed in reaching heaven in these or any other ways. It is only by God's great mercy that anyone can hope to be saved. It is only through God's electing love that his mercy can be received.

We experience the new birth when we acknowledge our sinfulness and ask the Lord for the desire and ability to turn away from our wrong-doing. That is the first step that must be taken if anyone is to receive eternal life. It is only by believing in the Lord Jesus Christ that anyone can be saved; and people can only come to Christ as individuals; there can be no 'block vote' to decide for Christ. We are born again when we come to Jesus in faith. That means believing that he died to take the punishment that is due because of our sins. When we become aware of the wonderful blessings of the new birth then we can say from the heart, 'Praise be to the God and Father of our Lord Jesus Christ!' We can enter into the experience of knowing Jesus as our own personal Saviour.

The blessing of a living hope

The new birth which we have been given leads us into **'a living hope'**. In everyday conversation we often say, 'I hope everything will turn out all right.' We mean that we are not sure that it will, but we have a strong desire that it should. However, the hope that Peter writes about here is nothing vague like that. It is a living hope. It is something sure and certain. It is a very positive thing. It is nothing less than the deliverance from sin and death which Christ has accomplished for his people.

The writer to the Hebrews describes the Christian hope as 'an anchor for the soul, firm and secure' (6:19). So when Peter says that God has 'given us new birth into a living hope' he means that through being born again we are secure in God's keeping. Just as an anchor holds a great ocean-going liner in place and stops it from drifting, so our new birth in Christ is something which can never be moved or taken away from us. 'In Scripture the use of the word hope always implies assurance, and he who hopes, patiently waits for that which he knows he shall attain.'[1]

The living hope is something which God has purchased for us by the precious blood of Christ. No one can ever take it away from us. No matter how far we may drift away from God in the stormy currents of life, he still has us in his care and his anchor chain will never snap, not even on the Judgement Day.

This new birth into a living hope is ours through the resurrection of Christ. Think what a hopeless state Peter was in just after the crucifixion of Jesus. He had denied his Lord when he had stated so vehemently that he would never do such a thing. He had let Jesus down in his darkest hour, and then he had been humiliated by the ear-piercing crow of the cock which shattered the stillness of the early morning air. He wept bitterly. He surely felt like committing suicide. He must have lost all hope of ever being able to hold up his head before God again. But when Jesus rose again from the dead what a difference it made to Peter! He was a new, forgiven man. Peter was especially mentioned in the message given by the angels to the disciples that Jesus had risen again from the dead.

So, from having no hope, Peter is transformed into a man with a living hope which has been brought about by a living Saviour who has come to life again from the dead.

We need to ask ourselves, 'What difference does the resurrection of Jesus Christ make to us?' It is amazing that we speak or think so little about the stupendous fact of the resurrection of Christ. Yet it is the foundation of our faith. Paul said, 'If Christ has not been raised, your faith is futile; you are still in your sins' (1 Corinthians 15:17). The early Christians made so much of this that people often assumed that Jesus and the resurrection were a pair of gods who were married to each other (Acts 17:18).

But Jesus did rise from the dead, and he is alive today. He says to us, 'I am the Living One; I was dead, and behold I am alive for ever and ever!' (Revelation 1:18). This means that because he is alive, he is with us wherever we go and whatever we do; and he is also in heaven interceding with God on our behalf.

What a great comfort the resurrection of Christ must have been to those of northern Turkey who were about to have tremendous trials unleashed upon them!

The blessing of an inheritance

God has not only given us new birth into a living hope, but this new birth is also **'into an inheritance that can never perish, spoil or fade — kept in heaven'**. The Jews had received a material inheritance — the land of Canaan. This was called

the promised land. It was a land flowing with milk and honey
(a land of plenty). Being given such a fertile land was a sign of
God's richest blessing upon his people.

What happened to this wonderful land? It fell into disuse
because God punished the Jews for their sinful ways by allowing them to be taken away captive into Babylon. Years later
it fell into defilement when the wicked Seleucid ruler, Anti-
ochus Epiphanes IV, desecrated the whole country and even
sacrificed pigs on the altar in the temple. After the heathen
Greek invasion, the land was spoiled by the Romans with
their multiplicity of gods (they always had room for one more,
provided he was not the only God). After the destruction of
Jerusalem in A.D. 70 the Jews were dispersed and it must
have seemed to them that the inheritance of the children of
Israel would fade away altogether.

What did Peter say about the inheritance that is given to the
new Israel of God? (By that is meant the whole company of
born again believers — see 1 Peter 2:9.) This inheritance can
never perish. Peter meant that, unlike our mortal bodies, the
inheritance that we have by being 'in Christ' can never decay
or be worn out with the passage of time.

Peter said that our inheritance can never be spoilt. He is
reminding his readers that 'Heaven is a place unpolluted by
sin and it contains nothing unworthy of God's approval.'[2]

Our inheritance will never fade because it is eternal and
'kept in heaven' for Christians. John Brown reminds his readers that 'Many a person, born to a rich inheritance, has never
obtained possession of it, but has lived and died in poverty;
but this inheritance is liable to none of the accidents of earth
and time. It is "in heaven," under the immediate guardian-
ship of divine power, wisdom, and love.'[3] And Archbishop
Leighton, writing in the seventeenth century says, 'It is a rich
and pleasant country where it lieth, it hath also this privilege,
to be the only land of rest and peace, free from all possibility
of invasion. There is no spoiling of it, and laying it waste, and
defacing its beauty, by leading armies into it, and making it
the seat of war; no noise of drums or trumpets, no inundations
of one people driving out another and sitting down in their
possessions. In a word, there is nothing there subject to decay
of itself, so neither is it in danger of fraud or violence.'[4]

Thieves cannot break in and steal it from such a glorious place. Our inheritance is safe in God's precious keeping.

Finally Peter says it is **'for you'**. Suddenly he changes from saying what God has given 'us' to what he has in store 'for you'. This again emphasizes the personal nature of the new birth.

The blessing of God's protection

God has not only given us new birth into a living hope, and into an inheritance, but Peter says that by faith we **'are shielded by God's power'**. The word 'shielded' 'means "kept safe", "carefully watched", and is frequently used in military contexts'.[5] Paul writes in a similar vein when he tells the Philippian Christians that the peace of God 'will guard your hearts and your minds in Christ Jesus' (Philippians 4:7). Therefore, we need not fear what danger may be looming on the horizon, nor dread the sufferings which God's enemies may inflict upon us. We need be afraid of nothing because God's power will shield us from all the attacks of the evil one. This confidence is ours because we have been brought to faith in **'our Lord Jesus Christ'** (1:3). The moment we believe in Jesus as our Lord and Saviour he becomes 'ours' by faith. God's elect people can have the assurance of the Lord's presence and protection day by day.

This protection, through God's guarding, is **'until the coming of the salvation that is ready to be revealed in the last time'**. Through belief in the Lord Jesus Christ we can enjoy a foretaste of our inheritance here and now, but the full reality of it is 'reserved in heaven' for us. We experience the benefits, the security and the assurance of salvation today, but the completeness of our salvation will only be made known on that great day when Christ comes again. The culmination of everything will occur at that moment and then we shall enter into the full possession of all the blessings of our redemption. Edmund Clowney sums it all up like this: 'Our hope is anchored in the past; Jesus rose! Our hope remains in the present; Jesus lives! Our hope is complete in the future: Jesus is coming!'[6]

4.
The blessings of suffering

Please read 1 Peter 1:6-9

Many people, perhaps some of you reading this book, know far more than the author what it means to suffer. Suffering comes in all kinds of forms. It happens for all sorts of reasons, and it comes in many different ways. Many people suffer as a result of some bodily illness, either through a temporary disease like the 'flu or chicken pox, or through more persistent sicknesses like asthma or arthritis. Some endure physical ailments of one form or another, while others are attacked by that horrible disease of depression.

Those who are ill know what agonies they have to endure through their affliction, but not many people who live in the affluent West know much about the kind of suffering the people of northern Turkey were undergoing, or were about to undergo, at the time Peter was writing to them. Believers were having to suffer purely because they followed Jesus. They were being persecuted 'for Christ's sake'. Malicious tales had been circulating about the new sect — those of the Way, people who were called by the insulting nickname of 'Christians' (Christ's ones). Like all minorities the believers discovered that people were suspicious of them, simply because nothing was known about them. Wherever there is a minority, who largely keep themselves to themselves, prejudiced behaviour against them is sure to follow. All kinds of stories will begin to be spread around concerning them.

Christians were different from the rest of society. They did not join in the worship of the various Roman gods. They often did not want to take advantage of the bargains which were on offer at the meat market, just because it was meat left over after a heathen sacrifice. The people of northern Turkey must have thought that there was something very suspicious about the followers of Jesus. Stories began to circulate about them. It was said that they worshipped a criminal — one who had been tried before a Roman proconsul, who had been found guilty and had been executed by the traitor's death of crucifixion. We can understand why people were highly suspicious of anyone who revered the memory of a traitor.

Then it was said that these Christians were cannibals. They all got up very early in the morning and gathered out in the open air, and after prayers, they ate their god. They said, 'This is his body that we are eating; this is his blood that we are drinking.'

And so, for these and other reasons, persecution broke out against Christians all over the then-known world. We can understand how dreadful it must have been for them to endure persecution. But there was something different about the way these people accepted their lot.

Rejoicing in suffering

Peter said that they were rejoicing in their sufferings. But the apostle does not say that they were rejoicing because they enjoyed the pain and the injuries of persecution. Anyone who enjoys inflicting or receiving pain is sick and needs urgent medical attention. What Peter is saying is that there are benefits to being persecuted for righteousness' sake. However, these benefits flow out as a result of the sufferings; they do not come purely because pain is being administered.

Christians who suffer today need to look beyond the trials, and remember what the Lord has done for them in granting them his great salvation. They are to remember also that sufferings only last for a while. When we get to heaven we will have no pain, affliction or sorrow. 'Weeping may remain for a night, but rejoicing comes in the morning' (Psalm 30:5).

The afflicted saint often looks forward to death because that is when we go to the realm where all suffering is removed completely. 'There will be no more death or mourning or crying or pain, for the old order of things has passed away'

(Revelation 21:4). The amazing thing is that every tear will be actually wiped out of our eyes; and God himself will do this (Revelation 21:3). So, despite the trials, worries, concerns and afflictions of this life, God's people should always remember the benefits that there are in being true believers.

Peter says that they were suffering **'all kinds of trials'** (1:6). These griefs were of various kinds. They came with different intensities and were sometimes very frequent, and at other times there was an uneasy waiting period — the lull before the storm.

Yet, despite all of this, God's people were to rejoice. They were to rejoice 'greatly' because the 'here and now' is not what matters ultimately. It is receiving the goal of our faith, the salvation of our souls (1:9), that counts in the long run.

Trials strengthen faith

In lands where Christians are persecuted, the church is strong. For many years, even when there was great oppression, there have been believers in Soviet Russia. There are many true churches and a good number of them have large numbers of young people in their congregations. The same can be said of other countries and other ages.

In eighteenth-century England the dissenters (or nonconformists) were sent to prison for preaching the gospel because they were not clergymen of the Church of England. That is why John Bunyan spent many years in prison. He never stole anything or murdered anyone. He just preached the gospel in meeting-houses or in the open air. This was against the law of the land. The law stated that the only legal place where church services could be held was the parish church. The only order of service allowed was the Book of Common Prayer and the only people licensed to preach were priests who had been ordained by a bishop of the Church of England.

Did these harsh restrictions stop the spread of the gospel? Rather than the work of the dissenters being curtailed, the number of preachers and new churches increased, so much so that in 1662 some 2,000 clergymen left the Church of England over the restrictions placed on the gospel. Many of these ex-ministers opened their own preaching-houses.

In verse 7 Peter gives an illustration of a fiery trial. He reminds his readers what happens to gold. This is a very precious and valuable metal. Yet to obtain the purest form of gold, it has to be refined to a high standard. Fire has to melt it so that it can be reformed. This fiery trial is necessary, otherwise many impurities will remain within the lump of precious metal. It is when the gold is put into the intense heat of the furnace that every trace of impurity is burnt up. If pure gold is wanted, then this smelting process must take place to remove every vestige of impurity. Only then will the gold be acceptable to a discerning owner.

Peter then speaks to the believers about their faith. He tells them that their faith is like gold which is being refined. But the faith of God's people is of much greater value than any precious metal. One day even gold will perish. This will be at the time when this present evil world will be utterly destroyed by fire (2 Peter 3:7). But the faith of true believers will endure right up to the culmination of all events. Suffering will be used to show the genuine nature of the faith of believers throughout this present age until the time when our blessed Lord himself returns. It is as though Peter is saying to his readers, 'Your faith will lead you right into the presence of God — into heaven itself.'

The apostle says that sufferings of various kinds are used by the Lord to prove that the faith of believers is genuine. Just as fire purifies gold, so trials cleanse our faith from all the filth of human works and effort. Trials leave us with a trust in God which is centred on him alone, because of what Jesus Christ has done for us on the cross. This salvation is gained for us by faith alone.

When we think of what some of God's people have to endure for the sake of the Lord it makes us wonder how genuine our faith is. Is our faith able to withstand all the afflictions of this life? If our world was to fall apart unexpectedly, would our faith remain strong? If we were to lose our marriage partner or our son or daughter, would our faith stand the test? If one of our loved ones contracted some dreaded illness, would our trust in Christ remain firm and steadfast?

All kinds of trials were already occurring to Peter's readers. What a comfort it must have been for them to read, **'These** [sufferings] **have come so that your faith may be proved genuine.'**

James also wrote in a similar vein, 'Consider it pure joy, my brothers, whenever you face trials of many kinds, because you know that the testing of your faith develops perseverance' (James 1:2-3). One Sunday evening I was listening to a sermon being preached on that text, little realizing that my own faith in God would soon be put to a very severe test. Not long after I returned home from church I received the awful news that my eighteen-year-old son had been killed in a road traffic accident a few hours earlier. At the time I could not honestly have counted it pure joy to be tested in such a devastating way, but I trust that my faith in God and his promises was strengthened because of it. 'Blessed is the man who perseveres under trial, because when he has stood the test, he will receive the crown of life that God has promised to those who love him' (James 1:12).

The joy of knowing Christ

Peter walked and talked with Jesus when he was on earth. Yet he says that those who never had the privilege of seeing Jesus in the flesh can rejoice because they see him now with the eyes of faith. The apostle means that when someone believes in the Lord Jesus Christ, the Saviour becomes a real and close companion to him or her.

One of the twelve said that he could never believe that Jesus had risen from the dead unless he could actually see with his own eyes the nail marks in the Lord's hands, and put his own finger where the nails had been in the Lord's hands and feet, and also place his own hand into the wound in Jesus' side. But when Jesus appeared to all the disciples, including Doubting Thomas, the Lord offered his hands to Thomas so that he could place his finger in the nail print. All that Thomas could say was, 'My Lord and my God!' 'Then Jesus told him, "Because you have seen me, you have believed; blessed are those who have not seen and yet have believed"' (John 20:29).

The Christians to whom Peter was writing were reminded by the apostle, 'Though you have not seen him, you love him; and even though you do not see him now, you believe in him and are filled with an inexpressible and glorious joy' (1:8).

This glorious joy is made available to those who are given a new birth, a new start, a new outlook on life. They now see everything from a different perspective. This is something which the unregenerate person cannot understand. We rejoice in Christ because we are given a living hope which is sure and certain. We are joyful because we are given an inheritance which is kept in heaven for us and we are full of gladness because we are shielded by God's power. We are given a greater love for Jesus. We believe in him and, as a consequence, we are filled with an inexpressible and glorious joy.

And, as in verse 5, Peter says that all of these things are leading to that time when Jesus Christ will be revealed in all his power and fulness. At that time our faith will result in praise, glory and honour for the Lord — and for us too. Although we have the assurance of our eternal salvation now, we shall, on that day, receive the goal of our faith, the salvation of the whole of our created beings — the salvation of our souls.

5.
The grace of God revealed

Please read 1 Peter 1:10-12

Salvation is the gift of God, and in these three verses Peter emphasizes the wonder of this salvation. He tells his readers, who were to prepare themselves for even greater suffering than they were then undergoing, that the prophets had foretold this salvation, the apostles were then preaching about the blessings of the gospel and even angels longed to look into these things. Peter spoke to these persecuted Christians of northern Turkey about the sufferings of Christ and the glories that followed him. Dr Clowney puts it like this: 'The Christ of glory is the Christ of the cross. The sequence of our lives follows the sequence of Christ's life. He suffered first, then entered into this glory. So must we.'[1]

Peter speaks of this salvation as **'the grace that was to come to you'** (1:10). The grace of God is a blessed gift. Grace is the free unmerited favour of God made available to undeserving sinners. There is nothing that any one of us can ever do which makes the Lord feel that he must do something to reward us. Salvation is free. It cannot be earned and it cannot be deserved. God is under no obligation to reward us for anything.

The prophets foretold this grace

Who are these prophets to whom Peter is referring when he said that **'The prophets ... spoke of the grace that was to come to you'**? He mentions no names but surely he is referring to those same prophets of whom Jesus spoke when he talked to the two disciples on the road to Emmaus. He explained to them what was said in all the Scriptures concerning himself. He did this by 'beginning with Moses and all the Prophets' (Luke 24:27). By this he meant all the prophets of the Old Testament, from Moses to Malachi.

On this same journey Jesus also spoke about his sufferings and glory. He said, 'How foolish you are, and how slow of heart to believe all that the prophets have spoken! Did not the Christ have to suffer these things and then enter his glory?' (Luke 24:25-26). And here in his first letter Peter takes up these same themes; first suffering, then glory.

The prophets said that this grace was to come for others. They desired it for themselves but it was not to be revealed in their time. They lived too soon. They saw it on the horizon. They searched for it **'intently and with the greatest care'**. They were trying to find out the time and circumstances when the coming grace of God would be made known. They 'took their task seriously, for their words concerned the salvation of man. And about this salvation, they wished to know as much as possible.'[2]

These prophets spoke of Christ. The whole of the Old Testament is full of Christ. He is not mentioned by the name 'Jesus', but he is there. The Old Testament prophets spoke of his suffering and of the glories that would follow. Sometimes these two were mixed up together. They could recognize the glories of Christ (the Hebrew word is 'Messiah'). They believed in the coming of one who would set the people free, and re-establish the kingdom of Israel so that it would be an everlasting kingdom like that of King David. But, like the Ethiopian eunuch, they were sometimes puzzled about so much talk of suffering. They were tempted to say, as he did, 'Who is the prophet talking about?' (Acts 8:34).

Often sufferings were spoken about in prophecy in connection with one who remained a mystery to the Jews, but whom Christians know as the Messiah. Psalm 22 has the words of this suffering one:

'I am a worm and not a man,
    scorned by men and despised by the people.
All who see me mock me;

they hurl insults, shaking their heads:
"He trusts in the Lord:
   let the Lord rescue him,
Let him deliver him,
   since he delights in him"'

(Psalm 22:6-8).

Another well-known example is in Isaiah 53:3:

'He was despised and rejected by men,
   a man of sorrows, and familiar with suffering.
Like one from whom men hide their faces
   he was despised, and we esteemed him not.'

These Old Testament prophets did not make up their prophecies. They were given them by the Spirit of Christ, who was in them, pointing forward to the sufferings and glories of Jesus Christ. This is clearly a reference to the Holy Spirit.

Why did Peter refer to the Holy Spirit as the Spirit of Christ? He did so because it is the Holy Spirit's task to testify about Jesus Christ. When Jesus was taken up into heaven he sent another Counsellor for his people. He said to his disciples, 'Unless I go away, the Counsellor will not come to you; but if I go, I will send him to you' (John 16:7). When Jesus commenced his earthly ministry we are told that he returned to Galilee 'in the power of the Spirit' (Luke 4:14). And Jesus, quoting a prophecy from Isaiah, said, 'The Spirit of the Lord is on me' (Luke 4:18). So we see that the Holy Spirit is the Spirit of Christ because Christ sent him and because he ministered through him.

This section not only teaches the unity of the Godhead but also the divine inspiration of the Scriptures. There is a unity about the Old and New Testaments. Not only are these prophecies concerning Christ's sufferings and glory fulfilled in Jesus but the same Spirit of God was at work guiding the sacred authors as they penned the Scriptures. Matthew Henry says, 'The revelations of God to his church are all perfectly consistent: the doctrine of the prophets and that of the apostles exactly agree, as coming from the same Spirit of God.'[3]

The Old Testament prophets did not just speak for their

own times. They did speak powerfully to their own people, but the prime purpose of these prophecies was for people who were to live hundreds of years after they were uttered. Peter says, 'The prophets ... spoke of this grace that was to come to you' (1:10). He says about the prophets that **'It was revealed to them that they were not serving themselves but you'** (1:12).

The apostles preached grace

The grace, of which the prophets had spoken in the past, has 'now been told you by those who have preached the gospel to you by the Holy Spirit sent from heaven'. These scattered Christians were receiving a message addressed to them, directly from heaven. This message was about the same grace of God of which the prophets had spoken much earlier. It was about the sufferings and glories of the Lord Jesus Christ.

It is also the same message which is being preached today, another 2,000 years further on in history. It is about Jesus Christ. This message is that 'God so loved the world that he gave his one and only Son, that whoever believes in him shall not perish but have eternal life' (John 3:16). It is that Christ 'bore our sins in his body on the tree [the cross], so that we might die to sins and live for righteousness; by his wounds you have been healed' (1 Peter 2:24). It says, 'Christ died for sins once for all, the righteous for the unrighteous, to bring you to God' (3:18).

Thirty years after Peter had seen the sufferings of Jesus at his trial and crucifixion, he now declares that our Lord had to undergo these sufferings before he could enter into the glories that would follow. This is still the pattern: the sufferings first, then the glory. Psalm 30:5 says, 'Weeping may remain for a night, but rejoicing comes in the morning.'

So it still is with anyone who comes to Christ for salvation. There has to be that time of sorrow, the time when we realize that we are sinners, in the hands of God. But after this period of sorrow there is glorification. Finally, after we have shared in his sufferings in this world, we shall share in his glories to come. Romans 8:17 tells us that 'We share in his sufferings in order that we may also share in his glory' — the glories of his resurrection, ascension and return (see Colossians 3:4).

Angels wonder at grace

Even angels desire to look into these wonders, says Peter.
The picture is of angels looking over the rim of heaven and
peering down to this earth. This is the same word which is
used of Peter and Mary when they 'bent over' to look into the
empty tomb (John 20:5, 11). 'As the cherubim bent down to
the mercy-seat, the emblem of redemption, in the holiest, so
the angels intently gaze, desiring to fathom the depths of "the
great mystery of godliness: God manifest in the flesh, justified
in the Spirit, seen of angels" (1 Tim. 3:16).'[4]

Why are the angels filled with wonder when they con-
template the glories of the gospel of God's grace? The angels
desire to look into these things because they have never
experienced such mercy themselves. They have never needed
mercy because they have always lived sinless lives. After the
fall of Lucifer from heaven, the angels in heaven have never
been tempted to sin. They have never wandered far off from
the Father's will for their lives. They have never needed to be
redeemed, because they are sinless beings.

But here Peter writes about them gazing with wonder at the
love of God in Christ Jesus. It truly is amazing that God
should make known such grace to men and women. We, who
are hell-deserving sinners, have been redeemed with the
precious blood of Christ. Think of the wonder of the gospel
message and silently praise God for all his love.

In the *Gospel Magazine* of 1777 an unknown author wrote
these words:

> Pause, my soul! adore and wonder!
>   Ask, 'O why such love to me?'
> Grace has put me in the number
>   Of the Saviour's family;
>   Hallelujah!
> Thanks, Eternal Love, to thee![5]

6.
Ideal Christian living

Please read 1 Peter 1:13-17

Doctrine is important. If we did not know the truths of Christian belief we would find ourselves living lives which were inconsistent with the teaching of God's Word.

So far we have been looking at the teaching which Peter gives at the beginning of his first letter. This forms the basis of everything which is to follow. All the practical instruction in the rest of the letter flows out of the doctrine which he has been giving in the first twelve verses. He will return again and again to these doctrines, but the foundation has now been laid for all that he wants to say to these scattered believers living in northern Turkey. Peter is writing to Christians who are going to be subjected to increasing persecution, and he is preparing them to endure this suffering for the sake of Christ. He reminds them that they are merely strangers in this world; they are just passing through. Their true home is in heaven. They have an inheritance reserved for them in glory. They may soon be killed, in which case they will be with their Lord in glory. But whatever happens to them, they are to live in the knowledge that the Lord Jesus Christ is coming again. In the meantime, because of their faith in Christ, they are shielded by God's power until the coming of the salvation which is ready to be revealed at the last time (1:5).

Be prepared

They cannot just sit back and wait for the Second Coming.

They must act as responsible Christians. 'The supreme purpose of redemption is to make men holy.'[1] Believers have a task to perform. 'The Church of Jesus Christ is not a dormitory for sleeping saints but rather a barrack bulging with spiritual soldiers eager to enter the battle.'[2] God's people must be prepared for action. But they must not just rush into the battle without thought. They must weigh up the opposition, but they must prepare their minds as well. If we are to live as God wants us to live then we must be right-thinking people.

The Authorized Version of the Bible says, 'Gird up your minds.' The picture here is of a person dressed in the long flowing robes of the day. If he is going to engage in positive action then he will have to do something about his clothing which might flap around his ankles and impede his progress. The only thing he can do is to bend down, pick up the hem of his robe, pull it between his legs and tuck it into his belt. It will then be out of the way. Peter then transfers this idea of clothing to the thought life. If a person is going to live correctly then he has to gird up his mind in a similar way to that in which the people of those days girded up their clothes. Only then will he be able to engage in strenuous activity and exercise an intelligent faith.

Next Peter says his readers must be prepared by being **'self-controlled'**. This reflects the idea of being sober. We know how a drunkard who is uncontrolled behaves. People under the influence of alcohol stagger from place to place and do not quite know what they are doing. Christians must never be like that, even if they are not drunk. God's people are to be in full possession of all their faculties, all of the time. Edmund Clowney says, 'Drunken stupor is the refuge of those who have no hope. But Christians who look for the coming of the Lord live in hope. They will not seek escape in the bottle, for they have already tasted the Spirit of glory.'[3]

Peter uses this same phrase elsewhere in his first letter. In 4:7 he says, 'The end of all things is near. Therefore be clear minded and self-controlled so that you can pray.' Jesus is coming again, so we need to keep clear heads, and watch. The Lord told a parable about servants waiting for their master to return from a wedding banquet (Luke 12:35-48). Peter is reflecting the Master's teaching when he tells his readers that if they want to pray properly then they must exercise self-control in every area of their lives.

The apostle again uses the same phrase in 5:8. Here he says, 'Be self-controlled and alert. Your enemy the devil prowls around like a roaring lion looking for someone to devour.' If we, in the course of our Christian life, doze off in regard to some aspect of doctrine or practice, the devil will try to consume us. The unregenerate person finds this kind of picture amusing. To him it is like harmless childish fun. But here Peter is warning us all that it is very dangerous to think of the devil like that.

Writing in a local church magazine, one of the elders explains how he has 'grown out' of the rather simplistic teaching he had received in his earlier Christian life. He says, 'Today the Church no longer believes in a personalized Devil orchestrating evil in the world.' He goes on to state that 'This view seems to be held in most of the established church denominations.' If that is true then it is no wonder that many are deceived into thinking that the Bible is no longer the inerrant Word of God when it speaks so clearly of a personal devil. Wayne Detzler says, 'Thousands of Christians doze through services every Sunday. Their devotional life is a mild anaesthetic. Peter warns that conflict with Satan is no place for sleeping saints. Satan is ever alert (as the story of Job reminds us), and he will snatch any sleeping saint.'[4]

We must not only prepare our minds for action and be self-controlled, but we must set our hope fully on the grace to be given us when Jesus Christ is revealed. We have seen that this hope is a living hope which has been given to us through the resurrection of Christ. It is new and it is alive. There is nothing vague about this living hope. (It would not be living if it was vague.) Peter goes on to tell us to **'Set your hope fully on the grace that is to be given you when Jesus Christ is revealed.'**

We are living today in tough times. It is not easy to be a faithful Christian or to prepare our minds for action. It is much easier to let our minds be lulled into inactivity. It is not so easy to be self-controlled. There are so many things to intoxicate us. There are many allurements to lead us into evil. But the best antidote to sinful action is right thinking. We need to bind up the loins of our minds and exercise spiritual discipline in our Christian lives. How can we do that? We can look to Jesus. He is coming again and when he returns it will be to give us such grace that we will be free for ever from sin and impurity.

Be obedient

Those of us who are parents are constantly saying to our children, 'Do what I say.' It is expected of children that they will be obedient to their parents. Parents have had more experience of life than their offspring and therefore, it is only sense that if they are wise, they will instruct their children on how to behave. And it is the natural thing for children to imitate their parents and do as they tell them.

Peter keeps urging his readers to be obedient. He says we have 'been chosen ... for obedience to Jesus Christ' (1:2). In chapter 1:22 he says that 'You have purified yourselves by obeying the truth.' He says that wives should be submissive to their own husbands, 'like Sarah who obeyed Abraham and called him her master' (3:6); and, speaking about the judgement that begins with the family of God, he goes on to ask, 'What will the outcome be for those who do not obey the gospel of God?' (4:17).

If we are to show our love for Christ, we must be like obedient children of our heavenly Father. We must not conform to the evil desires of our pre-conversion days. Then we were largely in ignorance and we indulged in unholy thoughts and actions. But now things ought to be completely different. We are under new management. We should not be living lives which conform to the standards of this world. The things we read should never contaminate our minds with sinful desires. We should remember that there is an off button on the radio and television sets. We should always ask ourselves, 'Is this the kind of thing I would like Jesus to find me doing when he comes back again?'

One of the clearest ways to tell whether a person has been converted is to see whether there has been any change of behaviour from his or her former way of life. A born-again believer will desire to do the will of his heavenly Father above everything else. He will gladly acknowledge that, however clever he was before his conversion, he now sees things with Christ-like eyes. In his unregenerate state his mind was darkened; he lived in ignorance as far as the truth of Christ and the blessings of the gospel were concerned. But knowing Christ as his Saviour has brought about the most dramatic change in the whole of his outlook. He has been called 'out of darkness into his [God's] wonderful light' (2:9).

Be holy

If we are trying to live holy lives we will not attempt to compare ourselves with anyone else, because every human being is sinful. Peter said that we should live copying God. Amazing though it is, this is the injunction: **'Just as he who called you is holy, so be holy in all you do'** (1:15). The holiness of God reveals God's absolute purity in every aspect of his being. Both the Old and New Testaments speak of God's holiness more than any other of his attributes. When Peter enjoined his readers to be holy he expected them to seek to imitate God in this respect. Jesus also gave similar commands in which believers are told to base their lives on God's attributes. He said, 'Be perfect, therefore, as your heavenly Father is perfect' (Matthew 5:48), and 'Be merciful, just as your Father is merciful' (Luke 6:36).

When Peter exhorted these scattered Christians to live holy lives he appealed to the highest authority. 'He offers confirmation of his teaching with words spoken by God himself.'[5] When Jesus was tempted by Satan in the wilderness he disarmed the devil with the formula, 'It is written' and appropriate quotations from Scripture (Matthew 4:4, 7, 10). It is not surprising that Peter turns to the book of Leviticus to appeal to the need for holy living. This book, more than any other, teaches that God's people ought to be holy, because God himself is holy. Look up the word 'holy' in a concordance. You will be surprised at the very large number of references there are to this word in the book of Leviticus. There are more there than in any other book in the whole Bible. In making his appeal Peter uses a direct quotation from Leviticus 1:44-45 where the command, 'Be holy, because I am holy' is given twice in the space of two verses.

The supreme standard for our lives is found in God alone, and we should try to live our lives like his. It is in the Lord Jesus Christ that we see God most clearly. One day Jesus borrowed a boat belonging to Peter and used it as a pulpit. Following his preaching to the crowds Jesus told the fishermen to 'Put out into deep water, and let down the nets for a catch.' Although they had been fishing all night (the correct time for fishing), they had caught nothing; but because Jesus asked them to fish they did so. The result was that they had a wonderful catch. 'When Simon Peter saw this, he fell at Jesus' knees and said, "Go away from me, Lord; I am a sinful man!"' (Luke 5:1-10). He did not want Jesus to leave him; but when he realized the holiness and majesty of Jesus he felt unworthy to be even near him. However, Jesus did not want to depart from Peter; he said, 'Don't be afraid; from now on you will catch men.'

When we become Christians our duty does not end with telling people that we have been forgiven and cleansed from our sin; that is only the beginning. When we are saved we should start to live an active life of opposition to sin and we should strive to live obediently to God's commands and thus demonstrate the meaning of the word 'holy'.

7.
Our great redemption

Please read 1 Peter 1:17-21

The non-Christian cannot understand heavenly realities. When we say that God's people have life abundant, he can only visualize worldly amusements and excitement. When believers talk of being redeemed, the unbeliever can only think in terms of 'What would that cost me?' When Christians talk of Jesus being raised from the dead and being glorified, the stranger to grace can only imagine a Hollywood-style heavenly choir and spectacular surroundings.

But the great redemption which is ours in Christ is something quite different from anything that the worldly person could ever think of.

We are God's children

This section starts with a statement which reminds us that we are God's children. We are God's children if we have obeyed the gospel. If we have listened to the good news of salvation in Christ, responded to that message, turned from our sin and believed in the Lord Jesus Christ for salvation, then we are God's children.

We are God's children if we have been born again. It is here, in verses 18-21, that Peter comes to the heart of the gospel. We need to weigh up everything that he says because this is still the gospel of salvation for us in these days, and it will continue to be until the last day of all time. The message is this: the only way that anyone can have any hope of eternal life is through believing in the gospel of our Lord Jesus Christ.

We need to start with the fatherhood of God. He is the one who created all things. He is Father of everything and everyone because he made all things out of nothing. He is Father and Judge of all people in that sense. But he is especially Father of those who have been saved.

In the Old Testament God is sometimes called Father (see Psalm 89:26; Jeremiah 3:19; Malachi 1:6). We see this truth even more clearly in the New Testament, where Jesus taught his disciples to pray, 'Our Father in heaven, hallowed be your name' (Matthew 6:9). In Romans 8:15 and Galatians 4:5-6 Paul speaks of Christians being adopted as God's sons. He says that God sent the Spirit of his Son into our hearts, the Spirit who calls out, 'Abba, Father'. We can see then that all those who know Jesus as their Saviour also know God as their Father. Indeed no one can truly say, 'Our Father' until he or she has been made one of God's own blood-bought children. No one can really believe in God without believing in the Lord Jesus Christ (1:21).

Robert Leighton, writing in the mid-1600s said, 'Christ is the medium through which we look upon God; for so long as we look upon God through our own guiltiness, we can see nothing but his wrath ... [When] God looks on us out of Christ, [he] sees us rebels, and fit to be condemned: we look on God as being just and powerful to punish us; but when Christ is betwixt, God looks on us in him as justified, and we look on God in him as pacified, and see the smiles of his favourable countenance. Take Christ out, all is terrible; interpose him, all is full of peace.'[1] God is fair and just in all his dealings with his children. We may well say, following some catastrophe, 'Why has this happened to me?' At other times we are tempted to complain and think that God is treating us badly. An old hymn goes:

> God shall alone the refuge be
> And comfort of my mind.
> Too wise to be mistaken, he,
> Too good to be unkind.[2]

Peter says that 'Since you call on a Father who judges each

man's work impartially, live your lives as strangers here in reverent fear.' He means that we should always remember that God is a loving Father. He is also our Judge but because we have been saved from the guilt and penalty of our sin we should not be frightened of him. However, we should remember that he is sovereign and we should live in holy awe of him. Even though he is all-powerful he always treats his children fairly, kindly and wisely. Because he is our heavenly Father, we should always live our lives here as strangers on this earth. The apostle has already hinted at this in verse 1. Now he says it more forcefully. In other words Peter is saying to believers, 'This is not your final home. You are just passing through this world. Therefore live your life here for God's glory, but remember you do not belong here. Always keep your eyes on your heavenly home.'

If we were always to live our lives like that then all the troubles of this life would fade into insignificance and we would want to show so much more love for God. When we recall where our true home is then we will want to live lives which display a reverent fear for God and love for his people.

The gospel message

Peter now sums up the whole of the gospel by reminding them of something which they already knew. He says, **'For you know ...'** (1:18). We should never tire of speaking about the good news of salvation in Christ. The gospel is old, yet ever new. But to the believer it comes with wonder every time we think about it. The pastor of the tiny village church where I was a member when I was a new Christian often used to pray before the morning service, 'Lord we don't ask that you will give us something new today; we just pray that it will come to us with a freshness as your Spirit lights up the Word.' Every time we hear the gospel preached in all its fulness it makes us thrill with the wonder of God's love.

Peter sums up the gospel in these verses under three headings. He speaks of redemption in verses 18-19, of revelation in verse 20 and of resurrection in verse 21.

Redemption

At one time trading stamps were very popular in this country.
You were given them at the supermarket and at the petrol
station whenever you bought any goods. The more you spent
in the shop or garage, the greater number of stamps you
received. You were encouraged to save them up until you had
a great number. You could then exchange them for a gift
described in the trading stamp catalogue. When you did this
you were said to have redeemed the stamps.

Likewise in the days of slavery it was sometimes possible to
redeem a slave. That was done by the slave, or someone else
on his behalf, paying a sum of money to the owner of the
slave. This would then mean that the slave could go free. He
had been redeemed, or had gained his redemption. So we see
that redemption has something to do with buying back.

All believers in the Lord Jesus Christ have been created by
God, like everyone else, but they have something greater
than the people of the world; God's people have been pur-
hased by the precious blood of Christ. He shed his blood for
them when he died on the cross for their redemption.

When Peter's readers became Christians, he said that they
had been redeemed from the empty way of life handed down
from their forefathers. We do not know whether they were all
Gentiles. Probably there was a mixture of Jews and non-Jews
in these scattered congregations meeting to worship God in
northern Turkey. Whoever they were, Peter says that before
they found Christ as their Saviour they were living empty
lives. Is that not a very clear description of non-Christians?
People who do not know that their sins have been forgiven are
living empty lives. They may pretend that everything is all
right. They may fill their lives with all kinds of entertainment
and activities (some of which may be very wholesome) but if
Christ is not the driving force within them, then they are living
empty lives. They have no real purpose in life. They have no
aim. They can find no lasting satisfaction in life. And when
they come to die they will have no joy and peace or hope for
the future. They will not be like the members of John Wesley's Classes and Societies. He said of them, 'Our people die
well.'

Peter continues by outlining what cannot be done to obtain
anyone's redemption. He says that **'It was not with perishable**

things such as silver and gold that you were redeemed' (1:18). He means that redemption cannot be purchased, as power and influence can sometimes be bought with money. He is saying, 'You can't buy God's salvation. Redemption is not for sale.' No doubt Peter was remembering the incident of Simon the sorcerer. 'When Simon saw that the Spirit was given at the laying on of the apostles' hands, he offered them money and said, "Give me also this ability so that everyone on whom I lay my hands may receive the Holy Spirit." Peter answered: "May your money perish with you, because you thought you could buy the gift of God with money!"' (Acts 8:18-20).

However, on the other hand, redemption is not cheap either. It cost the Lord Jesus Christ everything to purchase his people for God.

The Father had to send his own dear Son to this earth. While he was here Jesus went about doing good and performing signs and wonders. He proved that he was God's Son. He demonstrated that he was without blemish or defect. He was just like a sacrificial lamb — pure in every way. And then he was offered on the altar of sacrifice. Just as a pure lamb was slain to cover up the sins of God's people of old, so Jesus, the Lamb of God (John 1:29), offered his precious blood on the cross to save his people from their sins. He did not just die as an example to us of self-sacrifice. He died because he was the only one who could pay the price of our sin. He was the only person who ever lived upon this earth who was 'holy, blameless, pure, set apart from sinners' (Hebrews 7:26). And he became the last sacrifice that was necessary to be offered for the removal of sin. He obtained, once and for all, eternal salvation for all who repent of their sins and turn to God in faith.

Revelation

This sacrifice on the cross was not an afterthought on God's part. He knew that man would sin. He was aware that a Saviour would be needed. We cannot understand how God allowed sin to enter the world. But he did, and we must accept the fact. This does not in any way diminish God's sovereignty. It is just one of those mysteries which we cannot understand. God knew that sin would enter the world, and he made provision for a Saviour. Christ 'was chosen before the creation of the world' (1:20). God chose the most precious one he could to die for us. He sent his only begotten Son to be the only sacrifice that could meet the demands of God's law. This law said, 'The soul who sins is the one who will die' (Ezekiel 18:4). The only human being who never sinned was the Lord Jesus Christ. Mrs Alexander sums it up so well:

> There was no other good enough
> To pay the price of sin.
> He only could unlock the gate
> Of heaven and let us in.[3]

All of God's wonderful provision was planned before time began. But it has been revealed in these last days for our sake. The Old Testament Jews did not know Christ. They only had a glimmering of his coming. They offered their sacrifices day by day as a foretaste of the one great sacrifice which was to come. But now, in the gospel age, God's plan has been revealed. Jesus of Nazareth has been shown to be the Son of God. He has been declared to be the Saviour of sinners. And God has revealed this to us by the Holy Spirit in the gospel. It is 'for our sakes'.

Believer, think of what it cost God, the loving Father, to send his Son to this poor sin-sick world. Think of the agony of soul and of body that Jesus had to undergo at his trial and his crucifixion. And remember that it was for you that he died, to redeem you from your sins.

Christ has been revealed as the Saviour and he will carry on saving men, women and children right throughout this gospel age. However, there is a time coming when the age of grace will have outrun its course. Revelation 22:11 tells us that when Jesus comes again there will be no more opportunity for repentance. The last person will have been saved and everyone else will remain in their sins.

Resurrection

The crucifixion was not the end. Jesus rose to life again. This was a great stumbling-block to many people in Paul's day. It made his preaching incredible and unacceptable to those who lived in Athens (Acts 17:32). But the facts are indisputable. Jesus died, truly died. And now he lives, truly lives. God has raised him from the dead and glorified him. Jesus is now sitting at the Father's right hand in glory. He is interceding on our behalf. He is speaking to God for us. He is pleading for us to be helped and blessed.

The resurrection of Jesus is the ground of all our hope. We do not live our lives based merely on the teaching of a great man. We do not press on blindly following the philosophy of a marvellous teacher. Our faith and our hope are in God. Because he sent Jesus to be our Redeemer, because he revealed his plan of salvation to us in his Word, and by his Spirit, because he has raised Jesus to life again, we may live in the joy and certainty of that resurrection life.

Paul said, 'If Christ has not been raised, our preaching is useless and so is your faith' (1 Corinthians 15:14). Believers will not only be raised to life again at the end of this age but, through Christ, we too will enter into glory on that day. Although these are blessings for the future there is an obligation laid upon all believers for these days also. The Bible says, 'Since, then, you have been raised with Christ, set your hearts on things above, where Christ is seated at the right hand of God. Set your minds on things above, not on earthly things. For you died, and your life is now hidden with Christ in God. When Christ, who is your life, appears, then you also will appear with him in glory' (Colossians 3:1-4).

Our response

What effect does this gospel message have upon us? It should move us. It should encourage us. It should strengthen us and help us. Above all it should cause us to make a positive response to Christ. If these truths are so marvellous why do we just sit around and live our lives in an aimless fashion? Should not we respond to the Lord Jesus Christ in love and obedience? He calls us to follow him and to serve him in his church. We need to ask ourselves what active response we are making to this wonderful gospel of salvation.

8.
The benefits of God's Word

Please read 1 Peter 1:22-25

I remember sitting in my cousin's small front room one week-day morning in the early 1950s. Quite a crowd of us were gathered around a small black-and-white television set. (Very few of our friends and relatives had such a luxury in those days.) We were watching the coronation of Queen Elizabeth II. Everyone was very excited and happy. But the thing that sticks in my mind most was the point where the queen was presented with a Bible. The person who gave it to her said something like this: 'This is the most precious thing that this world affords.'

We all need to ask ourselves, 'How important is the Bible to me and my family?' Is it just something that we hunt for each week so that we can take it to church to make us look religious, or do we read it as regularly as we eat our meals?

Peter has a great deal to say to us about the importance of the Word of God in these four verses at the end of the first chapter of his first letter.

God's Word must be obeyed

Peter talks about being made pure by obeying God's Word. Everyone who is in his right mind wants to be made pure. No one really likes to be mucky for very long. All of God's people wish to live a life of holiness in mind and purpose. We desire to live close to God. It is as we obey God's Word that we are made pure. Peter calls God's Word 'the truth' in verse 22.

God's Word is true. There is nothing false about it. It is when we obey the Word of the gospel that we are purified. We are made clean through God's Word. When he realized the awfulness of his sin, David cried out to God,

> 'Have mercy on me, O God,
>   according to your unfailing love;
> according to your great compassion
>   blot out my transgressions.
> Wash away all my iniquity
>   and cleanse me from my sin ...
>   wash me, and I shall be whiter than snow'
>
> (Psalm 51:1-2, 7).

God heard David's prayer and cleansed him from his sin, and we too are cleansed when we obey the teaching of God's Word.

How can we show that we have been cleansed from the defilement of our sin? We demonstrate the fact of our cleansing by being different; and the root meaning of the word 'holy' is 'different'. The call for God's people to live holy lives is one of the important themes of Peter's first letter.

Peter goes on to talk about the fact that Christians should have love for all people. This is one of the marks of a true Christian. When a person has been born again he or she is no longer characterized by selfish lusts. He has a new aim in life. He desires to show to everyone that God has cleansed him from his sin and given him new desires. He wants to show God's love to everyone he meets.

But the believer should have *a special love for God's people.* John said, 'We know that we have passed from death to life, because we love our brothers' (1 John 3:14). A Christian should not only love his fellow believers, but he should want to be with them as often as possible. This does not mean that the only time that he is in the same place as them is when he spends an hour or so twice on a Sunday looking at the back of their heads! If we have a deep love for one another it means that we are prepared to sacrifice ourselves for our fellow believers. It means that we want to give up our precious time to listen to other Christians; and it means that we should have as our best friends those of the Christian fellowship to which we belong. This is how the Word of God should affect us. God is love and we, too, should be marked out as those who display love. Larry Crabb asks the question: 'Why do sincere believers rise early in the morning for time in the Word and then live their days with neither power in their ministry, peace in their struggles, nor love in their hearts?'[1] If we live like that then we are not benefiting from God's Word.

Our love should have a threefold nature. It should be *sincere*. There should be nothing unholy about it. We should never show love to our fellow believers just because we expect to get something in return. Jesus speaks about the folly of that in Luke 6:32-36: 'If you love those who love you, what credit is that to you? Even "sinners" love those who love them. And if you do good to those who are good to you, what credit is that to you? Even "sinners" do that. And if you lend to those from whom you expect repayment, what credit is that to you? Even "sinners" lend to "sinners", expecting to be repaid in full. But love your enemies, do good to them, and lend to them without expecting to get anything back. Then your reward will be great, and you will be sons of the Most High, because he is kind to the ungrateful and wicked. Be merciful, just as your Father is merciful.'

We should love other Christians solely because Christ's love so fills our hearts that we want to reflect that love to all others who are joined to the Lord by faith. We may well not agree with them about some things, but if they are united to the Lord and we belong to him also, then we should show sincere love to them for Christ's sake.

Our love too should be *deep*. We should not have a shallow love for others. It should be rich and full and bountiful. We should not be stingy, but we should give it to the full, for Christ's sake. The day after my eighteen-year-old son, Simon, was killed in a car accident, his Bible was found by his bedside. When it was opened it was found that he had only underlined a few passages in it, but each of them had to do with God's people loving one another. The one in 1 Peter 4:8 seemed to sum them all up perfectly: 'Above all, love each other deeply, because love covers over a multitude of sins.' Simon did not know much about theology but he longed that people should love each other more. I wonder if we would get so many hard, cold, critical statements in our Christian magazines if we always remembered that the Bible commands us to love our brothers very deeply.

Our love should be *from the heart*. We ought to show how seriously we mean our love. It should come from our innermost being. John said, 'This is how we know what love is: Jesus Christ laid down his life for us. And we ought to lay down our lives for our brothers ... Dear children, let us not love with words or tongue but with actions and in truth' (1 John 3:16, 18).

God's Word is for ever

God's Word is powerful. God spoke at creation. He said, '"Let there be light," and there was light' (Genesis 1:3). God's Word produced the universe and everything in it.

God spoke to Abraham. He said, 'Sarah your wife will have a son.' And because Sarah was ninety years old she laughed in unbelief. But God said, 'Is anything too hard for the Lord?' (Genesis 18:10-14).

God also spoke to Mary, through the angel Gabriel. But Mary did not laugh when she, a virgin, learned that she was to have a child. The angel said, 'For nothing is impossible with God.' And Mary replied, 'I am the Lord's servant ... May it be to me as you have said' (Luke 1:37-38).

Peter tells us that God's Word grants new birth. We are born again, made real Christians, by the work of Christ on the cross. If we are genuinely true children of God then God's only Son died instead of us. He paid the punishment that we should have endured. And through his death on Calvary our sins have been washed away. Peter says that we have been **'born again, not of perishable seed, but of imperishable, through the living and enduring word of God'** (1:23). In the parables of Jesus the Word of God is often likened to seed that is planted in the ground, which apparently 'dies' and then has new life springing from it. However, Boice says that Peter emphasizes that God is the 'Father of his children by likening the word of God to human sperm. The Latin Vulgate makes this clearer than our English versions, for the word used there is *semen*.'[2]

The Holy Spirit applies the precious cleansing blood of

Christ to our hearts and consciences. We cannot be saved unless the Holy Spirit works out that salvation within us. Titus 3:5 says, '[God] saved us, not because of righteous things we had done, but because of his mercy. He saved us through the washing of rebirth and renewal by the Holy Spirit.' When we speak of salvation we are not referring to something like a mouth-watering delicacy, placed in a cafeteria display cabinet just waiting for us to open up the glass front and take it out. We are talking about the new birth, which needs the mighty moving of the Holy Spirit working out Christ's salvation in our hearts. He gives us the desire and the power to reach out by faith and receive the salvation that is offered us in Christ Jesus.

Being saved is not a 'take it or leave it' affair. We can only be made aware of these blessings through the living and enduring Word of God. Do we praise God enough because we have God's Word, the Bible, available for us to read and meditate upon? If we know Christ as our Saviour then we have been born again by this Word of God which is imperishable.

Peter quotes Isaiah 40:6-8 to demonstrate the permanence of God's Word, He says,

> 'All men are like grass,
>   and all their glory is like the flowers of the field …
> The grass withers and the flowers fall,
>   but the word of our God stands for ever.'

The passage says that *all* men perish like grass. There are no exceptions. Even the most glorious and important of people only bloom for a brief while. Their statues might still stand in our parks and their musty books might remain on library shelves in stately homes, but they themselves have very soon died and faded away. However, in contrast to men and women, *the Word of God stands for ever*.

How important is the Bible for us?

How we should value the Bible! The psalmist declared that this was the case for him. He says, 'How sweet are your words to my taste, sweeter than honey to my mouth!' (Psalm 119:103). It ought to be so vital for us to want to read and meditate on its meaning every day of our lives. To get the best understanding of the Word of God many find that systematic Bible-reading notes are very helpful. As Christian people it is so important to discover what God is saying to his people in these days.

We ought to value the Bible highly because Peter said, **'This is the word that was preached to you.'** This is the word through which we are saved.

The Bible is a very valuable ancient book. But it is far more than that. God's people know how precious this book is to their spiritual lives. It is the means by which God reveals himself to us. It is the way in which we are fed with spiritual food. It is more precious than anything else in the world. No wonder the queen was presented with it at her coronation, and it was said to her that this is the most valuable thing the world affords — the 'lively oracles of God'.

9.
Keep on growing up!

Please read 1 Peter 2:1-3

'Why don't you grow up?' is something we say to people who are behaving in an immature way. We long to see them thinking and acting more responsibly.

Or to give another example, think of a person who, for some medical reason, has not grown up. He or she has the body of an adult but the mind of a little child.

Growing up is so important for everyone, and especially for Christians. If we remain children throughout our Christian life, then we have no stability. We cannot think or act as mature Christian men and women. We can so easily be diverted from the true Christian pathway and start following unhelpful and wrong doctrines and life-styles.

Paul speaks about the need for believers to be mature. He says, 'Then we will no longer be infants, tossed back and forth by the waves, and blown here and there by every wind of teaching and by the cunning and craftiness of men in their deceitful scheming' (Ephesians 4:14).

Peter has been writing to the Christians who were living in northern Turkey and reminding them of the glorious gospel of Christ. He has told them that they have been 'born again, not of perishable seed, but of imperishable, through the living and enduring word of God' (1:23). Now, in 2:1-3 he puts before them the need for them to grow up in their salvation.

Get rid of unhealthy practices

One of the first steps to physical fitness is to start living a much healthier life-style. There must be the removal of habits which are harmful to the body.

We hear a great deal about the need to give up smoking. The tar and nicotine contained in cigarettes and cigars can easily clog up the lungs. Research has shown that not only bronchitis but cancer can be caused, or aggravated, through smoking. So when a person goes into hospital with a heart attack, he is urged to give up smoking when he recovers.

The excessive consumption of alcohol can cause many health problems. The drunkard sometimes dies through cirrhosis of the liver. Studies have revealed that throat cancer is very prevalent among those who drink more than a few pints of beer each week.

Regularly eating an unhealthy diet causes many problems too. An excess of fatty food can cause overweight, thus placing extra stress on the heart, legs and other parts of the body. Too little fibre in the diet fails to flush out the unhelpful mess which collects in our bodies.

Finally, we hear about the harm which can be caused when too little physical exercise is taken. The body becomes flabby. Excess calories are not burnt off, and the over-fat person becomes lethargic and dull.

Now, as we turn to the spiritual side of the child of God, we read that Peter tells us about all the things that have to be removed from our lives before we can make real progress in the Christian life. He uses a figure which is similar to saying, 'Take off your old clothes.'

Paul uses this expression a number of times. One of them is when he writes to the Ephesian church. He says, 'You were taught, with regard to your former way of life, to put off your old self, which is being corrupted by its deceitful desires; to be made new in the attitude of your minds; and to put on the new self, created to be like God in true righteousness and holiness' (Ephesians 4:22-24). Peter figuratively tells his readers to take off the garments of malice, deceit, hypocrisy, envy and slander.

Peter does not tell them to resist these sins, or to fight against them. He says that believers are clothed with these things and they must take them off; 'Get rid of them' he says. Notice the three times that the little word 'all' occurs in this list. The apostle writes about **'all malice'**, **'all deceit'** and **'slander of every kind'**. There are similar lists to these elsewhere in the New Testament letters (e.g. Romans 1:29-31; 2 Corinthians 12:20; Ephesians 4:31; Colossians 3:8; 1 Timothy 1:9-11).

'Malice' is a desire to inflict pain, harm, or injury on our fellow man'.[1] Paul used the word **'deceit'** when he spoke to the sorcerer Elymas on the island of Cyprus. He rebuked him and said, 'You are full of all kinds of deceit and trickery' (Acts 13:10). Both **'hypocrisy'** and **'envy'** are plural words in the original. Jesus accused the Pharisees of being hypocrites, for they pretended to be what they were not. It is the old Greek word for an actor — someone who acted out a part which was likely to be quite different from his real self. **'Envy'** is a cruel desire which makes us want for ourselves what belongs to another. Slanderous talk comes about when the tongue is misused, as when Christians talk behind one another's backs.

What is common in all these things? They are all poisons in social life. Dr Clowney tells us that 'They are easily identified as poisons . . . [but] they are not so easily set aside![2] Every one of these sins is aimed at harming other people.

If it was necessary for first-century believers to do something about these harmful things, it is certainly true that God's people today should examine their lives for any trace of them. We should ask ourselves, 'Are the things that I do and say likely to lead to others being benefited and helped, or to their being hurt and upset?' Peter orders believers to get rid of these hurtful things. They are inspired by the devil and they are harmful to others and to ourselves as well. They will hinder our growth in the Christian life.

Crave spiritual milk

Having dealt with the negatives, Peter now says what his readers should do to aid their spiritual development. To a baby, milk is that nourishment without which there could be no growth. How lovely it is to jump out of bed at 2 a.m. on a cold winter's morning to meet the needs of a crying new-born baby! It may well not exactly be a delight, but the crying of a hungry baby is certainly a healthy sign. It shows that the baby has a craving for its natural food.

Peter says that if we are to grow up in our spiritual lives we are to be like babies. We are to keep on desiring **'pure spiritual milk'**. The word **'crave'** is very strong. 'The unrestrained hunger of a healthy baby provides an example of the kind of eager desire for spiritual food that ought to mark the believer.'[3] Those who are practising deceit, envy or slander will not really be able to long for pure spiritual milk. We have an example of the person who has a craving for God in Psalm 42, where the writer says,

> 'As the deer pants for streams of water
>   so my soul pants for you, O God.
> My soul thirsts for God, for the living God'
>
> (Psalm 42:1-2).

The milk referred to in verse 2 is the Word of God — the Bible. This is what Peter had been speaking about at the end of the previous chapter. That is why he starts off this chapter with the word **'Therefore'**. He says, 'This is the word that was preached to you' (1:25). God's Word stands for ever: it is 'living and enduring' (1:23).

The milk spoken of here *has no additives in it.* There are no 'E's in it! (Although when it comes to the Bible some people seem to add all manner of things with great ease!) God's Word does not need anything to sweeten it. It does not require any preservatives. It certainly ought not to be watered down in any way. Unscrupulous traders used to do that to wine in the New Testament days. Peter is concerned that the same thing does not happen to God's Word. He says that it is pure, and it must remain so if it is to be of spiritual sustenance to God's people.

This milk is *pure.* Peter means that it is wholesome, unadulterated and good for people. There is an absence of fraud or deceit about it. He uses the word which Jesus spoke concerning Nathanael, when he saw him sitting under the fig tree. The Lord said, 'Here is a true Israelite, in whom there is nothing false' (John 1:47). The Bible is just like that. There is nothing unwholesome about it and God's people need to make sure that they are not deceived into thinking that it contains errors, legends and myths which may, or may not, be true.

The milk spoken of here is also *'spiritual'*. This is a word related to *'logos'*, the Word (Christ). It is only used in one other place in the New Testament. That is in Romans 12:1 where Paul speaks of 'spiritual ... worship'. Peter is here showing that he is not speaking of literal milk, but he is describing that which sustains the soul.

Feeding on the Word leads to growth

It is only when we feed upon the Word of God that we can become mature Christians. Peter is not saying that God's people are to remain babies. Elsewhere in the New Testament we read about the need to progress from milk to strong meat (1 Corinthians 3:2; Hebrews 5:12-14). But here Peter is making the point that the pure Word of God must be the believer's staple diet.

In a natural sense, two or three times a day we need to stop what we are doing and have a meal. Those who do not do this eventually become ill. A hastily eaten sandwich while sitting at a desk, continuing to work, is not good for anyone if it continues day after day. Just as it is bad to over-indulge in food, so it is detrimental to health to fail to eat proper meals regularly.

In the same way, we need regularly to take in the Word of God. It should be our staple spiritual diet. As bread and water sustain our physical bodies, so prayer and the reading of, and meditation upon, God's Word keep our souls in good shape.

It might well aid our spiritual growth if we were to stop and ask ourselves if we read and think about God's Word as frequently as we have a meal. What about family prayers? Are they a thing of the past? To gather the family together at one time in one place may be difficult for many, but where there are two or more believers living in the same home it is a great blessing to read the Bible and pray together at least once a day. It is a joy when everyone present takes some part in such a daily act of worship in the home.

Psalm 34:8-9 says,

'Taste and see that the Lord is good;
  blessed is the man who takes refuge in him.
Fear the Lord, you his saints,
  for those who fear him lack nothing.'

Peter echoes these words in verse 3. He says that his readers **'have tasted that the Lord is good'**. Perhaps those to whom
Peter was writing had known the Lord for some time. He says
to them, in effect, 'Think about babies; once they have got a
taste for their mother's milk, they don't usually lose it. They
know what is good for them. And they go for it, until they are
filled.' In the same way believers who have once tasted God's
Word will continue to crave it until they are satisfied. If they
do not thirst for God's Word then they are ill spiritually and
need to be healed.

In this short third verse Peter also implies that Jesus is God.
In Psalm 34 'the Lord' means JHWH, or Jehovah. In 1 Peter
2:3 **'the Lord'** means Jesus. Peter goes on to speak about the
Lord Jesus Christ in the verses that follow. So Peter has no
problem at all in applying the name 'God' to his Master; Jesus
and God are one.

This section ends with the word **'good'**. The apostle says,
'The Lord is good.' This word can also be translated 'kind'.
'Peter wants to say that when the believer reads the Bible, he
meets his personal God in Jesus Christ, who grants him
numerous blessings. The child of God, then, joyfully exclaims
that the Lord is good and kind.'[4]

Where does this leave us?

Do we find reading the Bible a drag? If that is the case then we
desperately need help. Do we find no sweetness in God's
Word? Then we should think of it as necessary milk and
eagerly long to be fed by it. Do we find the Scriptures mean
very little to us? Then we should ask ourselves, 'Why is the
Bible called the Word of God?' We can find the answer to that
when we think about what a word is. A word is something
which we use to communicate with one another. We convey
the message which is in our minds to the mind of another person or persons by means of words. God speaks to us in Jesus.

He is sometimes called 'the Word'. God speaks to us when we read and meditate upon the Bible. He speaks to us when the Holy Spirit lights up the sacred page. Then we discover that it is God's word to us. And it is just as up-to-date as tomorrow's newspapers!

10.
A picture of the church

Please read 1 Peter 2:4-8

There are many pictures of the church in the New Testament. Sometimes it is described as a vine with many branches. Sometimes it is shown as a shepherd with many sheep. Sometimes it is a holy city being ruled over by a king. On occasions it is seen as a mighty army with its captain at its head. But here, in chapter 2, it is described as a spiritual house — a temple having a chief cornerstone.

We need to remind ourselves that Peter is not talking about the literal temple of the Jews which was in Jerusalem. He is writing about a spiritual temple which is still being built today. Indeed the Bible never means a physical building when it talks about 'the church'; it always means the whole of God's people or a group of them in a particular area.

The foundation of the church

Jesus is called **'the living stone'** in this portion of Scripture. 'The Stone' was one of the titles used to describe the Messiah. What are the qualities of stone? When we think of stone the idea of permanence comes into our mind. The mountains and hills stand certain and sure. Until the end of all things they will remain as a reminder of the certainty of God. We sing, 'Rock of ages, cleft for me, let me hide myself in thee.' God is like that and his Son, Jesus, obviously has the same attributes, for he is God.

But this stone is not dead. It is a 'living stone'. Jesus is the one who died to pay the punishment of our sins. However, he did not remain in the grave; he rose up, victorious over sin and death, and he is alive for evermore.

God the Father has appointed Jesus to be the foundation-stone of the church. Peter quotes three Old Testament scriptures to substantiate this (Isaiah 28:16; Psalm 118:22; Isaiah 8:14). God says, **'I lay a stone in Zion.'** By Zion the Lord means the church. The Lord has done this. Jesus Christ has been given this task by God the Father — to be the cornerstone. Jesus Christ is the head of the church by God's divine decree.

Peter tells us that Jesus has been **'chosen by God'** (2:4-6). Therefore anyone who rejects Christ's authority is a fool. Anyone who says, 'I will not have this man to reign over me' is rejecting the Lord God Almighty himself.

Next we read that Jesus is **'precious'** (2:4, 6). This means that he is valuable. He is highly prized. Anyone who sees nothing precious in the Lord Jesus Christ is to be greatly pitied, because if he carries on in this same frame of mind then Jesus will see nothing valuable in him on the Day of Judgement.

Verse 6 tells us that Jesus is the cornerstone, or foundation. The cornerstone was the first, and most important, stone to be selected and laid in place when a building was being erected. It was laid at the intersection of the corner and the other foundation-stones were placed alongside it, and at an angle to it, on the same level. As the building grew all the other stones were put in place in relation to the cornerstone. Each course of stones was built up from these main foundational ones. If the chief cornerstone was 'out of line' then the whole building would be unsound. We can understand, then, why Jesus is called the foundation-stone, the head of the church.

The members of the church

They are people who have come to Jesus, and who keep on coming to him. Peter says, **'As you come to him'** (2:4). 'Coming' is a term used for approaching the place of worship in the Old Testament. Therefore the members of the church are those who want to draw near to God. They are prepared to leave their own ways and submit to God's way. They are willing to give up their independence and surrender everything to God and to his purposes.

In other words, they want to be like Jesus. Peter says that Jesus is **'the living Stone ... chosen by God and precious to him'**. Then he goes on to say, **'You also, like living stones ...'** It is as though Peter were saying to these believers, 'Everything that Jesus underwent "you also" want to experience. You want to suffer with him. You want to share in the work of the kingdom. You want to be part of the living church of Jesus. You want to be prepared even to give your life for him.' I wonder if Peter wanted to say to them, 'Do you remember I once said that I would never let Jesus down, and a few hours later I was even cursing and swearing and denying that I ever knew him?'

These scattered Christians of the early church may well have been feeling very feeble at the time when Peter was writing to them, but he says, 'You are like living stones.' Peter was saying, in effect, 'Jesus saw me as a weak, impetuous fisherman; and he turned me into a rock.' Jesus had said to Peter, 'I tell you that you are Peter, and on this rock I will build my church' (Matthew 16:18). Peter did not believe, just because he had been given the name Peter, the rock, that Jesus meant that he would be head of the church. This could not have been, because Jesus Christ himself is the head of the church. And, in any case, why does Peter say here that God's people too, are living stones being built into the church? Peter realized that Jesus meant that it was the kind of faith that Peter displayed upon which Jesus would build his church.

God's people were like dead stones before they were born again. Before they became Christians they were dead to the things of God. Jesus held no beauty for them. He was not precious to them. They would not give up anything to serve him. This was all because, spiritually, they were dead towards him. They were just like cold, hard stones lying deep down in the darkness under the ground. They needed to be quarried and shaped before they could be of any use to God. However, having once 'come to him' — to Jesus in repentance and faith — they had been born again and made living stones in his spiritual temple.

Jesus often used this figure of something which is alive when speaking of himself. He has life in himself (John 1:4; 5:26). He is living water (John 4:10-14; 7:38). He is living bread (John 6:51) and the living way (Hebrews 10:20). And now these people, who were once dead in trespasses and sins, have been turned into living stones. They have been made alive. They have been changed by God himself.

As living stones, they are being built into a spiritual house. They do not remain as isolated believers. They did not just say, 'Isn't it wonderful to know Jesus as my Saviour? Isn't it great to feel no condemnation because my sin problem has been dealt with by Jesus?' and leave it at that. No, they are cemented together with many other believers. They are 'being built' by God into a spiritual house.

The moment anyone is converted he or she becomes part of the universal church of Jesus Christ. That does not mean that that person's name is necessarily written in the book of a particular church, but it does mean that his or her name is written in the Lamb's book of life. That is the most important thing of all and is what secures the person's salvation.

But the New Testament nowhere gives the impression that a believer can just be content to be a member of the universal church and never link up with a local church. It is important to join a local church which is alive to God. No one will find himself left to his own devices in heaven. No one will be able to say, 'Oh, I am thrilled to be a follower of Jesus, but I don't want to be tied down to a particular body of Christian believers.' All those who have been redeemed by the precious blood of Christ should become part of a local church fellowship. They should join it and they should be active in it. They should seek to become involved in the life of the church because they are living stones being built into a spiritual house.

God's people are to be **'a holy priesthood'**. Every true believer is a priest. This passage teaches the priesthood of all believers. Churches run upon New Testament lines do not have priests in charge of them. They have ministers or pastors, but every born-again believer who is a member of the church is **'being built into a spiritual house to be** [part of] **a holy priesthood'**.

In what sense are believers priests? They are like priests

because they are to reflect the holiness of God and their High Priest — Jesus (1:15). Christians are to offer spiritual sacrifices (2:5). Christians are to intercede for man before God and to represent God before man.

If we are seeking to live a life which is holy and pleasing to God, then we are doing priestly work. If we are offering to God the sacrifice of praise and thanksgiving, then we are performing priestly duties. If we are praying for our fellow men and women, then we are engaging in priestly work; and if we are explaining God's plan of salvation to people whom we meet, then we are doing priestly work.

Peter is concerned that these sacrifices which are being offered to God must be undertaken seriously. He says that they must be **'acceptable to God'**. And they will be if they are offered **'through Jesus Christ'**. Paul says a similar thing in Romans 12:1: 'I urge you, brothers, in view of God's mercy, to offer your bodies as living sacrifices, holy and pleasing to God — this is your spiritual act of worship.'

Are Christians different?

What is the difference between Christians and non-Christians? There most certainly is a difference and that difference ought to be evident to everyone who pays close attention to religious people. So often everyone is thought of as a Christian. But a Christian is not just someone who has been baptized as a baby. A Christian is not just someone who says his prayers, or who attends church services regularly. A Christian is someone who has had a personal encounter with the Lord Jesus Christ, and has come to believe in him for salvation. This must result in a clear change of attitude and lifestyle.

A Christian finds Jesus precious. **'Now to you who believe, this stone is precious'** (2:7). Sadly, many people reject Jesus. Psalm 118 gives us a picture of builders who reject a stone. They look at it and they say it is not good enough. It does not suit their purposes. This is how men treat the Lord Jesus Christ. He does not measure up to their standards. He does not meet their need. The reason for this is because they only think about the here and now. They are only looking

for material blessings. They have a 'live now, pay later' mentality. Because of this, they reject Christ as being irrelevant to
them, and what they want out of life. However, the amazing
thing is that God has chosen the one whom men rejected and
elevated him to be the capstone, or cornerstone.

How sad it is that people stumble at the Lord Jesus Christ!
He is the foundation stone and yet, instead of seeing that he
is the basis for the whole of life and eternity, they trip over
him and fall.

What does Peter mean when he says, **'They stumble'**?
Unbelievers do this when they disobey the gospel call. Just as
God was at work before the foundation of the world choosing
a people for himself, so the stumbling and fall of those who
disobey the message of God was also destined beforehand.

We all need to re-examine our own personal lives and ask
ourselves some fundamental questions about the Lord Jesus
Christ. We must not go through our lives thinking that we are
part of the church of Jesus Christ when all the while we may
be those who are stumbling. This passage raises some very
important questions. Is Jesus precious to us? If he is then are
we following him and obeying his commands as we should? Is
it our constant delight to serve the Lord and do we desire to
do this all our days? Have we ever gone back to basics and
asked ourselves if we have ever 'come to him'?

11.
The purpose of the church

Please read 1 Peter 2:9-10

Why is the church on this earth? Some people think the church is here just to provide them with a service when they want their baby christened, or their daughter married, or their father buried. Some people think the church is here so that children, old ladies and effeminate men can have somewhere to go on a Sunday and a weekday afternoon. Some people think the church is here merely to be able to give support when sudden tragedy hits the locality.

All of these things have some truth in them. But they are not the main reason why the church has been established. Peter addresses verses 9 and 10 especially to God's people with the aim of reminding them who they are and telling them what they should be doing.

God's people are different

This has been the constant theme of the letter. God's people are different because the Lord has chosen them. He has called them to be separate from the world. He has reminded them of his own holiness and he is concerned that they should hear God's call for them to be holy too (1:15-16).

God's people are different because they have a different view of the Lord Jesus Christ from the people of the world. He is precious to them and they rejoice in the wonders of who Jesus is and what he has done.

Peter starts verse 9: **'But you …'** He wants to remind them of the contrast which exists between them and the people of the world. He says, 'You believe; they do not believe. You have come to Christ for salvation; they have found him to be unacceptable. They have rejected him. You find Jesus altogether lovely; he is precious to you. They find no beauty in him at all. They come to this rock of salvation, and they do not see him for what he is. They stumble over Jesus and they fall. And in doing so, they fulfil the destiny of all disobedient people: they are cast out of his presence.'

The people of the world have no idea about the reality of Christ and of God; and sometimes God's people themselves need to be instructed in the wonder of the blessings that are theirs in Christ. Peter says, 'You need to be reminded of what you are. You are not a hotch-potch of individuals. You are a people, a nation. You are a collection of God's people. You have been brought together to stand together and to live for God together.'

Peter has been using the figure of stones. He says, 'You have been excavated from the cold, dark ground. You have been dug out of the rock. God himself has stooped down and lifted you up out of the horrible pit; out of the miry clay; and he has set your feet upon a rock' (Psalm 40). That rock is the Lord Jesus Christ himself.

What Peter says to these members of the early church in the first century applies equally to believers today. Right now God's people are being built together into a spiritual house — a temple for God's glory. Each of God's people is a separate stone. They have all had to be quarried specially. They have had to be shaped individually to make them fit into God's plan for them. Sometimes this shaping takes a very long time and, in fact, it is being carried out throughout the whole of their life on this earth. Sometimes this shaping activity is very painful for the believer, for there are many rough edges to be knocked off his or her personality. This task is the sanctifying work of the Holy Spirit. He is busy moulding all Christians into God's plan and purpose for their lives. And today each believer in the Lord Jesus Christ is being made to fit into God's building — the church. This is part of what it means to be 'made holy'. We can imagine how much careful chiselling has to be done to rough stones by a master mason in order to make them fit into exactly the places planned for them. In a spiritual sense believers need to have much work done in them in order to ensure that they fit into the places that the Lord intends them to occupy in his spiritual temple, his church.

There is a very interesting point to notice here. God does not use bricks in his building. Bricks all tend to be made in the same way. They all have the same dimensions. They all look the same. When God planned his church he decided to use individual stones for it. These have all been hand-picked by him. They are all shaped individually to fit into the exact place in his house for which they have been chosen. No man, woman or child comes to Christ in exactly the same way as another. God does not mass-produce his children nor does he expect them all to perform the same kind of service. Each has a role to perform in the church which is unique to him or her. However, each individual is carefully selected and shaped to blend together with the chief cornerstone and with all of the other stones to form the called-out people of God, the church.

Four descriptions of the church

A chosen people

Peter says, **'You are a chosen people.'** God's chosen people were the Jews of old. They were chosen especially for God. He did not choose them because there was anything superior about them. In fact, the Sumerians were probably ahead of them in civilization. The Egyptians were certainly much better builders than they were, but God chose them solely because he loved them. He chose them because he kept his promise, which he made to them when he brought them out of the slavery of Egypt (Deuteronomy 7:7-8).

Some people get very worked up about this doctrine of election of God's people to salvation. They say, 'It isn't fair that God should choose some and not others.' But the way to look at it is to ask, 'Is it fair that God should choose anyone?' No one *deserves* God's mercy. Every one of us deserves to be punished for our sins. If we believe in the Lord Jesus Christ and have been truly born again then we have been chosen by

him to salvation. Does this make you feel proud when you
realize that God has chosen you from the mass of mankind to
be his child? No one has the right to feel like that. Listen to
what Edmund Clowney says on this point: 'God does not
choose an élite. Israel is a chosen people, but not a choice
people. God's elect have no grounds for pride ... God chose
the foolish, the weak [and] the despised. No one may boast
before him.'[1]

Peter is saying to all Christian believers, 'You are a chosen
people.' Before Christ met with them they were a mixture.
Some were Jews and some were Gentiles. In the letter to the
Ephesians Paul had spoken about the Gentiles also becoming
part of God's people: 'Remember that formerly you who are
Gentiles by birth and called "uncircumcised" by those who
call themselves "the circumcision" (that done in the body by
the hands of men) — remember that at that time you were
separate from Christ, excluded from citizenship in Israel and
foreigners to the covenants of the promise, without hope and
without God in the world. But now in Christ Jesus you who
once were far away have been brought near through the blood
of Christ. For he himself is our peace, who has made the two
one and has destroyed the barrier, the dividing wall of hostility, by abolishing in his flesh the law with its commandments
and regulations. His purpose was to create in himself one new
man out of the two [Jew and Gentile], thus making peace, and
in this one body to reconcile both of them to God through the
cross, by which he put to death their hostility. He came and
preached peace to you who were far away and peace to those
who were near. For through him we both have access to the
Father by one Spirit' (Ephesians 2:11-22).

Wayne Grudem sums it up like this: 'God has chosen a new
race of people; Christians, who have obtained membership of
this new "chosen race" not by physical descent from
Abraham but by coming to Christ (v. 4) and believing in him
(vs. 6-8).'[2]

A royal priesthood

In the previous chapter we looked at the truth that we are all
priests as individuals. Now Peter says that as a group we are

'**a royal priesthood**'. The task of offering spiritual sacrifices to God is one of the duties and privileges of God's people.

Israel had been called to be 'a kingdom of priests' (Exodus 19:6). 'But Israel broke God's Law, and the priesthood was limited to the family of Aaron, so that Israel really became a kingdom *having* priests.'[3] The church is called to serve the King of kings and the High Priest of God, Jesus Christ, by being his obedient and worthy servants. John says that Christ 'has made us to be a kingdom and priests to serve his God and Father' (Revelation 1:6).

A holy nation

Most nations in the world behave pretty badly at times; they certainly cannot be thought of as holy. They are out for what they can get for themselves. Sometimes patriotism means 'advancing the interests of my country regardless of who gets trodden underfoot in the process'. When we look at the exploitation of poor countries by rich ones, we have little difficulty in believing that few nations could justify being called 'holy'. Yet Israel was called by God to be '**a holy nation**' (Exodus 19:6). Peter is saying the same thing here about the church. He is implying that God's redeemed people are the Israel of God. God has chosen the citizens of his nation to be set aside for works of service for his glory.

A people belonging to God

Malachi tells us that God's people are his treasured possession (Malachi 3:17). What is your most treasured possession? Do you not want to do all that you can to protect it? You want to care for it. You want to preserve it for the future. When we think about the church we realize that it belongs to God, and it is precious to him. If you belong to God, then you will want to acknowledge his ownership of your whole being. And the people of the church should willingly declare that they belong to the Lord and they want to spend all their days pleasing him.

Verse 10 underlines the change that has taken place through the Lord Jesus Christ. Once these believers were not

a people. They were lost. They were useless. They were like
Israel of old, which was signified in the name of Hosea's second son, 'Lo-Ammi' ('Not my people' — Hosea 1:9).

Once they had not received mercy. They had no hope.
They were like their forefathers, destined for captivity in
Babylon. They were like Hosea's daughter, 'Lo-Ruhamah'
('I will no longer show love to the house of Israel' — Hosea
1:6).

However, in the second chapter of Hosea's prophecy a
wonderful change comes about. God says, 'I will make the
valley of Achor [trouble] a door of hope.' There is a time coming, says Hosea, when the Lord will make a covenant with his
people. The Lord says,

> 'I will show my love to the one I called "Not my
>   loved one".
> I will say to those called, "Not my people", "You are
>   my people",
>   and they will say, "You are my God"'

(Hosea 2:23).

When we come to New Testament times we see how all this
is brought about through the atoning sacrifice of the Lord
Jesus Christ upon the cross of Calvary. Paul says in Romans
9 that these great blessings apply to Gentiles just as much as
they do to Jews.

What should the church be doing today?

God's people should be declaring the praises of their God.
They should not be taken up with their own pomp and ceremonies, or their own problems. They should be taken up
with their Lord. The praise of God should be in their hearts
and on their lips. They should be showing forth the praises of
God to everyone around them. How much time do you spend
declaring the praises of God? How much effort do you put
into telling others of your wonderful Lord? Is your prayer life
taken up with a catalogue of your wants and needs? It should
be filled with the praise of God. Try underlining in your Bible
every place in the book of Psalms where the praises of God

are declared. It will surprise you how much ink you will use.

Why should God's people praise him so much? Because he has called them out of darkness into his wonderful light. God's call is not something that can be treated lightly. It is an effectual call. It is nothing less than the sovereign work of God. Peter had a graphic illustration of this truth. Once he was imprisoned in a very dark cell. But God brought him out into the glorious light; he sent an angel to lead him out and set him free (Acts 12:1-11).

Charles Wesley put this experience so beautifully in his lovely hymn which starts with the line, 'And can it be ...':

> Long my imprisoned spirit lay
>   Fast bound in sin and nature's night;
> Thine eye diffused a quickening ray —
>   I woke, the dungeon flamed with light;
> My chains fell off, my heart was free,
>   I rose, went forth and followed thee.

Each of us should remember what we are, and praise God for it. Each of us should remember what we should be doing, and get on with this wonderful task of declaring his praises.

12.
How a Christian should behave

Please read 1 Peter 2:11-12

We have now finished the first part of Peter's letter. So far the apostle has mainly been laying down the basic doctrines which he wants to teach to the scattered Christians of northern Turkey. He has been exhorting them to live a life of holiness (1:15), love (1:22) and trust in God (related to 'hope' in 1:13). Now, for the rest of his letter (right up until 5:11), he intends to give some practical examples of how believers can live holy lives, filled with love and trust in God.

What Christians are

He says that they are his beloved friends. He commences verse 11 with, 'Dear friends'. We can learn from this that these Christians were dear to Peter. He knew them, or he knew about them, because they had become true followers of Jesus. Because both Peter and they were joined to the Lord, these Christians were, therefore, Peter's dear friends. He does not say, 'You are not as important as I am.' He says, in effect, 'We are all sinners saved by grace. I have an apostleship role to fulfil, and you have other duties, but that does not make me more important than you.' He goes out of his way to point out to the elders among these believers that they should 'not lord it' over those entrusted to their care (5:3).

These Christians were dear, not just to Peter, but to the Lord also. Jesus had died to cleanse them from their sins. He had died to give them new life and bring them into the body of Christ (his people). He had died to make them servants of God.

Peter next says that these believers were **'aliens'**. Aliens are people who do not belong in the country where they are residing. They have no citizenship rights in that land. They cannot make any demands upon the rulers of the place where they are living. The simple fact is that they are not part of that country at all.

Because believers are aliens in the world, they have to remember that this is not their true home, nor is it their final resting-place; they are just passing through. They are temporary residents on this earth and they are to remain here only for a little while. They really belong somewhere else. Their true home is where their Lord is; and he dwells in heaven.

Peter then adds that these believers are **'strangers in the world'**. In 1:1 he greets them as such. He does not mean that it is wrong for them to have friends where they live. There is no reason to infer from Peter's statement that God's people can act as though they were superior to the citizens of this world. Verse 12 makes it clear that Christians, although they are strangers on this earth, are called to live exemplary lives. They must always remember that they are 'in the world', even if they are not 'of the world' (Jesus gave his disciples this teaching in John 17); God's people must respect and obey the conventions and laws of the land in which they live, provided that these do not contravene God's law.

Peter calls them strangers because this world is not their real home. They may be citizens of this world, but their true citizenship is in heaven (see Philippians 3:20). Their treasure is in heaven and that is where they will spend eternity.

Things Christians should not do

There is a negative as well as a positive side to holy living. The Scriptures make it clear that, in order to live holy lives, God's people must stop doing certain things and must start doing other things.

Peter deals with the negative aspect first, when he warns his readers **'to abstain from sinful desires'**, (or 'fleshly lusts'

AV). He says, **'I urge you ...'** These sinful desires are the things which are contrary to godliness and Peter speaks most strongly against them. He lists some of the things he is referring to in chapter 4: 'For you have spent enough time in the past doing what pagans choose to do — living in debauchery, lust, drunkenness, orgies, carousing and detestable idolatry' (4:3).

All of these evils are 'public' sins and Christians must never indulge in them. Each of them refers to over-indulgence. As an example of one of the things in Peter's list, we could point to something which has recently been identified by many in authority as a great cause of much trouble — the imbibing of too many alcoholic beverages. While many people feel that it is right for Christians to abstain from these altogether, we have to admit that nowhere does the Bible teach that believers should never drink any alcohol. However, it is clear that if a Christian does 'drink' he should never over-indulge himself. If any Christian is ever in danger of becoming drunk at any time, then he or she should seriously consider whether it is right for him or her to drink any alcoholic beverage *at all.*

Or, to take another of Peter's examples, if there is a danger of a Christian making an idol of anyone or anything — be it a favourite singer or sportsperson — then it is better for that believer not to be a 'fan' of that performer at all. When we give greater affection or praise to anyone or anything than to the Lord, then we are making an idol of the object of our affection.

The apostle speaks most forcibly when he says that believers must abstain from these sinful desires. He means that they should have nothing to do with them. Paul, writing to young Timothy, put it like this, 'Flee the evil desires of youth' (2 Timothy 2:22) Wayne Detzler very graphically describes the kind of action required. He says, 'When a massive juggernaut lorry is bearing down on the driver of a motor-cycle, it is highly advisable for the cyclist to flee from the lorry.' He draws out the lesson by saying that Christians 'do not lightly enter into battle with evil desires; they flee from them'.[1]

These sinful desires must be avoided because, Peter says, they **'war against your soul'**. Christians are in a battle here in this world. Satan is constantly trying to lead us astray. He is waging war against our souls. Whenever anyone declares war, then he intends to do all in his power to win that war. Let us never be deceived into thinking that Satan does not mean business. He is certainly out to trap us.

If we are true Christians then Satan will never be able to snatch us from our Father's hand, but he will do everything he can to make our lives a misery. He will play upon our selfish natures. He will encourage us to look inwards. He will trick us by making us think that no one cares about us, or how we feel. He will make us think that there is only one side to any question, and that is, 'How does this situation affect me?' William Gurnall says, 'Satan designs every temptation to bring as much discomfort as possible to the saint, hoping to rob him of his peace, and create self-doubts about his sincerity.'[2]

What Christians should be doing

Peter warns his readers that living among the world will cause them problems. When worldly people see real Christians, they recognize that there is something different about God's people. It is as though Peter were saying to these Christians, 'You will seek to live a life of holiness. You will try to put God's laws first in your lives. You will try to serve Christ where you live. But non-believers will find this all very strange. They live their lives in order to get as much for themselves as possible. They may not cheat, steal or murder anyone, but their basic desire is their own happiness and that of their children and their fellow men and women. They will find it very strange that, while you desire and work for these things too, God's people have an even higher aim in life. You serve the risen Christ.'

Wherever people live lives which are different, then suspicion is bound to arise. If you were to have a Hindu family move next door to you, then you would be suspicious of their offerings to their deities each day, especially if this was done in their garden where you could see it. If you were to have a Muslim family move near you, then you would be suspicious of their devotion to Allah and the teachings of the Qu'ran.

We cannot understand why gypsies prefer to live as they do, but that is the life-style they choose. Wherever there are different customs being observed, then prejudiced behaviour against such people is likely to follow. Customs and ceremonies which we cannot understand cause us to be wary of the people who perform them. When it comes to some of the ceremonies and traditions of evangelical Christians then we can imagine that the people of the world find them very difficult to comprehend.

History tells us that Nero wanted to redesign Rome but there were many old houses in the way. Because the owners of these houses would not give their consent, Nero had them set alight, and then he falsely blamed the new sect called Christians for their destruction. This accusation gained acceptance because the Christians had such strange rituals, and they refused to let their God, Christ, be lumped together with all the Roman gods, upon an equal footing with them. Inevitably this led to much persecution for God's people. Many believers were thrown to the lions and numbers of them were sewn into animal skins and then left for wild dogs to pull to pieces. Things like this were done to provide entertainment for the crowds. Many Christians were crucified, had boiling oil poured upon them and were then set alight, just to make a torchlight avenue leading to Nero's palace. There were dreadful tortures inflicted upon God's people, just because they were different from the people of the world — the people whom Peter calls 'pagans' or 'Gentiles' (AV). He means that unbelievers are not the true Israel of God.

If such persecution should befall us, how ought we to react to it? We should do as Jesus did. He never said a word. He never spoke up in his own defence. He allowed himself to be ill-treated. He suffered death, never once opening his mouth in his own defence.

To counteract the opposition which Christians were already beginning to face, Peter gave the believers these injunctions: 'Be positive. Live good lives among them ... Let them see your good deeds.' Christians should be those who 'overcome evil with good'. The word 'good' in verse 12 means 'beautiful' or 'attractive'. That is how our lives ought to be. Jesus said, 'Let your light shine before men, that they may see your good deeds and praise your Father in heaven' (Matthew 5:16).

What does Peter say will happen as a result of Christians living holy lives? Unbelievers will 'see' their good deeds.

Christians today are watched very closely by the people of the world. They will take special notice, over a long period of time, of how you behave. They will be influenced by the way in which you cope with problems and troubles. And one day some of them will come to glorify God. They will do that on the day he visits them with his salvation.

Some questions we should ask ourselves

What do these instructions of Peter's have to do with Christians today? Perhaps the following list of questions will help us to sum up what is being taught in these two verses.
1. Do I always try to live a holy life?
2. Do I try to abstain from harmful desires?
3. If I find the first two questions difficult do I keep looking to Jesus and ask him to create a greater desire in my heart for God than the longings I have for worldly things?
4. Do I always seek to live a life which will force people to see the inadequacies of their own selfish attitudes?
5. Do I long that more people will be converted through the witness of my life lived for the glory of God?

13.
The Christian's attitude to governments

Please read 1 Peter 2:13-17

One important decision that the people of Britain had to make in 1988 and 1989 was whether they were going to fill in their registration forms for the country's new Community Charge or Poll Tax. The prime minister said that everyone should complete it and the leader of the main opposition party also said that people must fill in the form. However, some politicians said that the whole scheme was unfair and that individuals should protest by refusing to register for the tax — even though to do so might mean that they would be imprisoned for breaking the law. Many of those who found out that they were likely to pay less money under the new tax discovered that they had no qualms about filling in the form, but people who were likely to pay more were tempted to ignore it.

In the days when Peter wrote his first epistle, Christians were facing a far worse predicament. For them, it was not just a question of, 'Do I obey a law which I don't think is particularly fair in every case?' It was 'Do I obey a wicked, vindictive, power-crazy emperor whose concern about the poor is virtually nil?'

As we study this portion of Peter's first epistle we can discover three vital principles in regard to civil authorities. The first one concerns their position.

Authorities must be obeyed

The Bible teaches that God's design for this world is one of order. Paul even went so far as to say, 'The authorities that exist have been established by God' (Romans 13:1). He meant that even if Christians do not like those who are over them, they should still submit to them. And for us today it means that even if we think the way in which our government is running the country is wrong, we should still accept its authority. We may object strongly to many of the laws which are on the statute book, but it is still our duty to obey them.

If Paul and Peter believed that the corrupt rule of Rome was not just allowed by God, but actually ordained by him, then we too should accept the authorities which have been instituted by men and are set in authority over us. We should obey the laws which they have made. Whatever we might think of any government which we may have, in free countries the rulers have been democratically elected and the 'powers that be' reflect God's plan of order in society. God's purpose is that there should be order, not chaos.

In the Roman world the king was the supreme authority. Nero, weak as he was, reigned by God's approval. The Christian believers must often have thought, 'Why does God allow such an unjust man to rule over us?' In the same way many Christians who were in occupied Europe during the Second World War must often have thought, 'Why does God allow Hitler to remain in power? Why doesn't he do something to remove this despot?'

What does Peter say our attitude should be towards our rulers? He tells his readers, **'Submit yourselves ... to every authority instituted among men.'** They might well not like Cæsar but the apostle says, in effect, 'Accept that the emperor is the supreme authority over you. And do it **"for the Lord's sake".**' By writing that he means that this is God's pattern.

Peter teaches that believers are not only to submit to kings, but they are also to obey those who serve under them — their authorized governors. The name of the Governor of Judea at the time of Jesus' death was Pontius Pilate. Similar officials were in power all over the Roman world. Their task was to represent the emperor and see that his wishes were carried out. Governors had a twofold function: to punish those who did wrong and to commend those who did right. Notice carefully the wording. Peter does not say that their job is 'to punish those who annoy the governor'. Nor does he say that they are 'to reward those who are men-pleasers'!

A wise governor would have realized that his power was a delegated one: he did not make the rules; he merely carried out the conditions laid down by Cæsar in Rome. But Jesus took the matter one stage further. When he stood before Pilate, at his trial, Pilate said to the Lord, 'Don't you realize I have power either to free you or to crucify you?' Jesus replied, 'You would have no power over me if it were not given to you from above' (John 19:10-11).

There is just one case where the Scriptures tell us that authorities can be disobeyed by Christians. We read about it in Acts 4. When the priests and captain of the temple guard heard that Peter and John were 'teaching the people and proclaiming in Jesus the resurrection of the dead', they had the apostles arrested. Because Peter and John had healed the crippled man, the authorities were in a dilemma. They could not deny that good had been done to the man, but they did not want Peter and John to keep preaching about Jesus. This contravened their view of the law of Moses. So they called the two apostles and commanded them not to speak or teach in the name of Jesus. 'But Peter and John replied, "Judge for yourselves whether it is right in God's sight to obey you rather than God"' (Acts 4:19).

So the teaching of the Bible is clear. God is a God of order. Authorities are ordained by God and people must obey those in authority over them (even if they are wicked men), but Christians must only do this so long as the higher law of God is not being broken.

There is an illustration of this principle in Corrie ten Boom's book *The Hiding Place*. She describes the way in which her family became involved with hiding Jewish people who were 'on the run' from the Nazis. When they first became engaged in this work of mercy, one of the people they had to smuggle out of Haalem was a Jewish mother and her young baby. As a Dutch Reformed pastor from the countryside was visiting them at the time, it seemed as though this was God's answer to the problem. When they broached the matter to him he went pale and said, 'Miss ten Boom! I do hope you're not involved with any of this illegal concealment and under-cover business. It's just not safe! Think of your father! And your sister — she's never been strong!'[1] In the film version of the book the minister tells Papa ten Boom and his daughters that Christians are required to obey all those who are placed over them. Papa replies, 'We will obey those who make the laws but not if they are against God's higher law.'

We must never obey the laws of men rather than the teaching of the Scriptures. We have God's laws clearly laid down in places such as the Ten Commandments or the Sermon on the Mount and these should be our guide at all times.

We now come to a second principle regarding civil powers.

False charges against Christians must be dealt with in God's way

Christians will be persecuted. Jesus said, 'If they persecuted me, they will persecute you also' (John 15:20) and Paul similarly tells us that 'Everyone who wants to live a godly life in Christ Jesus will be persecuted' (2 Timothy 3:12). Bad treatment, for no good reason, was already happening to the believers in Peter's time. They were suffering, solely because they were followers of Jesus. Peter says in 4:12-14 that Christians should rejoice in the privilege of sharing in Christ's suffering: 'Dear friends, do not be surprised at the painful trial you are suffering, as though something strange were happening to you. But rejoice that you participate in the sufferings of Christ, so that you may be overjoyed when his glory is revealed. If you are insulted because of the name of Christ, you are blessed, for the Spirit of glory and of God rests on you.'

People who persecute Christians are very foolish. They are foolish because they do not believe in God. Psalm 14:1 says, 'The fool says in his heart, "There is no God."' It is a very stupid thing to persecute God's servants. Unbelievers do not realize that God's people mean no harm to anyone. True Christians are messengers of peace; they are not those who cause wicked things to happen.

Peter says that people who speak against Christians are guilty of ignorant talk. Ignorant talk is very dangerous. We often hear the people of the world speaking against the Lord, and what they say is utter rubbish. Every time they open their

mouths they display their ignorance of God's Word and his
plan for mankind.

So how should believers deal with **'the ignorant talk of
foolish men'**? They should obey God's will in combating persecution. What God wants is what matters above everything
else. 'Your will be done on earth as it is in heaven' (Matthew
6:10), Jesus said — and we repeat it in the Lord's Prayer.
Obeying God's will in every area, and in every respect, of our
lives should be our main concern.

Believers should silence the ignorant talk of foolish men by
doing good. This is what Peter has been speaking about in
2:12. When 'pagans' are all around us, and they are trying to
cause us to stumble, we should react to their opposition by living good lives.

However badly we are treated, we should return good to
those who attack us. Goodness always overcomes evil in
the end, just as light always banishes darkness. Jesus said,
'Blessed are you when people insult you, persecute you and
falsely say all kinds of evil against you because of me'
(Matthew 5:11). He did not retaliate when he was arrested.
He did not utter a word in his own defence. Paul puts it like
this: 'Do not be overcome by evil, but overcome evil with
good' (Romans 12:21).'

We now come to the third principle on how to behave in
regard to civil authorities.

Christians have a duty to live pure lives

The problem that we all have is that we cannot completely live
up to all of God's laws. No one, except the Lord Jesus Christ,
has ever been able to keep every one. Paul puts it very suc-
cinctly when he says, 'All have sinned and fall short of the
glory of God' (Romans 3:23). The outcome of this is that
everyone, on the Day of Judgement, should be banished from
God's presence, because they have broken his law. However,
the good news of the gospel is that Christ has died to set
people free from their sin. If they have experienced the new
birth then they have been set free: they no longer fear the
punishment of God. When Jesus died on the cross he died to
set his people free from the guilt and the power of their sins.

He took the punishment which was due to be laid on them and cast it upon his dear Son.

Peter says that believers are to live **'as free men'** (2:16). They have been set free from their sin by the shedding of the precious blood of Jesus, and they are meant to enjoy the liberty of the gospel of Christ. Saved sinners are no longer under the bondage of the law. They do not cringe when they think about their sinful past, fearing God's punishment. Christ has already paid for their sins. He did that when he died for them on the cruel cross. They are now set free from the bondage of their sin.

We should ask ourselves, 'Do I feel free? Do I appreciate the wonder of what Christ has done for me? Can I sing, "No condemnation now I dread, Jesus and all in him, is mine!"?' Do we live as though we have been freed from the great imprisonment of sin? Do people observe how we conduct our lives and say of us, 'They are behaving as though they have been given a royal pardon from some dreadful sentence'?

Do you abuse your freedom? As a believer in the Lord Jesus Christ you still have a duty to try to obey the Old Testament law. God still means it when he says, 'You shall have no other gods before me ... You shall not murder. You shall not commit adultery,' and so on (Exodus 20:1-17). This all still applies to Christians today. We have been freed from the penalty of our sin, but we are still required to keep God's law. Because of the sacrificial death of Christ we no longer live in fear of it, but we honour and respect the commandments of our God.

Just because Christ has set us free, that does not mean that we can live a life of lawlessness. We cannot 'get away with murder' when it comes to living as believers. We must live as servants of God. We must be slaves of God. We must remember that he is our Master, and we must always obey him in everything. A slave has no rights of his own. Likewise the believer is not his own; he is 'bought at a price' (1 Corinthians 6:20).

Because believers have been redeemed by God's gracious act of salvation (they did not deserve to be saved) they must live humble lives. They must show proper respect to everyone. That means they must honour everyone who is over them, in any sense of the word. It also means that they must respect everyone who may be 'under' them in their daily employment, or elsewhere.

It is a salutary thing to ask ourselves if we always show proper respect to everyone. James gave some teaching on this as it affects churches. He said, 'My brothers, as believers in our glorious Lord Jesus Christ, don't show favouritism. Suppose a man comes into your meeting wearing a gold ring and fine clothes, and a poor man in shabby clothes also comes in. If you show special attention to the man wearing fine clothes and say, "Here's a good seat for you," but say to the poor man, "You stand there" or "Sit on the floor by my feet," have you not discriminated amongst yourselves and become judges with evil thoughts?' (James 2:1-4).

Christians must love the brotherhood of believers. That means we should love our fellow Christian whether we like him or not; whether we feel like it or not; whether he likes us or not. It was a characteristic of the early Christians that they 'loved one another'. This love proved to be a very effective witness. The people round about noticed how they cared for one another. We have already looked at what Peter said on this subject in 1:22: 'Have sincere love for your brothers, love one another deeply, from the heart.'

Believers must also **'fear God'** and **'honour the king'**. Peter is very careful about the order in which he places his words. He speaks of God first, then the king, even though the king might have the power to say, 'Off with his head!' We must have a greater fear of God than we do of the king. But we must honour the king as well because he is fulfilling God's purposes.

So what should we do about any law of the land which we do not like? We should obey it. Why? Because we must submit ourselves to every authority instituted among men. This is for the Lord's sake. We should do everything we can to please God. Our Lord himself said, 'Give to Cæsar what is Cæsar's, and to God what is God's' (Matthew 22:21).

14.
The Christian's attitude to society

Please read 1 Peter 2:18-20

'It would be much easier to live as a Christian, if I wasn't in my present situation.' That is something we are all tempted to say from time to time. When we look at so many of our friends it appears that they have a very much easier time of it than we do. We think, 'If only I could find a different job, I think my life would run much more smoothly.' 'If only I didn't have such difficult home circumstances, I believe I could cope so much better.' 'If only I didn't have such awkward neighbours, my life would have much less hassle.'

We can go on and on thinking, 'If only...' Yet the facts of life are these: we are where we are. We cannot go through life thinking that the grass is always greener on the other side of the fence. We may be able to choose our home, but we cannot choose our neighbours. We may feel love for our relations, but we may hate their illnesses or indispositions. We love our children, but sometimes we detest their choice of music — and the loudness of it.

We are where we are because God has placed us there. We may long to be elsewhere, but if the Lord wants us to remain where we are, then, if we are going to be obedient to him we shall have to stay. There can be no move for us until God calls us to leave our present location.

Slaves and masters

Peter calls upon slaves to live in submission to their masters.

The slaves to whom Peter was referring were household servants. It has been estimated that there were over 60,000,000
slaves in the Roman Empire. 'They were employed in every
occupation, ranging from menial manual labour to pro-
fessionals such as doctors and teachers.'[1] These slaves were
not usually treated like whose who, several hundred years
ago, had been captured in Africa and were transported to
work in the cotton fields of the Southern States of America.
Roman slaves, on the contrary, were reasonably well looked
after. They had a well-defined role to fulfil in society.

But they were not free. Some of them lived quite comfort-
ably. They were often paid for their services, and occasionally, towards the end of their lives, some found themselves in
a position where they could buy their freedom. However, the
fact still remained that, until they were set free or were able
to purchase their liberty, they could not do as they wished;
they were slaves.

This all seems to be very wrong to us, but nowhere in the
Bible are slaves urged to rebel against their masters. Paul had
a great deal to say about the slave/master relationship (Ephesians 6:5-8; Colossians 3:22-25; 1 Timothy 6:1-2; Titus 2:9-
10); yet he never told slaves to escape from their masters. In
fact, in the case of Onesimus, who had run away from his master, Philemon, Paul sent him back after his conversion (see
the Epistle to Philemon).

Paul neither condemns nor approves of slavery. He just
accepts it as a fact of life for those times. He knew that if the
slaves were to rebel against their masters, then a bloodbath
could follow. This is exactly what did happen when all the
slaves rose up against their masters at the time of Spartacus.

However, the principles upon which the emancipation of
slaves was drawn up are laid down very clearly in the pages of
Holy Scripture. The time came when Christian people, under
the influence of William Wilberforce and others, finally had
slavery outlawed. Today, no self-respecting nation will allow
men, women or children to be slaves. But sadly, the debt trap
still binds some human beings to slavery in certain Third
World countries. Even in so-called civilized countries people
are often treated like slaves by their parents, children, wives,
husbands or others.

In verse 18 Peter, once again, uses the word **'submit'**; this time in connection with slaves. He had said that all Christians, whatever their status, must submit themselves to every authority instituted among men (2:13). Now he says that Christian slaves must submit to their masters. They must do what their owners said. Paul wrote in Colossians 3:22-24, 'Slaves, obey your earthly masters in everything; and do it, not only when their eye is on you and to win their favour, but with sincerity of heart and reverence for the Lord. Whatever you do, work at it with all your heart, as working for the Lord, not for men, since you know that you will receive an inheritance from the Lord as a reward. It is the Lord Christ you are serving.'

This teaching is also applicable to every employee in modern times. Many will work hard only when they are being watched so that their boss will give them a good bonus or promotion. Others will do everything they can to get out of working when they are not being watched. But Christian employees must always remember that they are employed, first of all, by their heavenly Master. As they do their work they must remember that in doing a good job, to the very best of their abilities, they are working to please God.

How are slaves to work? They are to submit to their owners **'with all respect'** (2:18). Their faith in Christ should not allow them to say, 'How can I respect someone who lets me slave my fingers to the bone, and yet never does anything to help me?' Peter says that Christian slaves should respect those who are over them. If this is the clear teaching of the Bible, then today, as Christian men and women, we should all gladly respect our 'masters', whether it comes naturally to us to do so or not. In fact, Peter said in verse 17 that respect should not only be given to those who are over believers but that God's people should 'show proper respect to everyone'.

But what about the case where a Christian slave has to serve a master whom he knows to be crooked? (Scholars tell us that the word 'crooked' is a better translation than 'harsh' which is used in the NIV in verse 18). Slaves could find themselves serving all kinds of masters. Some owners could be good and considerate and some could be utter crooks. Whatever the case, Christian slaves must remember that God has placed them where they are so that they might live good lives among their masters (2:12). One of the purposes of this is so that their masters might come to the point of knowing the Lord as their Saviour and so glorifying God themselves.

These principles have a bearing upon us today. The employer/employee relationship has some similarities to the master/slave relationship of New Testament times — especially when both of them are Christians. The employee has a duty to serve his employer well. He should do a fair day's work, because he remembers that he is serving the Lord. He should also remember that he is doing his work to please God.

The employer too, has a duty to see that good working conditions prevail and fair wages are paid to everyone. The Christian employer should not be like the Scottish shipbuilder of the last century, of whom it was said that he gave many thousands of pounds away to missionary work while, at the same time, a number of his workers starved to death! The employer should not try to cheat his workers out of their fair wages. He should see that when extra profits are made his workers are not forgotten when the 'share out' is made. Kistemaker says, 'In disputes, both employers and employees should settle their differences through arbitration and conciliation.'[2]

Paul says of Christian employers, 'Masters, provide your slaves with what is right and fair, because you know that you also have a Master in heaven' (Colossians 4:1). The apostle also says of workers, 'If a man will not work, he shall not eat' (2 Thessalonians 3:10). This does not mean that a disabled person should starve. Nor does it mean that someone who cannot get employment should receive no benefit. Paul means that those who blatantly refuse to work should not be given money.

It seems to be coming to light more often in these days that there are a great number of crooked employers. Their workers, especially if they are accountants or those who handle cash, are expected to 'fiddle the books'. Should Christian employees keep quiet about this and do as they are told, because the employer is their master and he has ordered them to keep quiet, or should they refuse to 'cook the books'? Paul said that slaves should do as they are told; should the same principle apply in modern times?

The answer clearly is, 'No'. We must obey God at all times and that means that we should be honest in *all* of our dealings.

Suffering for the gospel's sake

Peter calls upon all Christians to be prepared to suffer for the sake of the gospel. Peter writes about **'a man'** in verse 19. He is no longer just writing to slaves. The situation he is outlining concerns anyone who suffers unjustly. The Bible has a great deal to say about justice; it is a vital matter. The Scriptures often speak, for example, about the iniquity of the poor being down-trodden. However, it is a fact that injustices do take place. In the face of that, how should a Christian behave when he is treated unjustly?

What did Jesus teach about this kind of situation? He said, 'If you love those who love you, what credit is that to you? Even "sinners" love those who love them. And if you do good to those who are good to you, what credit is that to you? Even "sinners" do that. And if you lend to those from whom you expect repayment, what credit is that to you? Even "sinners" lend to "sinners", expecting to be repaid in full. But love your enemies, do good to them, and lend to them without expecting to get anything back. Then your reward will be great, and you will be sons of the Most High, because he is kind to the ungrateful and wicked' (Luke 6:32-35).

In other words the Lord is teaching that we should not be quick to speak up for our own rights. We should certainly stand up for the rights of others and do what we can to see that they get a fair deal. But when it comes to our own unjust treatment, Peter says that we should **'bear up under the pain of it'**.

It is a gracious thing for a Christian to **'[bear] up under the pain of unjust suffering'**. The Scriptures teach that God will reward us if we suffer for him; and that is a far better reward than any praise that we can receive from men. In the days when Queen Victoria ruled the British Empire the well-known preacher F. B. Meyer wrote, 'The hero-explorer may be thanked by his country and his Queen; but the weakest and obscurest saint may receive the thanks of the Almighty.'[3]

But there is a danger for the believer, when it comes to suffering unjustly. We can be tempted to behave like martyrs, but we must not. However, we should never have the attitude that implies, 'Look at me. See how I am suffering. Notice the way I put up with my affliction. Observe how humble I am.' The truly humble Christian keeps quiet about his suffering and gladly accepts whatever the Lord allows to come his way. He quietly rejoices because he is counted worthy of participating in the sufferings of Christ' (4:13).

Peter says that the Christian bears up under unjust suffering because **'he is conscious of God'**. Just as God saw the misery of his people in Egypt (Exodus 3:7), so he sees the affliction of his people today. For the Lord to know about a believer's suffering is a blessing for the Christian because he knows that God himself enters into the pain and trial. There was this aspect in the messages sent by Jesus to the seven churches in Asia. He said to the Ephesian church, 'I know your deeds, your hard work and your perseverance' (Revelation 2:2). He said to the church at Smyrna, 'I know your afflictions and your poverty' (Revelation 2:9). And he said to the church in Philadelphia, 'I know that you have little strength, yet you have kept my word and have not denied my name' (Revelation 3:8). J. Oatman Jr wrote,

> Jesus knows all about our struggles,
> He will guide till the day is done:
> There's not a friend like the lowly Jesus,
> No, not one! No, not one!

Peter says that when we suffer punishment we should make sure that it really is for injustice. Suffering is no credit to us if we are being punished for some wrong that we have committed. We should always endeavour to live exemplary lives. If we disobey the law of the land, then it is right that we should suffer for it. We should **'receive a beating for doing wrong'**. This is only right, fair and just. Christians should never expect to be let off anything just because they are followers of Jesus Christ. Some would say that believers should be punished even more severely than non-Christians, because God's people should know better.

Some while ago a British judge was caught driving a car a few yards while under the influence of alcohol. He was given a comparatively small fine but his driving licence was not taken away. This caused an outcry in the press at the time. Many felt that, as an upholder of the law, he should have known better and ought to have received a far heavier sentence than an ordinary member of the public would get.

Christians should be prepared to suffer for doing good. This is commendable. In both verses 19 and 20 Peter uses this word which is translated 'commendable'. It is the word 'grace'. Peter is saying that it is a gracious thing to suffer for the cause of Christ. This is what Christ did. 'Christ suffered for you, leaving you an example, that you should follow in his steps. "He committed no sin, and no deceit was found in his mouth." When they hurled their insults at him, he did not retaliate; when he suffered, he made no threats. Instead, he entrusted himself to him who judges justly. He himself bore our sins in his body on the tree, so that we might die to sins and live for righteousness; by his wounds you have been healed' (2:21-24).

This is the attitude Christians should have towards suffering. This is how we should behave. Ask yourself, 'Does the world treat me badly?' And then remember how it treated Jesus Christ, the Son of God; he received far more punishment than any of his people do. If you endure suffering, this is commendable to God. He knows, he cares, he understands. And he is with you in it all.

15.
Why Christ suffered

Please read 1 Peter 2:21-25

In the previous chapter we thought about how Christian slaves were sometimes called upon to suffer for no good reason; indeed, they quite often suffered unjustly. We examined the teaching on this subject given by both Peter and Paul. We saw that they said that if any Christian is badly treated, even though he has done nothing wrong to deserve this punishment, he must bear it without complaining. That is his Christian calling.

It seems a very strange thing to say that Christians are called upon to suffer, and to be punished when they are not to blame. Yet this is Peter's clear teaching here. To illustrate it the apostle draws our attention to the way in which the Lord was treated.

Christ is our example of suffering

Peter first of all reminds us that all believers have been called by Christ. This means that if we truly know the Lord as our Saviour, then we have been called by him. If we have been called by the Lord, God has done something for us; he has taken the initiative, and his call must be obeyed because he is sovereign. Jesus said that when the shepherd calls his own sheep by name they listen to his voice and follow him. This teaching on God's call runs throughout this letter, and indeed throughout the New Testament. Believers in the Lord Jesus Christ have been born again because they have first of all been 'called by grace'.

In the first verse of this letter Peter describes believers as 'God's elect' (1:1) In the next verse he gives us more details about our calling. He says, we 'have been chosen according to the foreknowledge of God' (1:2) and, because of this gracious act, we are true Christians. God himself has called us to repent of our sin and he has granted us the gift of faith (Ephesians 2:8). We have, therefore, been enabled to cast ourselves upon Christ alone for eternal salvation.

The same theme of calling is taken up in chapter 2. In verse 9 Peter says that we have been 'called ... out of darkness into his [God's] wonderful light'. True believers have been called to leave the darkness of sin and evil. Who does this calling? The triune God, the second person of the Trinity, the one who describes himself as the Light of the world (John 8:12). Peter teaches that all Christians have been called into that wonderful light, and their task in this world is to reflect the glorious light of Christ so that it shines into the darkness which is all around us. That is our calling.

Then in chapter 3:9 Peter says that we are called to respond positively when people treat us badly. 'Do not repay evil with evil or insult with insult, but with blessing, because to this you were called so that you may inherit a blessing.' It is not always easy to remember our calling when we are suffering unjustly; but we should seek to respond in God's way. Believers should always give a blessing in return for an insult, however cruelly they are treated. To behave like this is neither natural nor easy; but it is what we are commanded to do by the Lord himself and, therefore, we should gladly try to do it.

The final time that Peter writes about our calling in this letter is in chapter 5:10. Here we are told that the God of all grace has called us 'to his eternal glory in Christ'. This means that God's people should not worry about how badly people treat them on this earth. They should recall how the Lord was treated. He suffered far worse than any of his followers have done. Believers should look upwards. They should rejoice in the knowledge of the blessing that is in store for all God's blood-bought people. Peter says that we are called to God's 'eternal glory in Christ'.

One of the reasons why Jesus suffered was so that he could be an example to us. When we first learned to write, many of us were given a copy-book. This might have letters printed very lightly on the page (perhaps in feint dots) and our task would be to go over them with our pencils or crayons; we had to trace them, filling in the outline of the letters. In another type of copy-book, a line of very beautiful lettering was printed at the top of each page. We had to use the blank lines which filled up the rest of the page to do our best to copy this copper-plate writing. The words which were written at the top of the page had to be used as a guide. They were our example which we had to follow as best we could.

Victorian schoolteachers did not invent this system. Children were taught by this system 1900 years ago, in the days when Peter wrote this letter. Perhaps the apostle had this in his mind when he wrote, **'Christ suffered for you, leaving you an example, that you should follow in his steps'** (2:21). In other words he was saying, 'When it comes to suffering unjustly just look at Christ. He is the example we should all follow. His life is the one we should try to copy.' Kistemaker puts it like this, 'As a child traces letters on a page, so the Christian traces the path of Christ.'[1]

Peter said that Jesus suffered for us, and we should follow in his steps. How can we follow Jesus, when it comes to suffering? He did not retaliate when they hurled insults at him (2:23); and he made no threats to anyone when they inflicted suffering upon him (2:23).

Another way in which Jesus was an example to us is his uncomplaining nature when he suffered. He kept silent when he was badly treated. When we read verses 21-25 it seems as though we are reading a personal testimony. But how did Peter know that Jesus had insults hurled at him? How did he know that Jesus issued no threats when he had unjust suffering laid upon him? The answer to those questions is found in chapter 5:1, where he described himself as 'a witness of Christ's sufferings'.

This is certainly a fulfilment of Isaiah 53, but we also have Peter's corroboration of the prophecy. Peter could write so definitely because he had seen it all happen. He was there when Jesus was arrested in the Garden of Gethsemane. He was rebuked by Jesus when he raised his sword and cut off the ear of the servant of the high priest (John 18:10-11). He was on the receiving end of Jesus' piercing look when he denied that he knew the Lord while he was in the house of the high priest (Luke 22:61). He knew about the soldiers mocking and beating Jesus while he was awaiting his various trials (Luke 22:63-64). He knew about the awful ridiculing and mocking of Jesus by King Herod and his soldiers (Luke 23:11). He knew about the dreadful flogging of his Lord before Pilate (John 19:1). He knew about the awful weals and wounds made in the body of his Master by those dreadful whips, with their jagged pieces of bones and metal tied into their ends. And he may well have witnessed, from afar off, the crucifixion of the Son of God. No wonder he wrote so graphically, **'When they hurled their insults at him, he did not retaliate; when he suffered, he made no threats.'**

One of the most amazing things about the crucifixion was that Jesus, the Lord of glory, could have escaped it all. He could have called 10,000 angels to his side. He could have reversed the scheming plans of the Jewish religious leaders. He could have caused Pilate to stick to what he knew to be right, and release Jesus as an innocent man. But he did none of these things. **'Instead, he entrusted himself to him who judges justly.'** He committed himself to the tender care of this loving Father. What an example this is to us! It shows us how to behave in the face of unfair and unjust treatment. Christ ought to be our example. We should be those who follow in his footsteps.

When we are badly treated, the best thing that we can do is to entrust ourselves to the mercies of our loving heavenly Father. We should not try to get our own back. Paul said, 'Do not take revenge, my friends, but leave room for God's wrath, for it is written: "It is mine to avenge; I will repay," says the Lord' (Rom. 12:19). God is the Judge of all the earth and 'judges justly'. We can leave our cause in his hands and know that it will be dealt with fairly.

Christ's death was far more than an example of suffering

There is a vast difference between the sufferings of the Lord and any pain that we can ever be called upon to endure. He was sinless. **'He committed no sin, and no deceit was found in his mouth'** (2:22). No one else can measure up to his righteous standards. Like so much in these few verses at the end of this

second chapter, here is another allusion to Isaiah 53. Jesus is
the only person who ever lived who was utterly sinless. If he
were not completely pure then he could not be our Saviour,
because God demands that the only acceptable sacrifice for
sin should be one that is perfect. Jesus Christ meets our need
because he is 'holy, blameless, pure, set apart from sinners,
exalted above the heavens' (Hebrews 7:26).

This verse also speaks of the manner of Jesus' death. Peter
says that Jesus **'bore our sins in his body on the tree'**. The word
translated 'tree' can also mean 'cross'. In Acts 5:30 Peter and
the other apostles addressed the high priest and the Sanhed-
rin. They said, 'The God of our fathers raised Jesus from the
dead — whom you had killed by hanging him on a tree.' And
in Galatians 3:13 Paul quotes from the Old Testament
(Deuteronomy 21:23): 'Christ redeemed us from the curse of
the law by becoming a curse for us, for it is written: "Cursed
is everyone who is hung on a tree."' When he died on the cruel
cross Jesus bore away the sins of each of his people.

We might not think that we have any serious sin, yet we do,
because even the slightest taint of wrong is enough to keep us
out of heaven (Revelation 21:27). Deep down in our consciences we all know that we are sinners. But the problem is that
we do not realize the awfulness of our sin. We cannot take it in
that God, in his perfect holiness, cannot even look upon sin
(Habakkuk 1:13). We do not really believe that if we die without having our sin cleansed, then we are lost for all eternity.

The Jews of old understood very clearly the need for an
atonement to be made for sin. They gave much money and
spent a great deal of effort in bringing many sacrificial lambs
to the temple. They did this year after year. They were so concerned about their sin against the holiness of God that they
would do anything to have their sin washed away. All their
lives they kept up the whole of the temple ritual. They so
feared the wrath of God against sin that they continued to
bring their spotless lambs to be sacrificed. They did this
because they wanted their sins taken away. But they also
realized that their religious offerings were not a permanent
answer to the problem of sin. The blood of bulls and goats did
not actually take away their sins (Hebrews 10:4) and, in any
case, the effect of their offerings only lasted for a short time.

They knew that their temple sacrifices would have to be repeated over and over again.

However, when Jesus died upon the cross, his death was a once-for-all sacrifice for sins. He himself bore our sins in his body so that our sins might be destroyed; the effect of his death is that 'we might be dead to sin'. An accompanying blessing is that we might be given new life in Christ; this means that we should henceforth 'live for righteousness'.

Do you realize that Jesus had to undergo all that pain and suffering to redeem you from the guilt and penalty for your sin? 'The wood of his cross could be put upon another; [but] the weight of sin was his alone to bear.'[2] If you know him as your Lord and Saviour then it is true for you that **'By his wounds you have been healed.'**

Christ's death grants us his loving care

Peter says Jesus is the Shepherd of his sheep. It is in the nature of sheep to wander astray. As sinners we have wandered astray from the paths of God. Isaiah 53:6 says, 'We all, like sheep, have gone astray, each of us has turned to his own way.' But, by dying for us, Jesus the Good Shepherd (John 10), Jesus the Great Shepherd (Heb. 13:20) and Jesus the Chief Shepherd (1 Peter 5:4) calls, feeds and cares for the sheep of his pasture. How wonderful it is to be able to say, with confidence, 'The Lord is my shepherd'! (Psalm 23:1).

Peter says that those who repent of their sin and come to Christ for salvation are like sheep returning to their shepherd.

Peter also says that Jesus is the overseer of his people's souls. When we come to Jesus for salvation he grants us many blessings. He calls us to himself. He bears away our sins. He enables us to die to sin. (That means that he gives us the desire to learn to hate sin and to turn away from it. This is a very difficult thing to do and it involves a life-time of sanctification.) Jesus also gives us new life, and grants us the desire to live for righteousness. He receives us when we come to him, or, if we have backslidden, when we return to him. He is a shepherd to us, and he is an overseer or guardian for us.

The Authorized Version translates verse 25: you 'are now

returning to the Shepherd and Bishop of your souls'. Commenting upon this verse, Wayne Detzler says that Christ is not like a bishop 'who sits in a palace and makes semi-royal visitation, but [he is] an overseer who supervises the life and work of believers as they labour for the Lord'.[3]

Our blessed Lord cares for his people and guides them throughout the whole of their lives. The writer of the Epistle to the Hebrews encourages Christians by saying, 'Let us fix our eyes on Jesus, the author and perfecter of our faith, who for the joy set before him endured the cross, scorning its shame, and sat down at the right hand of the throne of God. Consider him who endured such opposition from sinful men, so that you will not grow weary and lose heart' (Hebrews 12:2-3).

16.
The responsibilities of wives

Please read 1 Peter 3:1-6

At the beginning of chapter 3 we have six verses which are directed particularly to wives. Peter has been writing to various groups of people telling them that they must be submissive to others in their attitude, and by the way in which they behave. In chapter 2:13 we saw that Peter was telling all Christians that they must submit themselves to 'every authority instituted among men'. In 2:18 he instructs Christian slaves to submit themselves to their masters; they must do this whether their owners are treating them well or badly.

Now, in 3:1-6, he tells Christian wives to be submissive to their husbands. The apostle says that they are to behave like this 'in the same way' that Christian believers are submissive to their governments and Christian slaves are to obey their masters.

Witnesses of the Christian message

What was the background to Peter's remarks about wives needing to submit themselves to their husbands? Most of the wives who had a problem over this question had recently become Christians. In Roman society it was the accepted thing that a wife should always have the same religion as her husband. This was felt necessary for the sake of order in each home; it was consistent with the Roman view of government. Everything in the whole of society should be neat and tidy.

The outcome of this practice was that if a Roman husband

became a Christian then it automatically followed that his
wife should abandon her old religion and 'take on board' all
the teachings of Christianity. However, if it was the wife who
became a Christian, while her husband remained a pagan,
then a difficulty arose. The husband would see this change in
his wife's religion as a threat to his authority as head of the
household. It was the husband's prerogative to decide which
religion the family should follow. He would reason something
like this: 'There are many different beliefs to choose from
here in the Roman world. You can worship as many gods as
you have time for, so why not add your worship of Jesus to the
religion which our family adopts?'

The thing that the unbelieving husband would find difficult
to understand would be the exclusive nature of Christianity.
If Roman religion allowed the worship of as many gods as a
person liked, why did Christianity insist on only one? The
unconverted husband would have a problem with the teaching of Jesus because the Lord declared, 'I am *the way* and *the
truth* and *the life*. No one comes to the Father *except through
me*' (John 14:6). This teaching would be hard for a Roman
husband to accept (in the same way as it seems to present
problems for many 'modern' churchmen today).

It is this difficulty that Peter is dealing with in these six verses. He outlines the situation by writing about a husband who
did **'not believe the word'**. He means the gospel message when
he refers to 'the word'. Obviously one of the first things a
newly converted wife would do would be to witness to her
husband about Jesus and his love for sinners. Her husband
might listen to the reasons for her change of religion, but it
was very likely that he would turn his back upon it; he would
refuse to believe the gospel. What should a Christian wife do
about a husband who would not believe the word?

In the first place we notice that Peter does not say, 'Ignore
him. He's had his chance to believe and he has turned his back
upon Christ. Make no more attempts to witness to him.' Secondly, Peter implies that a believing wife should not 'nag' her
husband. What he says in effect, is 'Instead of nagging him to
Christ, [you] should love him to Christ.'[1]

This is only one of the things that Peter means when he says
that wives should be submissive to their husbands. He writes,
'If any of them [the husbands] **do not believe the word** [then]

they may be won over without words [or talk], **by the behaviour of their wives, when they see the purity and reverence of your lives'** (3:1-2).

It is important to notice that Peter does not say that 'They may be won over without *the* word.' Christian wives with unconverted (or backsliding) husbands should certainly use the Word of God to speak to their spouses. However, they should also know when to keep quiet. But all the time they should seek to live a life which displays the beauty of Christ. This holy life would be likely to attract the unbelieving husband to the Saviour.

When we read these verses we are reminded that it is dangerous for a Christian to marry someone who is not a believer. Paul gives a clear command when he says, 'Do not be yoked together with unbelievers' (1 Corinthians 6:14). This is all right when the person is not yet married but what should a woman do if she is converted to Christ after she has married? Should she leave her husband because he is not a Christian? Paul says, in 1 Corinthians 7:13, 'If a woman [already] has a husband who is not a believer and he is willing to live with her [even though she is a Christian, then] she must not divorce him.' To God the marriage relationship is very precious and it should not be dispensed with easily, but naturally it is so much better if husband and wife can be 'one in the Lord'.

Declaring the beauty of Christ

Not only should Christian wives seek to win their unconverted husbands to Christ by living holy lives, but they must also be careful how they dress.

Christian wives should not set out to draw attention to themselves. Peter speaks of the worldly 'beauty' of those days. He writes about the **'outward adornment'** of women. He means that the cosmetic additions of the world should not be the things that matter most to women. 'The "outward adorning" is the Greek word *kosmos,* from which we get the word cosmetics.'[2]

Women in Roman times spent many hours producing ornate hairstyles, which often had gold and silver jewellery plaited into them to hold the marvellous 'creation' together. The acquisition of elaborate jewellery for the woman's body, as well as for her hair, would cost a great deal of money. Also her display of fine clothing would probably cause a stir when others saw her wearing an expensive dress, which was in the latest fashion.

Peter does not seem to be favourably impressed with this slavery to fashion. It would have taken a great deal of time to dress in keeping with the then current trends. (It still does sometimes today.) It would have cost a great deal of money to purchase the necessary adornment for a well-turned out lady of Roman society. (It can still do so today.) Besides it would be likely to provoke a great deal of admiration (or jealousy) when others saw it. We all know of the fuss which is sometimes caused at weddings and other functions, when a lady turns up wearing a dress in the same material and of the same design as someone else!

What does all of this mean for Christian wives today? Is Peter saying that Christian wives should look frumpish? Does he mean that Christian women should take no care over their appearance? Is he saying that it is always wrong for believers to spend time and money on perms or jewellery or clothing? I do not believe that the argument that Peter is using here can be interpreted like that. He is not giving a complete ban on make-up and beautiful clothing.

What he is speaking about in this passage is the great danger that can happen if a woman becomes obsessive about fashion. He is speaking about an over-indulgence in these things. One door-to-door seller of cosmetics, who called at my house on our council estate, told me that she took orders of between £250-£300 each month! Peter is saying something like this: 'You should always try to look nice, but make sure that you get your motives right.'

This means that no Christian woman should set out to make herself attractive just to tease other men. Neither should any Christian wife set out solely to please her husband. Wuest says of the Roman wives, 'These women were making the mistake of thinking that if they dressed as the world dressed it would please their unsaved husbands, and the latter would be influenced to trust the Lord Jesus as Saviour. It is true that they would be pleased — pleased because the appearance of their wives appealed to their totally depraved natures and pleased because the Christian testimony of their wives was nullified by their appearance.'[3]

Every Christian woman should have it as her motive to please God in everything she does, says and thinks (and the same goes for men, too). Peter implies that one day 'hair, jewellery and fine clothes' will all perish. What Peter is writing about is something which is far more precious, something which is unfading (like the inheritance of God's people in 1:4). He said that the beauty of God's people should be that of 'their inner selves' (3:4). When we think of real beauty we should remember what God said to Samuel when he sent him to anoint a new king for Israel: 'The Lord does not look at the things man looks at. Man looks at the outward appearance, but the Lord looks at the heart' (1 Samuel 16:7).

What does Peter say about our inner selves? He implies that for Christian men, as well as women, what should be inside of us is **'the unfading beauty of a gentle and quiet spirit'**. The word translated 'gentle' is only used a few times in the New Testament. Mostly it describes the attitude of Jesus. But in Galatians 5:22 it speaks of the way in which Christians ought to live their lives. There 'gentleness' is listed as one of the fruits of the Spirit.

Each Christian should ask himself, 'Is the Holy Spirit so active in my life that I am being made gentle?' Paul prays for the Ephesian believers that '[God] may strengthen you with power through his Spirit in your inner being' (Ephesians 3:16). Do we have a kindly, caring attitude to others? Are we those who do not insist on our own rights? Grudem says that 'If we are gentle we are not pushy, not selfishly assertive, not demanding our own way.'[4] If we have a gentle and quiet spirit then our attitude will be seen as something which is beautiful to other people (and certainly to the husbands of believing wives). That gentle and quiet spirit is, most importantly of all, **'of great worth in God's sight'** (3:4).

There is an old chorus which we used to sing in Sunday school years ago. It is in the form of a prayer and it sums up the attitude that God's people ought to be seeking:

Let the beauty of Jesus be seen in me,

All his wondrous compassion and purity,
Oh, thou Spirit divine,
All my nature refine,
'Till the beauty of Jesus be seen in me.[5]

The example of holy women from the past

Peter alludes to all those godly women in the Old Testament
who put their hope in God. There are many holy women that
we can read about in the Scriptures. They were sometimes
called 'mothers in Israel'. That means that these holy women
lived out their lives with the sole aim of honouring God. They
set an example to the other women as to how they should conduct themselves. And one of the ways they did this was by
being submissive to their husbands.

Peter cites the example of Sarah and Abraham. She obeyed
her husband and called him master. Does Peter mean that
Christian wives should bow and scrape to their husbands
today? Do the Scriptures teach that wives should behave like
that in these times of Women's Lib.? No. Peter is using an
example. Sarah was submissive to Abraham in accordance
with the customs of her day. It would certainly cause Christians to be a laughing-stock if wives were to behave like that
in our day and age. How did Sarah show her submission to
Abraham? She accepted that he was responsible to take the
decisions in their family life.

How does that apply to us today? The Scriptures nowhere
teach that wives are inferior to their husbands. However, the
New Testament does teach that husbands and wives have different roles to fulfil. Galatians 3:28 speaks of the equality of
male and female in Christ, and 1 Peter 3:7 tells husbands and
wives that they are 'heirs together of the grace of life' (AV).
Christian wives should take Sarah as their example in their
relationship to their husbands. They should **'do what is right'**
(3:6). That means that they should obey God first of all, and
also that they should support their husbands in everything
that they do, provided that it is wholesome and good. Finally,
they should **'not give way to fear'** (3:6). Wayne Grudem sums
it up like this: 'A woman with a "gentle and quiet spirit" who

"continues hoping in God" will not be terrified by circumstances or by an unbelieving or disobedient husband.'[6]

It is not only wives who can benefit from this advice. All of us need to see that our inner life is right with God and that we are displaying 'the unfading beauty of a gentle and quiet spirit'.

17.
The responsibilities of husbands

Please read 1 Peter 3:7

Several times I have heard various ladies complain about their pastor's treatment of passages such as this one. One of them said to me on one occasion, 'Our pastor preached at great length on the duties of wives; once he preached a whole series of sermons on the role of women in the church and in the home. Then when he came to deal with the responsibilities of men, he just dismissed them with a few remarks at the end of one of the sermons on women.'

I nearly made the same mistake. When you read the opening of 1 Peter 3 you notice that Peter, like Paul, devotes a great deal of space to the women's responsibilities, and only tacks on to the end of the passage a few words about how men ought to behave towards their wives. When I prepared the chapter on wives, I noticed that Peter spent six verses on women and only one on men. So I thought I would not spend too much time on the duties of husbands and merely add on a few remarks regarding them at the end of that chapter, until I thought more deeply about the subject. Then I saw that there is a great deal here which is of vital importance, and just because it does not occupy much space in 1 Peter 3, that does not mean that we can hurry over the subject.

One day my wife was turning out her cookery magazines and, knowing I was soon to reach the subject of the responsibility of husbands in my Sunday morning preaching, she passed on to me a page from *Home and Freezer Digest* which was headed 'Men according to women'. Here are some of the things which women sent up to that magazine about their views on their husbands. They said, 'Men are different because they lose things and ask you what you've done with them. They take shirts off without undoing the buttons. They take jumpers off by yanking at the back of the neck. They insist they can pack a car boot/suitcase better than you. They think that sport is news. They wash up — but leave the sink dirty. They think houses are self-cleaning and fridges self-replenishing. And they don't cook unless it's a barbecue — which is macho.' So what does Peter say about husbands?

Respect for wives

Husbands are exhorted to treat their wives with respect. The word translated **'respect'** carries with it the idea of honour and preciousness. A husband should always respect his wife. Why is this? Because he has been given his wife by his father-in-law. When her father gave his daughter away he entrusted her to the care of his new son-in-law, and the new husband accepted that responsibility. From that moment onwards he has to look after his wife as her father and mother once did.

Even if the husband did not receive his wife from the hand of her father, if he is a Christian then he should always show proper respect to everyone (2:17). And if that is how he should treat people whom he does not know particularly well, then how much greater respect should he give to his wife! In other words, he should never take her for granted. He should never treat her merely as a servant or a play-thing.

A Christian husband should remember that his wife is precious. This means that he is to respect and honour her as someone who is very valuable. Whenever the television *Mastermind* trophy is presented at the final of that TV quiz programme I always think, 'Wouldn't it be terrible if that beautiful glass bowl were to be dropped?' Peter says that husbands should respect and care for their wives in the same way. Like her husband, the wife is one of those living stones which are being built into the spiritual house for God's glory (2:5); and as Jesus is precious to the believer (2:7) so a wife should be precious to her husband (3:7).

The apostle goes on to explain how Christian husbands are to treat their wives with respect. They are to do so by being

considerate to them. Wives are exhorted to obey their husbands. Peter has said that they are to be submissive to them
(3:1). Therefore, they should always talk in a respectful way
about their husbands. This does not mean that they will never
have disagreements with each other, but these should always
be in private; they should never be aired publicly. Otherwise
the wife is undermining her husband's position as head of the
household.

Consideration for wives

Husbands should be considerate of their wives. They should
consider their *views* on all things. The husband is the head of
the household and the wife must submit to him. But the husband is not always right. Christian husbands should listen to
the views of their wives, and be prepared to adjust their own
ideas in the light of what their wives say.

Husbands should also consider their wives' *feelings*. A husband who truly loves his wife will be considerate of how she
feels. He will not make demands on her which are unreason-
able. Colossians 3:19 says, 'Husbands, love your wives and do
not be harsh with them.' A husband will not force his wife to
do something which she does not particularly like. He will
always take into account her emotions and her desires before
he makes a decision which affects the whole family.

Husbands should remember that women are the weaker
partners in marriage. This does not mean that the wives are
inferior in status. Galatians 3:28 says, 'There is neither ...
male nor female, for you are all one in Christ Jesus.' It does
not mean that women are weaker in intellect. It does not
mean that women are weaker in their ability to plan and
organize things. It is not only in modern times that women
have become successful business people. Listen to this:

> 'A wife of noble character ...
>   selects wool and flax
>   and works with eager hands.
> She is like the merchant ships,
>   bringing her food from afar.
> She gets up while it is still dark;

she provides food for her family
and portions for her servant girls.
She considers a field and buys it;
out of her earnings she plants a vineyard.
She sets about her work vigorously;
her arms are strong for her tasks.
She sees that her trading is profitable,
and her lamp does not go out at night.
In her hand she holds the distaff
and grasps the spindle with her fingers'
(Prov. 31:10, 13-19).

So what does Peter mean when he says wives are the weaker partner? It seems to mean that, by and large, women are weaker physically — and also sometimes emotionally. 'Wives are often more likely to be hurt deeply by conflict in their marriage or by inconsiderate behaviour on the part of the husband.'[1] And therefore, this is a further reason why husbands should treat their wives with respect.

Notice that Peter does not say that wives are weak. He says, **'Treat them with respect as the weaker partner.'** Archbishop Leighton put it like this, 'The husband, who is generally ... the stronger, yet is weak too; for both are vessels of earth, and therefore frail; both polluted with sin, and therefore subject to the multitude of sinful follies and frailties.'[2]

Peter also says that husbands should live with their wives. This does not mean that husbands should never be absent on business. Sometimes it does happen that husband and wife are parted for a while, but this should never be by design; it should only be of necessity. It should never be a relief to be separated from one another, but rather it ought to be an unavoidable pain which should be put right at the earliest possible moment.

A husband should never find the company of others more congenial than the company of his wife. A husband should want to spend as much time with his wife as possible. Work should not be more important, nor more interesting than his home life. The company of friends should not be more enjoyable than the company of wife and children. The pursuit of hobbies or social activities should not be more valuable than the time which is spent at home. John Brown says of a wife, 'Her presence will make [her husband's] own mansion, however humble, far more agreeable to him than any other which he may occasionally visit.'[3]

Finally, the phrase **'live with your wives'** has the same meaning as 'to know' in the Old Testament. In other words, it means to show and to give love. A husband is to be considerate of his wife and to respect her when it comes to the most intimate moments of love in marriage.

A lovely picture of the biblical relationship between husbands and wives is found in Ephesians 5:23, 25-26: 'The husband is the head of the wife as Christ is the head of the church, his body, of which he is the Saviour ... Husbands, love your wives, just as Christ loved the church and gave himself up for her to make her holy, cleansing her by the washing with water through the word.' Hendriksen describes this love as 'spontaneous and self-sacrificing'.[4] This is how husbands are to love their wives. Husbands are to love their wives, 'just as Christ loved the church and gave himself up for her' when he died upon the cross at Calvary.

The gracious gift of life

Marriage is a partnership. It should not be one where each goes his or her own way. Obviously one partner might well have some interest which does not capture the imagination of the other. But, by and large, husband and wife should demonstrate their unity and their partnership in marriage.

Each has a special function to perform in the partnership. Usually the husband is the better handyman about the home, and the wife is better at the more domestic duties. But that does not mean that they cannot share one another's responsibilities. In our home, generally speaking, whoever gets in first cooks the evening meal.

Marriage is a partnership with an aim in view. The Authorized Version says, we are 'heirs together of the grace of life'. This life on earth can be very enjoyable. It is a joy to have the company of a loving husband or wife; and when they are taken from us in death then it is a strength to be able to look back to so many happy times spent together. It is a joy to bring up children and to see them making good progress in life. But the greatest joy of all is to realize that together we are heading towards the joy of heaven. Life here is nothing compared with the joy that awaits those who trust in Jesus for salvation. Eternal life is not just something which goes on for ever and ever. If it were, then the question, 'Won't you get bored there?' would be valid. But life eternal is to know and see Jesus face to face — to enter into the joy and wonder of his presence. By writing 'the gracious gift of life', Peter is not just thinking about the joy that children bring; he means the joy of life eternal which awaits every believer in the Lord Jesus Christ.

The blessing of praying together

There is an old saying which has a great deal of truth in it: 'The family that prays together stays together.' Those who have the privilege of family relationship should highly value their times of prayer together. Barbieri says, 'Partnership in the physical realm will produce children, and partnership in the spiritual realm will produce answered prayers.'[5]

Prayer is very important in anyone's life. If we are not in close touch with our Creator and Redeemer, then our life will be very barren. If husband and wife are not able to approach the Lord together in unity then somewhere there is a serious lack of commitment to one another. If a husband does not treat his wife with proper consideration and respect, and a wife does not submit herself to her husband as head of the family, then prayer will go unanswered.

If a husband fails to shoulder the responsibilities as head of the household and the wife always 'wears the trousers' then, not only is there disharmony in the home, but this lack of unity will 'hinder [their] prayers'.

How important it is for us all — husbands, wives, widows, single people or children — to move together as the family of God seeking God's face in prayer and living to please him in all that we do, say and think!

18.
The ideal church fellowship

Please read 1 Peter 3:8-12

We have been seeing how various groups of believers ought to behave in relation to others. Now we come to a summing up of the way in which God's people should react to each other and also how they ought to behave towards their enemies.

Many a young soldier has boasted that he was not going to have any fear in the heat of conflict. He saw only the glory of war and he genuinely looked forward to being able to lead his men into the battle. But when the time comes, and the dreadful slaughter begins, all his courageous words start to turn to jelly. He is a very different person when he is actually 'under fire'!

So it is with some Christians. They are full of advice for others. They speak of what they will do and what they will not allow others to do, but when they find themselves criticized, when things do not go in the way they have planned, then their bold words prove to have a hollow ring about them.

We need to be very careful in our behaviour towards others; otherwise we could easily find ourselves acting in an un-Christlike way. Wayne Detzler gives the example of the difference between a prayer meeting and church business meeting. He says, 'It is so easy for us to appear humble in a prayer meeting, but church members' meetings with their uninhibited debate often strip saints of pretended humility.'[1]

This section starts, **'Finally, all of you'**. Peter does not mean that he is coming to the end of his letter. He means that he is summing up this section, which started at 2:11. He began this part of his letter by addressing all believers. Then he gave particular instructions to specific groups of people, and now he draws it to a conclusion by saying, 'Finally, all of you'.

How Christians should act towards each other

Peter details five ways in which Christians are to behave in regard to their fellow believers. In verse 8 we see true ecumenicity outlined. If we all followed the teaching of this verse to the letter, then we would have genuine Christian unity in action.

First of all, he says that believers are to **'live in harmony with one another'**. Ths does not mean that we are all to be the same in every way. If that happened there would not be harmony but unison. When we talk about harmony in music we do not mean that everyone has to sing or play the same note at the same time. This is quite acceptable in short passages of music but if it carries on throughout the whole score then it would almost certainly sound monotonous long before the end was reached.

Until recently the modern ecumenical movement behaved as though Christians were all the same. They are not, nor are they expected to be. The differences among us bring out the richness of Christian fellowship. When a Christian church is made up of believers from many different backgrounds then there can be a beautiful fulness as each one blends together in the life of the church. In the church of which I am pastor, at the time of writing, we have thirty-six members, about two-thirds of whom are drawn from nine different denominational backgrounds — plus about a third who have had no previous church affiliation. This adds a great richness to our fellowship. I cannot remember ever hearing the phrase which is sometimes heard in churches, 'We've never done it that way before.'

Paul illustrates the way in which Christian fellowships should work by drawing from the example of the human body. He says that the body is a picture of how the church should be — a unity made up of many parts, all vastly different from one another, yet each one blending together in a unity (see 1 Corinthians 12:12).

Despite the fact that we are not all the same in our

appearance and our ideas, we are all meant to 'live in harmony with one another'. How can we attempt this very difficult task? We can try to carry it out by seeking to have the mind of Christ. 'Peter ... wants Christians to be governed by the mind of Christ, so that differences do not divide but rather enrich the Church.'[2] Paul said, '[Be] likeminded, having the same love, being one in spirit and purpose' (Philippians 2:2). Paul also said that God's people should display the attitude that Jesus had to suffering on the cross. He said, 'Let this mind be in you, which was also in Christ Jesus' (Philippians 2:5 AV). Also the beautiful hymn of Kate B. Wilkinson says,

> May the mind of Christ my Saviour,
>   Live in me from day to day.
> By his love and power controlling
>   All I do and say.

Secondly, Peter says that God's people should be **'sympathetic'**. Christians are to be concerned people. So often we are greatly concerned about ourselves — concerned about our own welfare, or that of our loved ones. But if we only have any real interest in the things that affect us (or our own Christian circle), then we are no better than unbelievers. We are exhibiting that worldly attitude of selfishness. The material, physical and spiritual welfare of others ought to be of great concern to us.

Christians are to be those who always seek to follow the example of Jesus. Hebrews 4:15 tells us that 'We do not have a high priest who is unable to sympathize with our weaknesses.' This means that Jesus knows all about us, and he enters into our sufferings with us. Christians are likewise to enter into the sufferings and the joys of other people. Paul told the Romans, 'Rejoice with those who rejoice; mourn with those who mourn' (Romans 12:15). And, in using the picture of the church as a human body, Paul says, 'If one part suffers, every part suffers with it; if one part is honoured, every part rejoices with it' (1 Corinthians 12:26).

Do people outside of the Christian church recognize us as those who sympathize with our neighbours' misfortunes? Or are we those who say, 'I won't help her; she never does anything to help me?' How do we show our sympathy? Sometimes words carry little meaning, if we do not engage in the practical deeds which show that we really mean what we say.

Thirdly, Christians are to **'love as brothers'**. Peter had already written about this in 1:22. There he said that we should 'have sincere love for [our] brothers'. He goes on to say that we should 'love one another deeply, from the heart'. This is one of the keynotes of the Christian faith. Paul says to the Roman Christians, 'Be devoted to one another in brotherly love' (Romans 12:10). He tells the Thessalonians that they have been taught by God to love each other (1 Thessalonians 4:9-10). And the writer to the Hebrews declares, 'Keep on loving each other as brothers' (Hebrews 13:1). Kistemaker writes that 'The Greek term is general, so it includes both brothers and sisters in God's household.'[3]

This call to love one another does not mean that we have to agree with everything that our fellow believers do and say. But it does mean that we should love them — and show love to them. There may well be some things that are done in the name of evangelicalism which seem, to us, to be contrary to the sense of Scripture, and unwise. Yet we must pray for our brothers and sisters in Christ and show love to them — even if we disagree with the way in which they are going about the preaching of the gospel. Paul said, even of those who preached Christ insincerely, 'The important thing is that in every way, whether from false motives or true, Christ is preached. And because of this I rejoice' (Philippians 1:18).

Fourthly, believers are to be **'compassionate'** in their dealings with each other. They are to be tender-hearted towards one another. That is not the same as being 'soft-hearted'. A soft-hearted person is one who does not have all his wits about him. A soft-hearted person is one who is easily fooled — he is 'soft in the head'. To be tender-hearted is something quite different. It is to be 'affectionately sensitive, quick to feel and show affection'.[4]

In these days, when our television screens are filled with terrible pain and cruelty, it is so easy to become immune to it all. We behave as though these terrible things do not happen. This is not the spirit of Christ. Christians ought always to have a tender heart towards those in need.

Fifthly, Christians are to be **'humble'**. This is something which Peter speaks about several times. The Greeks regarded humility as a stupid thing. They did not see any virtue in being humble. They wanted to be assertive all the time. Courage was what really mattered to them! If anyone was humble he was showing weakness as far as the Greeks were concerned. But Jesus displayed humility and taught that his followers should be humble people. He said, 'I am gentle and humble in heart' (Matthew 11:29). In the upper room it was he who took the towel and basin (the task of a servant) and washed his disciples' feet (John 13:4-5).

This was the spirit taught by Peter. In chapter 5 he speaks to young men about humility. He says, 'Clothe yourselves with humility towards one another' (5:6). In the same verse he says, 'Humble yourselves ... under God's mighty hand.' 'Others can humiliate us, but only we can humble ourselves.'[5]

Charles Swindoll said in one of his radio services, 'You can fake love, you can fake patience, you can fake tolerance, you can fake wealth or poverty but you cannot fake humility.' 'Humility is the fairest flower that blooms; but display it once and it withers into pride.' 'There is no way you can write a book called, *How I achieved humility,* or a sequel entitled, *How I regained humility.*'

How Christians should behave towards their enemies

Peter says, **'Do not repay evil with evil or insult with insult, but with blessing, because to this you were called so that you may inherit a blessing'** (3:9). Jesus had already taught this in the Sermon on the Mount. There he said, 'Love your enemies and pray for those who persecute you' (Matthew 5:44). Alan Stibbs wrote, 'We shall enter increasingly into the full enjoyment of the blessing of God's forgiveness and good will only if we learn ourselves to extend similar forgiveness and good will to others.'[6] How did Jesus behave when his enemies attacked him? 'When they hurled their insults at him, he did not retaliate; when he suffered, he made no threats. Instead he entrusted himself to him who judges justly' (2:23).

Peter ends this section by quoting from Psalm 34. In these verses we have a prescription for a happy life. But Peter is not saying that those who obey these injunctions will be rewarded with the gift of eternal life. This passage is addressed to believers and is sound advice to all those Christians who **'would love life and see good days'**.

On many occasions, in both Testaments, we are bidden to use our tongues wisely. James 3:6 tells us that the tongue is a world of evil, and without proper constraint it will destroy both those who speak and those who listen. Christians must be true to their word and be free from falsehood and deceit.

However, it is not only the word, but the deed of the believer which is to be wholesome. He must avoid even the appearance of evil (1 Thessalonians 5:22) and remember that peace can easily be broken; it must not be taken for granted. We must actively seek it and pursue it, and live at peace with all men (Romans 12:18). Believers should always remember that the eyes of the Lord are on the righteous. He is watching over them.

Peter also reminds his readers that God's ears are attentive to his people's prayer. They are not alone in their suffering; their heavenly Father hears them. And God's face is against those who do evil; he sees everything that is happening.

So what should we do when evil hangs over us? (The word **'evil'** appears three times in the quotation in verses 10-12.) God's people should trust him, and leave everything to his care and keeping.

> **'Whoever would love life**
> **and see good days**
> **must keep his tongue from evil**
> **and his lips from deceitful speech.**
> **He must turn from evil and do good;**
> **he must seek peace and pursue it.**
> **For the eyes of the Lord are on the righteous**
> **and his ears are attentive to their prayer,**
> **but the face of the Lord is against those who do evil'**
>
> (3:10-12).

19.
Submitting to suffering

Please read 1 Peter 3:13-17

Why am I here on this earth? This is a question that many thoughtful people ask themselves. It seems as though we live our lives 'as a tale that is told' (Psalm 90:9 AV).

> 'The length of our days is seventy years —
>   or eighty, if we have the strength;
> yet their span is but trouble and sorrow,
>   for they quickly pass, and we fly away'
>
> (Psalm 90:10).

The psalmist says, 'We finish our years with a moan' (Psalm 90:9). What, then, is the point of life?

Some people answer the question by saying, 'I am here to do good to others.' This is an excellent reason for the purpose of our existence. If our purpose in life is to be **'eager to do good'** (3:13) then what have we to fear?

Peter has just quoted from Psalm 34: 'The face of the Lord is against those who do evil' (3:12). Now he poses the question, **'Who is going to harm you if you are eager to do good?'** And the answer must be: 'No one — or very few people.'

But life is not always as simple and clear-cut as that. Evil people lurk everywhere, especially where you do not expect them; and they seek to trap God's people in any way they can. Take the question of suffering, for instance.

The Christian attitude to suffering

Suffering will come even to real Christians. God's people do often suffer. Sometimes we think of suffering purely in regard to illness. Christians do not escape sickness. It comes upon them, as it attacks all kinds of people — good and bad alike. God does not just send illness to those who, from our point of view, deserve it. He sometimes allows people to suffer who have been kind and thoughtful all their lives.

For the Christian there can be a positive side to suffering. Suffering often brings great blessing with it, and blessing means real deep-down joy. One Christian believer in our fellowship said, 'My Lord suffered so much for me, why shouldn't I suffer for his sake?' The afflicted Christian can often witness more effectively to his or her faith than the person who is always hale and hearty.

Suffering throws life, with its joys and sorrows, into perspective. Some people say that the music of composers who endured a great deal of suffering is very much richer than that of those who had a smooth pathway through life. Maybe this is the reason why I find the works of Beethoven and Mozart far more moving than those of Mendelssohn, who counted Queen Victoria and Prince Albert among his friends.

David Cook says, 'Suffering ... is an opportunity to do good. This means that it creates the possibility of serving and helping others. It gives opportunity to show the love of Christ ... Often clergy, who visit those who are suffering extreme pain, come away talking of a sense of peace and glory there. They feel that the sufferer has been more help to them than they have been to the sufferer. It is an opportunity for God to be with us in our suffering.'[1]

Peter says, **'Even if you should suffer for what is right, you are blessed'** (3:14). Possibly he means that it does not seem likely that such trouble would come upon those to whom he was writing — but maybe it would. Perhaps he is saying this in such a diffident way in order to reflect their lack of concern about the danger of their facing persecution. Perhaps he wants to prepare them for something they are not expecting. But, whatever the reason, he wants them to be prepared for suffering.

All through the letter he has been hinting at the coming of

persecution of believers by unbelievers (1:6; 2:12, 15, 19; 3:1,
9). Now he goes into details of how the believers should meet
this affliction. He says, 'Whatever happens, you are going to
be blessed — provided that you suffer for righteousness'
sake.' In 3:17 he says with bluntness, **'It is better, if it is God's
will, to suffer for doing good than for doing evil.'**

He seems to be reminding them of the words of Jesus in the
Sermon on the Mount, a sermon which he himself had heard
Jesus utter: 'Blessed are those who are persecuted because of
righteousness, for theirs is the kingdom of heaven. Blessed
are you when people insult you, persecute you and falsely say
all kinds of evil against you because of me. Rejoice and be
glad, because great is your reward in heaven, for in the same
way they persecuted the prophets who were before you'
(Matthew 5:10-12).

Then Peter quotes from Isaiah 8:12: 'Do not fear what they
fear, and do not dread it.' In the days when Isaiah said those
words the inhabitants of Jerusalem were scared stiff. They
had been dreading an invasion from the Assyrians. They had
heard about the terrible cruelty these people inflicted upon
their captives. And their minds were filled with nothing but
dread of their enemies. It was just then that Isaiah received
this word from the Lord.

What does this verse mean? The word **'fear'** can mean, 'be
afraid,' or 'hold in holy reverence and respect'.

Isaiah looked at those cringing, frightened inhabitants of
Jerusalem and he received this from the Lord — both a negative and postive word. He said, 'Do not fear what they fear,
and do not dread it' (negative).' The Lord Almighty is the one
you are to regard as holy' (positive). The negative meaning is
the one which we normally associate with the word 'fear'. The
positive aspect is the same as what we declare when we say in
the Lord's Prayer, 'Hallowed be your name' (Matthew 6:9).

Peter takes up Isaiah's words and applies them to Christians in the present gospel age. He says, 'There is no need to
be afraid.' Who is going to harm you? The devil will try. But
if you trust in the Lord he will protect you. After these words
he says, **'In your hearts set apart Christ as Lord.'** He means
that the Lord Almighty who spoke to Isaiah is exactly the
same holy one as the Lord Christ. The apostle says, in effect,
'Just as Isaiah regarded the Lord as holy, so you are to

sanctify Christ in your hearts as Lord.' As the heart is the centre of your personality and being, so Christ should be set apart to rule and reign there as your Lord, Master and King.

Carolyn M. Noel, in her hymn, 'At the name of Jesus', puts it like this:

> In your hearts enthrone him,
> There let him subdue
> All that is not holy,
> All that is not true.

The privilege of witnessing for Christ

There will come times when our faith in Christ will be challenged. Peter says that believers should be prepared for that. How are believers to be ready for testing times? First of all, people who claim to be Christians must be those who know the saving grace of the Lord Jesus Christ in their hearts. That means we should make certain that we have repented of our sin and cast ourselves upon the Lord. We cannot help anyone else in a spiritual way until we are sure of our own salvation. Secondly, we can be prepared for coming affliction by making sure that we are living in a right relationship with the Lord. That means that we should have a healthy prayer life and a genuine concern that our lives are being lived in accordance with God's will. Thirdly, we can be prepared by knowing the gospel itself. We should know why we have been saved. We should be able to explain to other people how we know we are saved for all eternity, and we should be able to lead others to faith in Christ. Finally, we should be prepared for suffering by being able to give a reason for the Christian hope which is within us.

Paul often had to give a defence of Christ before his accusers (Acts 22:1; 25:16; 1 Corinthians 9:3; Philippians 1:16). We, too, should be ready to speak up for Jesus. Peter says we should **'*always* be prepared to give an answer to *everyone* who asks [us] to give the reason for the hope that [we] have'**.

The hope of the gospel is not something airy-fairy and vague. We do not have a 'hope-so' religion. If we truly know Christ as our Saviour then we have a 'know-so' salvation. The

Christian hope is something which is firm and sure. In 1 Corinthians 13 Paul spoke of three Christian virtues: faith, hope and love. And the writer to the Hebrews says, 'Let us hold unswervingly to the hope we profess' (Hebrews 10:23). Ernst Hoffman describes the Christian hope as 'patient, disciplined, confident waiting for and expectation of the Lord as our Saviour'.[2]

However, under what kind of circumstances might we be called upon to 'give a reason for the hope' that we have? It may be that an official tribunal will some day call us before it to explain our Christian beliefs. There are those who are militantly atheistic in the world today. Professor A. J. Ayre once said, 'My God, my God, I shall die a happy man if I can make one person disbelieve in God.'[3]

But it is more likely that Peter was referring to those occasions when Christians are challenged by ordinary people to explain their belief in Christ as their Lord and Saviour. Wayne Grudem says, 'The inward hope of Christians results in lives so noticeably different that unbelievers are prompted to ask why they are so distinctive.'[4] Later in the letter Peter writes about unbelievers who challenge Christians about their holy living. He says, 'They think it strange that you do not plunge with them into the same flood of dissipation, and they heap abuse on you' (4:4). But God's Word says that Christians should be different from the people of the world. To live a holy life means to be different from the crowd. That is why Paul called upon the Corinthians to 'Come out from them and be separate' (2 Corinthians 6:17).

How should we react when our faith is challenged? Peter says that we should behave in a Christ-like way. We should speak with gentleness and respect. There is no reason for a Christian to preach the gospel in an arrogant way. We should never have the self-righteous attitude which indicates, 'I've done my duty in preaching to you, but I don't really care about what happens to you. You have refused to accept Christ as your Saviour so I wash my hands of you.'

That kind of attitude can be counter-productive. It is certainly not how Jesus sought to win people to God. Christian people should always act like gentlemen and gentlewomen before the world — and before everyone else as well. We should show proper respect to everyone (2:17).

We should also keep a clear conscience. Our conscience is that little voice within us that tells us whether we are doing right or wrong. Anyone who has not silenced his conscience will automatically know whether he is trying to deceive God and his fellow men and women. My dog used to know it was wrong to steal food off the draining-board; that's why she always hid under the table to eat it. But human beings have been given the precious gift of a conscience, not just an instinct, to tell them the difference between right and wrong.

Peter says that God's people should be those who are **'keeping a clear conscience'**. He means that we should not knowingly do that which would mar our testimony. If we take unnecessary risks when we drive our cars (and especially if we have biblical texts on the back window) we will not have a clear conscience as we continue our journey.

We should also have **'good behaviour in Christ'**. If we do we will not need to defend ourselves. Peter says, **'Those who speak maliciously against [us] ... [will] be ashamed of their slander'** (3:16).

God's people today need to ask themselves, 'Am I eager to do good?' We must not be like those zealots in the time of Jesus who engaged in action which was politically extreme. Peter does not mean that Christians should be 'eager to do what is right by the standards of their own political party'. He says, instead, 'Engage in good works, doing always what is right.' And that includes always being prepared to witness for our glorious Lord.

20.
The wonder of being saved

Please read 1 Peter 3:18-22

Dr Martyn Lloyd-Jones often used to say that the amazing thing about Bible commentaries is that they go into great detail explaining all the things that are perfectly clear and understandable to you, but when you reach something which you cannot understand they gloss over it completely.

I looked up a number of commentaries on this passage. All of them said of verse 19, 'It is difficult to understand.' I had already discovered that! You can imagine how 'helpful' I found those comments!

First of all, let us look at the passage in its entirety. As I prayerfully read it several times, these words jumped out of the page at me: '... **to bring you to God**' (3:18); **'A few people ... were saved'** (3:20); **'now saves you also'** (3:21); **'It saves you ...'** (3:21).

Think how wonderful it is to be saved. It is a joy and comfort to know, for certain, that Christ has washed us from our sins and made us his own children. It is a great blessing to have the assurance that when we die we will go to be with the Lord Jesus Christ in heaven.

Christ's death

His death was unjust. That is why Peter starts verse 18 with the word **'for'**. He had been saying that Christians often suffer for no good reason. They are persecuted for righteousness' sake. Therefore, if we suffer for doing something wrong then that is nothing to be proud of; rather we should be ashamed. 'It is better ... to suffer for doing good than for doing evil' (3:17). Jesus never did anything wrong. He is the only person who ever lived who was sinless. That is why nothing but his death could atone for our sins. He, the righteous one, suffered and died to bring us, the unrighteous ones, to God.

Consider the wonder of the statement that Jesus died to bring us to God. No one else could do that. No priest, or even bishop, can bring us to God — although he might be able to give us much helpful guidance. No saint, however holy, can bring us to God — although he or she may set us a good example to follow. No religious ceremony or continually offered prayers (it matters not how holy the person is who prays for us) can bring us to salvation. Only Jesus, the Son of God (he is God himself), could achieve such a tremendous act. He is the one person who ever lived who has never committed any sin. Only the atoning sacrifice of his death can bring us to God. That is why he had to die such a cruel death.

Then Peter tells us that Jesus died **'once for all'**. In the Old Testament it was necessary that many sacrificial lambs be offered to God, again and again, to keep on cleansing the people from their sins (because people keep on sinning again and again). But since Jesus died, a full atonement has been made for sin, and his cleansing lasts for ever. 'Christ was sacrificed once to take away the sins of many people' (Hebrews 9:28). And he went through all that pain and suffering to bring his own people to God. There is now no further need of any sacrifice for sin.

Jesus died and rose again. **'He was put to death in the body.'** He actually died. He did not just pass out on the cross. Nor was it someone else who died in his place. He, the Lord Jesus Christ, was put to death in his body.

Then Peter continues, **'... but made alive by the Spirit'**. This refers to his resurrection from the dead. Sometimes the Bible says that the Father raised Christ from the dead (Acts 2:32; Galatians 1:1; Ephesians 1:20). Sometimes the Son is said to have raised himself from the dead (John 10:17-18); but here Peter says that 'the Spirit' raised him from the dead.

In the NIV (like the AV) the word Spirit has a capital 'S', which implies that the passage refers to the Holy Spirit. But not every translation of the Bible has a capital 'S', so it may mean that Jesus was raised from the dead by his own spirit. However, as Father, Son and Holy Spirit are one God in three persons, we should not argue about which member of the Trinity raised Jesus from the dead. Suffice it to say that he rose by a mighty power.

Christ's preaching

While on earth, during the first century A.D., Jesus preached a great deal. He preached the Sermon on the Mount. He taught the Lord's Prayer. He told very interesting stories called parables and, as a result, he gathered large crowds about him. One of the things that Jesus often taught was the need for people to repent.

This is fundamental in all biblical preaching. Jesus said, 'No one can see the kingdom of God unless he is born again' (John 3:3). He meant that people need to repent of their sins as an important part of the process of being born again. He also said, 'I have not come to call the righteous, but sinners to repentance' (Luke 5:32).

This is what true Christian preachers do. People are not aware of the danger they are in. The only way to reach God is by repentance from sin and faith in Jesus Christ alone for salvation. Several stages are involved in repentance. First of all unconverted people must be convicted by the Holy Spirit of their sin. They must be brought to see their own utter helplessness and hopelessness without Christ and his salvation. This is the part that people do not understand. In their natural state they do not wish to admit that they are sinners. To be bowed down under deep conviction of sin is something which they find degrading and undignified. They do not mind being sorry for their foolish ways, but they do not desire deep soul-searching. They do not mind admitting that they have a need of Christ, but to repent in sackcloth and ashes, as it were, is asking a bit too much.

Then there must be a true sorrow for sin. Sinners must desire to turn away from it. That act of repentance will lead them to turn towards God in faith. They do that when, by the Spirit's aid, they are brought to trust in Christ's atoning death. Then he will bring them to an awareness that he has washed their sins away. Salvation is of the Lord from start to finish.

Peter tells us that Jesus also did some preaching in the time before he was born as a baby at Bethlehem. Many people believe that 'the angel of the Lord' in the Old Testament is a pre-incarnate appearance of Jesus. He appeared to Hagar in Genesis 16:7, and to others in Genesis 19:1, 21; 31:11, 13; he is mentioned in Exodus 3:2, 4, and in Judges 2:1-5; 6:11-12, 14, and then throughout Judges 13. He is also found in Zechariah 3:1-6; 12:8.

Peter says that Jesus went and preached to the people of Noah's day. We know that these ancient people were very wicked (Genesis 6:5); and we know that Noah preached to them (2 Peter 2:5). He no doubt reminded them of their wickedness and their need to repent of their sins. 1 Peter 3:19 tells us that Jesus also went and preached to these people, presumably through Noah.

All the time the people were being called to repentance God waited patiently for them to repent. But it is clear that they did not turn from their sinful ways, because we know that only eight were saved. Everyone else was drowned under God's judgement — the flood. So where are those disobedient people now?

Peter tells us that they are in **'prison'**; they are in captivity. Their spirits are suffering bondage and eternal punishment in the place that Jesus calls 'hell'. What a sad thing it is when anyone refuses to obey the gospel message! Those people had the opportunity to repent, but they turned their backs upon it. As a result only a tiny number were saved.[1]

Christ's salvation

These eight people were saved from judgement by means of the ark. In the ark they were safe and secure. God had sealed them in, from the outside. It mattered not how fierce the storm was outside; they were safe on the inside of the ark. It mattered not how high the flood waters rose; the ark bore them above those waters of judgement. It mattered not what terrible havoc was being wreaked outside; they were safe inside the ark. That is a picture of what it is like to be saved.

The ark is a picture of the Lord Jesus Christ. Today all of those who abide in Christ are as safe as the family of Noah were during the flood. The onslaughts of hell cannot harm them for they are 'in Christ'. They may experience the frightening roar of the devil, and even be scared by it; but they are in no real danger, for they are inside the Lord Jesus Christ.

Peter uses the figure of baptism to symbolize the security that there is in Christ. Those eight people in the ark were lifted up out of the water. So also those who have been saved, and have testified to their faith in Christ, have been raised up with him that they 'might live a new life' (Romans 6:4). Notice that it is not baptism that saves us, but that which baptism symbolizes. When we are baptized we are buried under the water (to symbolize that we are dying with Christ and are, therefore, dead to sin) and we are lifted up out of the water (to symbolize that we now intend to live a new, resurrection life).

Baptism itself does not wash away our sins. It is the work of Christ on the cross which does that. When we are baptized we show, in picture form, that Christ has already washed away our sin and given us new life. Our obedience to baptism is **'the pledge of a good conscience'**. We do not have to be baptized to go to heaven, but baptism is necessary in order for us to have a good conscience before God.

On the Day of Pentecost when all the crowds were convicted of their sin they cried out, 'Brothers, what shall we do?' Peter replied, 'Repent and be baptized every one of you, in the name of Jesus Christ for the forgiveness of your sins' (Acts 2:37-38).

Peter says here that the ceremony of baptism does not wash away our sin, as a bath removes the dirt from our bodies. It is what baptism stands for that saves us. Jesus washes away our sins when we turn to him in repentance and faith.

It is very interesting to notice that it takes quite a lot of water to wash dirt from someone's body. Therefore, I personally believe that baptism requires rather more water than my youngest son uses to wash himself in the morning; that amount of water often leaves his face flannel bone dry!

At the end of this section Peter reminds us that Jesus is now in heaven. The resurrection of Jesus is a sign of our salvation. Jesus is now at God's right hand. This is the place of power and authority. He has authority over all the beings in heaven. They are in submission to him. And so should we be.

21.
Living for God

Please read 1 Peter 4:1-6

What is your purpose in life? What do you hope to achieve? How do you measure success in life?

Many people think they have been successful when they have a good job, a big car (or cars), a happy, well-fed and well-clothed family — in short, when they have everything that money can buy.

We need to ask ourselves, 'Is this the sum total of our ambition?'

Some preachers today, especially in the U.S.A., encourage their followers to believe that success and prosperity are the rights of everyone in the kingdom of God. But David Cohen has answered these views very forcefully by writing, 'There is no doubt that God, our heavenly Father, does own the cattle on a thousand hills. Nor is there any doubt that he wants to bless his people, to give them life in all its abundance, to heal the sick, to care for the oppressed, and to set the captives free from debt and bondage of spirit, as well as of the body. But the trappings of success seem to fit uneasily with the followers of one who had nowhere to lay his head, and who invited those who would come after him to take up their cross daily and do so.'[1]

Each of us needs to ask ourselves, 'What do I want out of life?' True Christians ought to have as their goal the desire to follow Christ wherever he leads them, to honour Christ in everything they do, and to give loving obedience to their Master throughout all their days.

Peter wrote his first letter to encourage these scattered

Christian believers to live their lives for the glory of God. But living for God is not as easy as it might sound at first. It involves a number of things which do not come easily to us.

Suffering for Christ

In chapter 4:1 Peter resumes the theme he left in 3:18. He directs his readers back towards Christ's suffering upon the cross. Jesus died as a righteous man, but he died to take away the sins of unrighteous people. He died to bring his chosen people to God.

Although Christ has always been the Son of God, that does not mean that he escaped the agony of the cross. He was also fully man. He really suffered. There was the excruciating pain of the nails which had been driven through the most sensitive parts of his hands and feet. There was the distress of knowing that one of his friends had betrayed him; and then there was the knowledge that another had denied him. (In fact the one who swore he never knew him was none other than the apostle Peter, who wrote this letter.) Jesus suffered the indignity of being rejected by those whom he came to save. On top of all that, he suffered the injustice of being given a false trial before he was put to death, even though he was entirely innocent of any crime.

Peter tells his readers that God's people should have the same attitude to suffering and injustice that Christ had. He says that Christians are to 'arm themselves'. They are to put on spiritual armour. Paul expanded on this concept when he wrote about the need for believers to be clothed with the whole armour of God (Ephesians 6:10-18).

Peter means that persecution is on its way. Not only were the believers of northern Turkey going to have to suffer for their faith, but Christians all over the world of those days were going to have to endure persecution. Paul said, 'Everyone who wants to live a godly life in Christ Jesus will be persecuted' (2 Timothy 3:12). These believers to whom Peter was writing must be prepared to suffer for Christ's sake. They would have to suffer unjustly. They would be abused, as their Saviour was. They must be prepared to suffer for doing good, just as their Lord did.

Some believers today know what it is to suffer painful afflictions of mind or body because of their love for the Lord. Some have to put up with difficult home or work situations because of their faith in Christ. But very few Christians in these days know what it is actually to be thrown to the lions — not because they have done something to deserve it, but because that is the accepted penalty for following the Lord.

However, there is a difference between us and our Lord. He was sinless. He never knew what it was to do anything wrong. He never did anything to deserve the suffering with which he was afflicted. Following his death on the cross, Peter says, **'He ... is done with sin'** (4:1). But we still live in our body of sin and death (Romans 7:24). We still have to battle against sinful desires. We are still tempted to do wrong and we still live our lives as though the whole world ought to revolve around us and do what we want.

Peter is saying that for Christians to live as though they were the most important people alive is the wrong kind of life-style. We need to arm ourselves against such things. We should try to combat such wrong desires by looking to Jesus. We ought not to live the rest of our earthly life seeking to gratify our own evil human desires. Rather, we should be living our lives as though we are seeking to follow the will of God.

Living a holy life

Peter reminds these believers of the way in which they lived their former lives. They chose to do what the pagans did. It is salutary to consider how the people of the world see us. Do they look at us and see no difference between the way we live our lives and the way they live theirs? So often Christians seem to try to justify their actions by saying, 'Oh, we mustn't let people think we are peculiar. We must do all the things that they do and so show them that we have liberty to enjoy ourselves because Christ has set us free.'

But Peter says, 'You should be seen as those who are different.' That is what it means to be holy. He says, **'You have spent enough time in the past doing what pagans choose to do'** (4:3). It is almost as if he is saying, 'You have wasted enough time in the past.' Time is going so quickly that it should never be wasted. In Chester Cathedral there is an old clock with this inscription:

> When I was a child I laughed and wept — time crept;
> When I was a youth I waxed more bold — time strolled;
> When I became a full grown man — time ran;
> When older still I grew — time flew;
> Soon I shall find in passing on — time gone.
> O Christ, wilt thou have saved me then?
>
> Amen.

Peter next draws up a list of the things these Christians had done in the past. The first word he uses is **'debauchery'**. This sums up all the rest. Before they had become Christians these people had lived their lives without any regard for restraint. Their own pleasure was all that mattered to them.

At the time of writing, many people in civil authority are stating that over-indulgence in strong drink is one of the causes of crime and violence on our streets. Notice, then, how many of the words in this list have to do with drinking too much alcohol. So often nice, quiet, well-mannered young people can be transformed into foul-mouthed louts when they have had several cans of lager inside of them.

The last item in Peter's list is **'detestable idolatry'**. This means worshipping the creature, rather than the Creator. We can so easily make an idol of something or someone, and our admiration can quickly turn to worship. 'In that time idol worship resulted in immorality and intemperance.'[2]

This list is very similar to the lists Paul uses in Romans 13-14 and Galatians 5:20-21.

Warning of judgement to come

Unbelievers cannot understand why Christians do not join them in their fun. They sometimes get the idea that Christians get no pleasure out of life. And if we are giving them that impression then there is something wrong with our lives. This is because a joyless Christian is a contradiction in terms. However, believers in the Lord Jesus Christ do not derive their joy from pleasures, however wholesome. The joy they receive comes from the blessing of God upon their lives. 'Happiness comes from basking in the knowledge of the redeeming love of the Father and the Son, and showing active loyal gratitude for it. You love God and find yourself happy. Your active attempts to please God funnel the pleasures of his peace into your heart.'[3]

Unbelievers find it strange that Christians have moral scruples. When I was in the army our drill corporal taught us that soldiers never got put on a charge for doing something wrong; they were only brought before the Commanding Officer 'if they were stupid enough to allow themselves to be caught doing something wrong'. The worldly person seems to think that sin is all right so long as no one finds out about it. But Christians know that God sees everything they do. It is possible to deceive our parents. We can fool our husbands or wives. We can even pretend to ourselves that everything is all right in our lives. But we can never hide anything from God. He sees everything — even our thoughts.

Because Christians do not join in the ungodly pleasures of those who do not put God first in their lives, the people of the world think that they are strange. For them, anything which is unusual is treated as suspect. This is a natural inclination with us all. That is why some schoolchildren make such terrible fun of a handicapped child. They taunt the poor wretch because they cannot understand how he can be like he is. It is the same kind of mentality which causes worldly people to abuse Christians just because they are different from non-Christians.

This does not mean that Christians can 'wash their hands of' unbelievers. God's people have a duty to the ungodly. It is so easy to think, 'Why should I do anything to help those who treat me badly?' But in Ezekiel 33:8 God says, 'When I say to the wicked, "O wicked man, you will surely die," and you do not speak out to dissuade him from his ways, that wicked man will die for his sin and *I will hold you accountable for his blood.*'

Christians have a solemn responsibility to preach the gospel to every creature and to remind them that there is a judgement day coming when we shall all have to stand before the Lord and give an account of our lives. We will be questioned then about our relationship to the Lord Jesus Christ. And the questioner will be Christ himself. T. S. Eliot, writing about the judgement day says, 'Be prepared for him who knows how to ask questions.'[4] Believers must warn unconverted people of the need to be right with God. They must tell them that it is very dangerous to leave such vital matters until a later date. None of us knows how much time we have left on this earth.

The important question for everyone concerns Jesus Christ and their relationship with him. John Newton put it like this:

> 'What think you of Christ?' is the test,
>   To try both your state and your scheme;
> You cannot be right in the rest,
>   Unless you think rightly of him.
> As Jesus appears in your view
>   As he is beloved or not;
> So God is disposed to you,
>   And mercy or wrath are your lot.[5]

There is a very solemn verse in Hebrews 9:27: 'Man is destined to die once, and after that to face judgement.' The Bible speaks of no second chance after death. Rather it says. **'The gospel was preached ... to those who are now dead.'** In other words Peter is saying that people who heard the gospel while they were alive are going to be judged after death. They were called to repentance while they were on earth but now they are dead it is too late to turn to Christ. Psalm 115:17 says, 'It is not the dead who praise the Lord.' The only ones who are at peace after death are those who came to saving faith in the Lord Jesus Christ before they departed from this life. The urgent thing for us all to realize is that 'Now is the day of salvation' (2 Corinthians 6:2). Tomorrow might be too late. And God's people have the solemn responsibility of telling everyone these things.

22.
Practical Christian living

Please read 1 Peter 4:7-11

How should Christians conduct themselves? What sort of things should characterize their behaviour? What do others expect of people who claim to be Christians?

We must remember that, like those to whom Peter was writing, God's people are a minority in this world — certainly as far as Britain is concerned. There are far fewer real Christians in the British Isles today than there are people who care nothing, or very little, for the commands of God. Similarly in many other countries in the world only a very small percentage of the inhabitants are born-again believers.

At this point in his letter, Peter gives some very straightforward advice on how believers should live their lives as individuals, and also how they should behave in the fellowship of God's people. Peter focuses his readers' thoughts on realities.

The end of all things is near

Peter reminds his readers that life, as they know it, will one day come to an end. This world will not last for ever.

It is so tempting to think that life, and the world around us, will carry on as it always has done. If we are living our lives with that attitude then there is something wrong with our thinking. If we look at what Peter wrote in his second letter we will see that he reminded his readers that the people of the world think like that. They say, 'Everything goes on as it has since the beginning of creation' (2 Peter 3:4). But anyone who knows what happened in history remembers that that is not true. Things have not carried on as normal ever since the creation of the world. There was that terrible time when God brought judgement on the earth through the instrumentality of the flood. At that time all who refused to enter into the safety and security of the ark were drowned. Peter shakes the people of the world out of their complacency by saying that severe judgement is going to be unleashed upon this world again. He states that there is a day coming when all people will be judged (1 Peter 4:6). He then says that it is important for Christians to be those who **'live according to God'** in the light of the coming judgement.

Peter is re-emphasizing one of his major themes. The end of all things is near. This was the constant hope of the early church, and we too should realize that we are now living in the last days. Christ is coming again and we must be ready for his appearing. This fact ought always to be in the forefront of our minds. We should be living our lives in the light of his return. We do not know when he will come back but we do know that when he does return he will come as the Judge of all people.

In saying, **'The end of all things is near,'** Peter is making it clear that his readers are living in the final age of redemption. And we today are living in those same end times. God's plan of redemption has been working through all of its stages. From the time of the creation of the world, right through until the resurrection and ascension of our Lord Jesus Christ, God's mighty plan of salvation was being carried out. It is mainly in the history of the nation of Israel (recorded in the Old Testament) that we see this wonder of God's plan being unfolded. But now, for Christians (who are a kind of new Israel of God — see 1 Peter 2:9-10), because of the work of Christ on the cross, these things are coming to fulfilment: 'The end of all things is near.'

We do not know when the end will come, but we do know how we ought to live our lives. Peter says, in his second letter, 'Since everything will be destroyed ... what kind of people ought you to be?' (2 Peter 3:11). He goes on to say, 'You ought to live holy and godly lives ... and speed its coming.' And in our passage Peter says, **'The end of all things is near. Therefore be clear minded and self controlled.'**

Prayer and love

Peter encouraged the people to pray more effectively. People so often see prayer as a duty or a ceremonial ritual. There can be a world of difference between saying our prayers and praying. Our prayers sometimes seem to reach no higher than the ceiling. But the Lord intends that our prayers should be much more than a way of ordering our thoughts. He wants us really to reach through to him when we pray. However, so often, there seems to be a barrier between us and God.

What is the cause of the blockage? So often it happens because of various things which are within us. We are not clear-minded; we do not seem able to clarify our thoughts. We do not know what we should ask for in prayer and our minds seem to be confused. A second thing that Peter mentions is that we are not self-controlled when we come to God in prayer. Our thoughts wander from one thing to another. We cannot seem to concentrate upon the things of God. Perhaps this is because we have allowed Satan to come in and cause confusion in our minds.

Prayer is a great problem to many Christians. Every time they hear a sermon on prayer it seems as if they are being rebuked for not praying long enough or hard enough. The result of such a sermon is not that they pray better but that they become more and more depressed. The more they read about the great saints of old who prayed for many hours at a time, the more worried they become about their own prayer life. 'I cannot pray for hours at a time,' they say. 'What is wrong with me?' I often felt like that until I learnt that the godly C. H. Spurgeon never prayed for more than ten minutes at a time because he had a problem over concentration. He found it much better to pray in short snatches, but often. Why do we keep listening to Satan who tells us that God will only listen to long, well-rounded phrases which are full of deep thoughts? The Lord hears the

> … burden of a sigh,
>   The falling of a tear,
> The upward glancing of an eye
>   When none but God is near.[1]

The sad fact is that if we have not got the vertical plane right (i. e. our prayer life with God) then we will not get the horizontal aspect right either (our relationship to our fellow men and women). But Scripture says that we should be those who love each other deeply. If we do not have a deep love for each other we shall soon start finding fault with our fellow believers. A Christian fellowship is made up of human beings, all of whom have imperfections. When we are converted we become saints, but that does not mean we put on haloes and thereafter live perfect lives. The sinful human nature with which we are all born still shows through. When we are converted we remain human and we still have our irritating little ways (or even irritating big ways!).

However, when there is true love in a fellowship of God's people **'Love covers over a multitude of sins'** (4:8). If we love each other deeply 'from the heart' (1:22) then we will be given the grace to overlook all the annoying habits of our fellow church members.

Peter goes on to speak about one of the ways in which we can show love for others, and that is by being hospitable. This is one of the most effective ways of showing Christian love and concern. God's people should ask themselves, 'When did I last offer real hospitality to someone?' The *Concise Oxford Dictionary* defines hospitality as 'the friendly and generous reception of guests or strangers'.

I shudder when I hear that some churches are so 'middle-class' in their attitudes that no one ever visits anyone else without first having a formal invitation. These churches have so taken on the culture of the people living in that area that the church fellowship has become contaminated with the thinking of the world. The result is that no one just drops in on somebody, because they fear that they will not be made welcome. If that kind of thinking pervades a church, hospitality is not being exercised.

In the days of Peter inns were dangerous and often immoral places. Therefore it was very important that Christians should open up their homes to believers who were passing through their district. If we can afford it our family tries to spend the summer holidays somewhere in Greece. One of the reasons we do this is because the Greek people are naturally hospitable. The Greek word for 'stranger' *(Xenos)* also means 'guest'. The implication of this is that Greeks are not afraid of strangers (they do not suffer from xenophobia) but they treat unknown people with honour, as welcome guests — even though they may never have seen or heard of them before.

However, when it comes to offering hospitality we, in places like south-east England, sometimes find that we have a problem. Sometimes certain people outstay their welcome, or they forget to say, 'Thank you for having me,' when they leave. Peter says of such situations, 'Do not grumble,' when that happens. If we feel that we have been taken for granted then we should remember how the friends of Jesus treated him on many occasions. We should not complain when we are treated in a similar way.

Living to God's glory

Peter also says that we should use our spiritual gifts so that others may be blessed and God will be glorified. The New Testament contains various lists of spiritual gifts which are available to believers. These gifts are listed in Romans 12:4-8 and 1 Corinthians 12:7-11. They may be natural gifts which are spiritually enhanced at conversion, or they may be specially bestowed upon a believer when he or she is saved. However, not every Christian has all of the gifts and no gift is more important than any other (although some might be more noticeable than others).

There are, however, some warning notes to be struck. We must never exercise our spiritual gift, or gifts, to benefit ourselves. Gifts should never be used to draw people's attention to the person using them, nor should they be used to show people how clever a person is. That is not why God bestows spiritual gifts. These gifts have been given for other reasons. Our desire should be to see that, through the exercise of spiritual gifts, others are built up in their faith (Ephesians 4:12). We should remember that we are here to help others and encourage them in the things of God.

We should always bear in mind that God's Word, the Bible, contains everything that we need. When we speak we should speak **'the very words of God'** (4:11). This obviously means that we should be very keen to pass on the words of

Scripture because they are sweet and wholesome. But also we should remember that when we teach God's Word or tell our acquaintances about the Lord, everything we say should be in line with the general teaching and principles contained in God's Word. Any preacher who speaks the very words of God to edify others experiences the power of the Holy Spirit at work within him enabling him to deliver the 'living words' he has received from God. In the same way anyone who serves the Lord as part of the life of the church will experience the strength of God helping him in his important work. Everything that any of us does should be done only for the praise of God, through Jesus Christ.

And we do these things in a prayerful spirit knowing that the end is near. We should always seek to live a life filled with love and concern for the welfare of others. We should do everything for the glory of God. So this section ends, as does 5:11, with a great crescendo of praise to God, a doxology: **'So that in all things God may be praised through Jesus Christ. To him be the glory and the power for ever and ever. Amen.'**

23.
Joy in suffering

Please read 1 Peter 4:12-19

'If ever a man suffered ...,' was a phrase my father tended to use whenever he could not get his own way. It was his way of expressing his exasperation with people or events which stopped him doing what he wanted to do.

We can get very annoyed when our plans are hindered. Often in our annoyance we feel very sorry for ourselves. But irritations of this kind are nothing in comparison with some of the sufferings which many of our fellow men, women and children have to go through. When we see how bravely some people suffer, then all our little pains fade away into insignificance.

In these last eight verses of chapter 4, Peter speaks about people suffering because they are Christians. We have noticed how he has taken up this theme of suffering time and time again. This is because the persecution started by Nero was drawing near for these believers in northern Turkey.

Suffering was nothing new for the Jews. They had experienced many times of suffering down through the ages. They had been slaves in Egypt and captives in Babylon. And since these New Testament times the Jews have passed through numerous periods of affliction. Throughout Europe they were very badly treated in the Middle Ages — and since. Hitler and Communist powers have done their worst to suppress the Jewish race. The anguish of the Jewish people has been expressed very sympathetically in pieces of music like the beautifully sad piece for cello and orchestra, *Schelomo* by Ernest Bloch.

But suffering had not been bred into the Gentiles like that. The Gentiles among these Christians would have needed special preparation and this is why Peter writes so tenderly to them. He does this, not so that they could grit their teeth and bear it, but in order that they could use their pain and benefit from it.

The blessings of suffering

The apostle tells them not to be surprised at their suffering. He calls them **'dear friends'**. He had used that same expression in 2:11. He writes like this because he wants them to know that he loves them and cares for them in their pain. He wants them to realize that he is standing with them in their sore affliction. So he says, 'Don't be surprised.'

It is a most natural thing for Christians to suffer. When this time of great persecution came upon them they were not to think that something strange was happening to them. After all, if their Master suffered, why should they escape it? If they delighted in being followers of the Lord then they must go all of the way with him and experience life as he did. That meant being misunderstood, bearing pain and even suffering a cruel death.

Peter says that when believers suffer unjustly they are to rejoice. These believers were to rejoice because they were participating in the sufferings of Christ. Peter had once rebelled against the idea that Jesus would suffer. We read in Matthew 16:21-23, 'From that time on Jesus began to explain to his disciples that he must go to Jerusalem and suffer many things at the hands of the elders, chief priests and teachers of the law, and he must be killed and on the third day be raised to life. Peter took him aside and began to rebuke him. "Never, Lord!" he said. "This shall never happen to you!" Jesus turned and said to Peter, "Get behind me, Satan! You are a stumbling-block to me; you do not have in mind the things of God, but the things of men."'

Just as Peter found it strange that the spotless Son of God should have to suffer, so these believers were no doubt tempted to complain about the sufferings they were experiencing, or were likely to undergo shortly. Peter seems to be saying to them, 'Don't think about your own troubles; rejoice that you have been counted worthy to suffer for Christ.'

Why do Christians suffer? Sometimes, like these early Christians, God's people suffer because they preach Christ. The people of the world do not understand the wonders of God's love. They cannot believe that anyone can come to God without making some great effort himself or herself. They cannot believe that it is simply a matter of repenting of their sin and turning to Christ. They will not believe that 'God so loved the world that he gave his one and only Son, that whoever believes in him shall not perish but have eternal life' (John 3:16).

Sometimes Christians suffer because they will not give up the knowledge that when God has hold of us, he will never let us go. There was a period in my life when I was undergoing a period of great trial. It went on for several years. I was even tempted, on occasions, to question whether it was worth carrying on living. Eventually the worst happened (the thing I had been dreading). During those long months several unconverted people asked me, 'Where is your faith in all this?' Being asked that was a kind of mild persecution. Without any hesitation or (I hope) false religiosity I replied, 'It hasn't diminished a bit. Although I am numb, my faith in Christ is now much stronger. I've nothing else to hang on to.' I could say that because I, and most believers who undergo trials, know that the eternal God is our refuge and underneath us are his everlasting arms bearing us up (Deuteronomy 33:27).

Painful trials do bring great blessings with them. Peter had already spoken to them in 1:7 of the value of gold being refined by fire. When precious metals are passed through the refiner's fire all the filth and impurities are burnt off. What is left is pure gold or silver. Likewise afflictions purify God's people. David Kingdon has said, 'Suffering prepares us for glory.'[1] Suffering helps us to see life in perspective. In our suffering we see that the most important thing for us is to put Christ first in our lives and to live for God's glory.

Whatever happens, suffering believers rejoice because they know that this world will one day come to an end. This means that one day suffering will cease. One day we will be overjoyed. This will come to pass on that day when Christ's glory is revealed, when he comes again. On that day, '[God] will wipe every tear from their eyes. There will be no more death or mourning or crying or pain, for the old order of things has passed away' (Revelation 21:4).

When we remember these things we find out that great blessings descend upon us every time we are insulted for the name of Christ. It is not a very pleasant thing to be spat upon. This used to happen regularly to some of the young men running our church coffee bar some years ago. All they were doing was trying to provide somewhere for the youths to go out of the rain, and to seek to reach them for Christ. But, as a result of their efforts, they were badly treated. They were doing this work **'because of the name of Christ'** (4:14); and those who were badly treating them were 'slandering the noble name of him to whom [these believers belonged]' (James 2:7). 'In the early Christian community the single word *name* was synonymous with the Christian religion.'[2]

Peter says something very wonderful about such situations. He says that when this happens, **'The Spirit of glory and of God rests on you.'** Jesus put it like this: 'If the world hates you, keep in mind that it hated me first. If you belonged to the world, it would love you as its own. As it is, you do not belong to the world, but I have chosen you out of the world. That is why the world hates you. Remember the words I spoke to you: "No servant is greater than his master." If they persecuted me, they will persecute you also. If they obeyed my teaching, they will obey yours also' (John 15:18-20).

No shame in suffering

There are things that we sometimes do of which we are ashamed. Peter says, **'If you suffer, it should not be as a murderer or thief or any other kind of criminal, or even as a meddler'** (4:15). We trust that we will never indulge in such dreadful crimes. If we did so, and suffered for it, these actions would not only bring shame upon us, but they would also discredit our church fellowship, and indeed, the whole of God's people everywhere. We should take great care that we live lives which are holy. The people of the world are constantly watching us and looking to see how they can trip us up.

Have you noticed that Peter includes meddlers with murderers and thieves? Jesus does the same kind of thing when he identifies pride with adultery and wickedness (Mark 7:20-23, AV). Peter is saying that it is not only the sorts of things that the world calls sins which are wrong; it is also many more subtle things that cause pain to God and mar our witness. The AV translates 'meddlers' as 'a busybody in other men's matters'. Do you know anyone who fits that description? We need to ask ourselves if we are guilty of such things.

Peter says that when **'you suffer as a Christian, do not be ashamed, but praise God that you bear that name'** (4:16). 'Christian' was a derogatory term, just as originally, the terms 'Methodist' and 'Baptist' were nicknames. The name 'Christian' only appears three times in the Bible (here and in Acts 11:26; 26:28). Peter says that, even though you suffer when people call you by that degrading name, do not be ashamed, but praise God that you bear the name of Christ.

Christians sometimes sing,

> Ashamed of Jesus, that dear-Friend
> On whom my hopes of heaven depend!
> No! when I blush, be this my shame,
> That I no more revere his name.[3]

Paul tells the church at Rome, 'I am not ashamed of the gospel, because it is the power of God for the salvation of everyone who believes; first for the Jew, then for the Gentile' (Romans 1:16).

Suffering according to God's will

Judgement is coming to all. We have seen this theme touched upon throughout this chapter. One day 'We will all stand before God's judgement seat' (Romans 14:10). Then 'Each of us will give an account of himself to God' (Romans 14:12). Jesus described the judgement of the end times as a separation of sheep and goats. The sheep will enter into their heavenly inheritance, and the goats will be cursed and enter into the eternal fire prepared for the devil and his angels (Matthew 25:31-46).

If God's people are to be judged (not punished) in order to 'prove' them, then **'what will the outcome be for those who do not obey the gospel of God?'** (4:17). They will be judged very severely for their rejection of Christ. Peter illustrates this by quoting from Proverbs 11:31: **'If it is hard for the righteous to be saved, what will become of the ungodly and the sinner?'** Peter is speaking about the difficulties Christians have in obtaining salvation; it is hard work. He knew that Jesus said, 'Small is the gate and narrow the road that leads to life, and only a few find it' (Matthew 7:14).

If believers have to 'work out' their salvation (Philippians 2:12) (even though they cannot earn it) what will become of 'the ungodly and the sinner'? The ungodly person neither worships nor loves God and the sinner transgresses God's commands. Peter does not supply the answer to his question; it is obvious.

What should those do who suffer according to God's will? They should **'commit themselves to their faithful Creator'** (4:19). This is exactly what Jesus did upon the cross. His last saying was, 'Father, into your hands I commit my spirit' (Luke 23:46). Because God is faithful, we can confidently commit ourselves to him knowing that he will never let us down.

Despite all the pain and difficulty that suffering Christians endure they should still **'continue to do good'** (4:19). Peter frequently urges his readers to persist in this task of doing good (2:15, 20; 3:6, 11, 17). We should show our commitment to God by carrying out acts of love and mercy towards all of our fellow men.

24.
The responsibilities of church leaders

Please read 1 Peter 5:1-4

Every so often we come to a portion of God's Word which is addressed to a particular group of people or a specific situation, and we say to ourselves, 'Oh, this doesn't concern me! I can switch off here and pay no further attention.'

At first glance this passage seems to have no relevance to those who are not elders in the church because Peter addresses the first four verses of this last chapter, **'To the elders among you ...'** But I believe that every Christian can learn something from this section. After all, we are told that 'All Scripture is God-breathed and is useful ...' (2 Timothy 3:16).

However, this passage does have special meaning for those who are elders, or those who feel that God may be calling them to this high office. It is not wrong to desire to be active in Christian leadership. Paul says, 'If anyone sets his heart on being an overseer, he desires a noble task' (1 Timothy 3:1).

Peter claims to be an elder

Peter was an apostle. He says so in 1:1: 'Peter, an apostle of Jesus Christ'. When I have been on holiday I have quite often attended Greek Orthodox Church services which have been held in village churches in various parts of Greece. Whichever church you go to, you will discover that they are all designed in the same way. The floor, where all the congregation walk or stand, represents the flat earth. All over the walls there are paintings depicting various holy people. The higher up the wall the person's picture is, the more important he or she is. Each church is built according to the Byzantine style with a large dome covering the centre. Painted on the inside of this dome you will always find a picture of God looking down from heaven on to his world. The saints are often painted in tiers, and nearer to the roof of the church there are pictures of the twelve apostles. Peter is one of them. Similar scenes are carved way up in the stonework of many ancient British cathedrals.

But when Peter writes this passage he does not wish to be thought of as far away from ordinary people. He tells the elders of the churches to whom he is writing that he, Peter, is also a **'fellow-elder'**. He implies that elders are to be among the 'flock that is under [their] care' (5:2). The phrase **'under your care'** literally means, 'that is among you'.[1] The point to notice is that Peter is not puffed up with pride because of the high office which he held. He is filled with humility because he realizes that it is a great honour to tend the flock of God's people.

Peter then says that he was **'a witness of Christ's sufferings'**. Again we see the way in which Peter expressed his humility. He could have said, 'I was privileged to see Jesus perform many marvellous miracles.' Or he could have spoken about the numerous wonderful sermons he actually heard Jesus preach. He could have highlighted that important occasion of the transfiguration, when only he, James and John witnessed that wonderful moment when Jesus met with Moses and Elijah. Instead of mentioning any of these events he points only to the sufferings of Christ.

This would remind Peter of his blackest hour, that time when he let his Lord down so very badly. 'We remember just what kind of "witness" Peter was: one whose courage failed and who, three times, denied that he even knew Christ.'[2] Yet Peter lived to receive the Lord's forgiveness and to be restored to a position of usefulness in God's kingdom.

This is a great comfort to those of us who have also failed the Lord grievously. We are conscious that we have sinned against the Lord and the work to which he has called us. When we consider our behaviour we feel sure that there can be no further usefulness for us in God's kingdom. But one of the wonderful things about God's grace and mercy is that he

uses failures. He takes notice of those who freely confess their
faults and truly repent of their sins and, sooner or later, he
brings them back into his service. These servants of God can
then sing with new meaning,

> Ransomed, healed, restored, forgiven,
>   who like thee his praise should sing?[3]

Next Peter says that he is **'one who also will share in the
glory to be revealed'**. He again identifies himself with ordinary people. He had seen Christ's glory on earth. He had
been a witness to these wonderful things. He had seen the sufferings of Christ and his entrance into glory, but he does not
say, 'Look at me. I am an apostle. I am going to have a special
place in the kingdom.' Instead he says, 'I will *share* in the
glory to be revealed.'

Again Peter looks forward to the glorious second coming of
Christ. At that wonderful time all of God's people will participate in his future glory, and Peter, in his humility, will be
glorified along with each of God's blood-bought people.

The work of an elder

Elders are to be shepherds of God's flock. The term
'shepherd' was used many times in the Old Testament.
Believers are 'his people, the sheep of his pasture' (Psalm
100:3). The leaders of Israel were to act as shepherds of the
flock of God. Through Ezekiel, God had to chastise the
shepherds of Israel who, instead of caring for the people of
God, only took care of themselves (Ezekiel 34:1-10).

Peter must have heard Jesus use this same figure of a
shepherd. The Lord had called himself 'the good shepherd'
(John 10:1-18). He had also alluded to himself when he told
the parable about the shepherd who left the ninety-nine sheep
which were safely gathered into their fold, and went out and
found the one that was lost (Luke 15:3-7).

After his resurrection Jesus had spoken to Peter about the
love that he had for the Lord. He said, 'Simon son of John, do
you truly love me more than these?' 'Yes Lord, ... you know
that I love you,' replied Peter. The same question was asked

of Peter three times. Each time his disciple replied in the same vein. After each of Peter's answers Jesus gave these commands: 'Feed my lambs,' 'Take care of my sheep,' and 'Feed my sheep' (John 21:15-17).

The apostle applies this teaching of the Master and says that the elders of the various churches to which he is writing are to be shepherds like that. He is saying that elders have the responsibility of caring for the people of God. The believers are 'under [their] care'. They have to protect them, feed them and generally look after their welfare. They have to do this by teaching and applying the Scriptures to their situations. Archbishop Leighton said that the food (he means by that the preaching) that these elders should give to the people should not be 'empty of subtle notions, nor light, affected expressions, but wholesome truths, solid food, spiritual things spiritually conceived, and uttered with holy understanding and affection'.[4]

Elders are also to be overseers. The word 'overseer' is sometimes translated 'bishop' (as in the AV). That is what a bishop does. He has the spiritual oversight of God's people. In the New Testament there were several overseers in each church. When Paul wrote his letter to the church at Philippi he addressed it to 'all the saints in Christ Jesus at Philippi, together with the overseers and deacons' (Philippians 1:1). The New Testament bishop does not appear to be a man who dressed in a special hat and wore a large ring which all the people stooped to kiss. He was one of a number of respected, humble brethren who had the special responsibility for running the affairs in the church.

We can see from this passage, and from Acts 20:17, 28 that the terms 'elder', 'shepherd' (pastor) and 'overseer' (bishop) were all used in ways which showed they were interchangeable. The word 'elder' seems to indicate the title of the man and the words 'shepherd' and 'overseer' describe the work which he did.

Did these elders do this job because there was no one else able to do it? I think not. When you consider the great dangers that elders (or any prominent Christians) had to face in those days you will realize that no one took on the office lightly. Elders had to have courage and to be willing to accept this difficult task. They had to want to place themselves in the front line of the battle against Satan. They had to be prepared for all the criticism which sometimes comes the way of church leaders. But also there were very severe troubles awaiting anyone who took on the office of an elder in those days. Edmund Clowney sums it up like this: 'The elders who received Peter's letter carried spiritual burdens that weighed heavier as they saw the darkening horizon of impending persecution.'[5]

Elders certainly did not do the job because of the stipend they received. However, Peter does not say that elders should not be paid. The Lord Jesus himself said that 'The worker is worth his keep' (Matthew 10:10). It is, therefore, perfectly in order for elders to be paid for the work they do, but Peter says that elders should **'not [be] greedy for money'**. No one should do the work of an elder just because the pay is good — indeed in many churches pastors are very poorly paid.

Finally, Peter says to these elders that they should not be those who are **'lording it over those entrusted to you'**. Elders should not go around with the attitude that demands respect from everyone; they have not been called to this task by the Lord so that they can throw their weight around and expect unquestioning obedience to their commands. Elders should be those who command respect rather than demand it. They should 'set an example for the believers in speech, in life, in love, in faith and in purity' (1 Timothy 4:12). By their gentle, but firm leadership they should be 'examples to the flock'.

The rewards of church leaders

Once again Peter refers to the second coming of the Lord Jesus Christ. He calls the Lord the 'Chief Shepherd'. Elders (including those called by the title 'pastor') are under-shepherds; Jesus is the Chief Shepherd. He is the one who cares for his flock in a way which is absolutely perfect, and one day he is coming again for his own.

At that wonderful time faithful elders will receive a crown of glory that will never fade away. Victors in ancient times were crowned with a garland of flowers. Sometimes these were made from 'everlasting' flowers. But even those much-coveted crowns passed away eventually.

When Philip of Macedon (the father of Alexander the Great) died in 336 B. C. his coffin was surmounted with a beautiful intricately made golden crown, the gold of which was beaten into the shapes of tiny wild flowers and insects — even a little butterfly. On 17 August 1989 I saw that same golden crown, still gleaming, in the Archæological Museum in Thessaloniki, northern Greece. It has lasted all these years, but one day, together with all earthly things, it will perish. (Peter speaks about this in 1:7.) But it is not only elders who will receive a crown. James 1:12 tells us that all believers will be granted a crown — a crown of life on that day, one which will 'never perish, spoil or fade' (1:4). Isaiah prophesies that this crown of life will be the Lord himself:

> 'In that day the Lord Almighty
>   will be a glorious crown,
> a beautiful wreath
>   for the remnant of his people'

(Isaiah 28:5).

We read in Revelation 4:10 of twenty-four elders in heaven. John describes them as those who are taking their crowns of glory and casting them before the throne of him who once wore the crown of thorns for them.

25.
The problem of humility

Please read 1 Peter 5:5-7

A few years ago there was a song which went something like this: 'It's awfully hard to be humble when you're perfect in every way.' I am sure the composer of this song had his 'tongue in his cheek' when he wrote it, but this does express the way many people act. They behave as though they were perfect.

We all know that we ought to be humble under God's mighty hand, but when we think about ourselves and what we have achieved then the devil tempts us to think that we are really pretty good.

A command to young men

Peter says that young men are to **'be submissive to those who are older'**. It is a characteristic of young men and women to behave as though they were the most important people alive. Young men often seem to be full of ideas. They are not 'backwards in coming forward'. To hear them speak, we would get the impression that there is no subject upon which they are not experts. They often show an impatience with other people, treating them as though they are inferior.

Perhaps with these views in mind, Peter says that young men who are members of churches should have a submissive attitude to everyone. There are times when they need to force their learning and knowledge to 'take a back seat'. They should submit to those who are older — even if the older people have never been to university or had such a wide experience of the modern world as they have. In writing to these churches Peter seems to be saying that young men should not always be given their head. Care must be taken in giving them leadership positions in the church of Jesus Christ. It may be true that they are likely to be better educated than their elders. They probably have more paper qualifications than older people. They may have travelled to a wider variety of countries than others, but it is unlikely that they have had more experience of life than their elders. The psalmist suggests that one of the advantages of being old is that the young only know what it is like to be young but those who are older have experienced both 'worlds'. He says, 'I was young and now I am old' (Psalm 37:25).

The Scriptures teach that young men need to show a great deal of humility and respect for those who are older. The complaint often made today is that young people are not humble. But 800 years before Christ was born a Greek poet called Hesiod wrote, 'When I was a boy, we were taught to be discreet and respectful of elders, but the present youth are exceedingly impatient of restraint. They have execrable manners, flout authority and have no respect for their elders.' He adds, 'What kind of creatures will they be when they grow up?'[1]

In this section Peter is continuing the theme he started in 5:1-4. He writes, **'in the same way'**. He used this phrase in 3:7 when he spoke of the responsibilities of husbands. There he said that husbands should act lovingly towards their wives, and their wives should be submissive to them. As young men must behave in a caring and considerate way to those who are older, so elders ought to behave in a loving and kind way to the people of God under their care.

Although this phrase 'young men' may include young women also, it does seem that the men (elder and younger) played important roles in the leadership of the church in Peter's day. Even those who were sometimes to the fore had to learn to be submissive to those in authority over them. Submission was due to the ruling authorities in government (2:13-17). Slaves had to submit to their masters (2:18-21). Wives had to submit to their husbands (3:1-6) and young men had to learn humility by being submissive.

A command to everyone

He says that **'all of you'** must **'clothe yourselves with humility towards one another'**. They were not just to humble themselves before important people, but also towards each other. Paul says that the Philippian believers should 'in humility consider others better than [themselves]' (Philippians 2:3). The message which is coming through is that everyone is important in God's sight and equal care and loving concern should be shown to all.

One of the responsibilities that church leaders have is to see that 'all of the flock' are being cared for. How sad it is when some church members do not humble themselves before others! They expect everyone to 'come up' to their intellectual level. It concerns me that sometimes those who are converted in their sixties, seventies and eighties are not treated gently enough. Some of them do not have the expertise to read long, closely reasoned theological treatises. Yet, when people are seeking the Lord we so often give them a book to read — quite often it is a long complicated book. They are treated as though they are intellectuals. Did most of the apostles spend hours each week studying religious books? We do not even know if some of them were educated beyond the rabbinical school, where their reading would have been confined to the Old Testament Scriptures. When we consider this we must realize that those who are younger must treat with great consideration those who may be less well educated than themselves. We must not expect too much from them. Those who write books like the Welwyn Bible Commentaries constantly have to bear this in mind.

How often it happens that there are people in a church service who are left sitting on their own, or standing waiting at the end of the service with no one talking to them! Sometimes this is because younger believers do not feel they have anything in common with older friends who may not be able to converse on their intellectual level. If this is the case then something is wrong and more thought, work and prayer needs to be put into the art of communication.

Peter says that his readers must clothe themselves with humility. The word 'clothe' means 'to tie a piece of clothing to oneself'. Slaves used to knot a white scarf or apron over their clothing to distinguish themselves from freemen. 'The suggestion is that Christians ought to tie humility to their conduct so that everyone is able to recognize them. Peter exhorts the readers to fasten humility to themselves once for all. In other words, it stays with them for the rest of their lives.'[2]

All Christians must ask themselves if they are prepared to let their humility be seen by everyone for the rest of their lives. How unscriptural it is to think, 'I'm happy to act humbly towards some people, but not to others. And I don't know whether I can keep this up for the rest of my life'!

It may well be that Peter had in his mind that scene in the upper room when the disciples had gathered with Jesus for the Last Supper. No one had taken upon himself the humble duty of washing the dirt from the feet of the guests. So Jesus set all of his disciples an example of humility by stooping down, taking a bowl of water and a towel and washing their feet. When Jesus came to Peter the apostle at first rebelled against such a thing, but Jesus said, 'You do not realize now what I am doing, but later you will understand' (John 13:7). Maybe this is why Peter wrote, 'All of you, clothe yourselves with humility.' Calvin comments that 'No ornament is more beautiful or more becoming, than when we submit one to another.'[3]

Then the apostle quoted from Proverbs 3:34: **'God opposes the proud but gives grace to the humble.'** This is a statement which is also used by James to teach the same lesson (James 4:6). God hates pride and he opposes those who display it. In any case what have believers to be proud of? If they have achieved anything of lasting value it is for the Lord's glory, not for theirs. The reason they were able to do something valuable is because the Lord has given them the wisdom, the ability and the strength to do it. 'Where, then, is boasting? It is excluded' (Romans 3:27), because all spiritual good is done only through the grace of God.

God's hand is over everything

We read a great deal in the Bible about the hand of God. God is not human, but to explain to us his power, the Holy Spirit uses human terms — as though God really had hands, eyes and a right hand. Jacob, speaking of the blessings given to Joseph, said that 'the hand of the Mighty One of Jacob' was upon him (Genesis 49:24). God told Moses that the children of Israel would be delivered from Egypt. He said, 'Because of my mighty hand [Pharaoh] will let them go' (Exodus 6:1), and Moses and the Israelites sang this song of deliverance: 'Your right hand, O Lord, was majestic in power. Your right hand, O Lord, shattered the enemy' (Exodus 15:6). This expression obviously speaks of the power and strength of the Lord.

God's people must humble themselves under God's right hand. With this statement we come to the culmination of all of Peter's exhortations about submission. We must submit to the authorities who are over us (2:13). We must also submit to one another (Ephesians 5:21). But most of all we must submit ourselves to God.

He promises that those who submit themselves to him will be lifted up. There are many examples in Scripture of those who humbled themselves before God, and were then delivered. 'Because Rehoboam humbled himself, the Lord's anger turned from him, and he was not totally destroyed' (2 Chronicles 12:12). 'Hezekiah repented of the pride of his heart ... therefore the Lord's wrath did not come upon [the people]' (2 Chronicles 32:26). After Nebuchadnezzer was humbled by God he was in due time restored to his position of authority (Daniel 4:34-37).

However, when it seems as if we are living under some dark cloud, we may have to wait for a long time before we experience that restoration which we seek. The Scriptures say that **'[God will] lift you up in due time.'** Peter means that he will intervene 'at the right time'. Only God knows when that will be. To those who are weary of waiting to be lifted up, the message is 'Do not despair.' God does have his loving hand upon his people and he will lift them *at the right time*. He will not leave them until it is too late. Peter's message is 'Humbly commit yourselves to the Lord who knows all about your trouble and concern.'

When Christians become over-anxious they must remember that they are failing to submit to God's loving care over them. Jesus said, 'Do not worry about your life, what you will eat or drink' (Matthew 6:25). He did not mean that

we should not be sensible with our resources. He was not saying that we should not take care over how we spend our
money. He was not advocating that we should never plan anything. Jesus meant that we should take no anxious care about
our life.

It is pride that makes us anxious. When we are proud we
are not prepared to hand everything over to God's control.
We say to ourselves, 'I've got to work this out without any
help from anyone at all.' When we get into that frame of mind
we should remember that God's mighty hand is over us and
that he will protect and provide for us.

Is it not a wonderful thing to know that we can cast (that
means 'throw') all of our anxieties upon God because he cares
for us? How stupid it is then to have the attitude that says,
'Why pray when you can worry?'[4] Peter says to these dear
Christian folk of northern Turkey, 'God does care for you and
he wants you always to cast your anxieties upon him.' The
same comforting news applies to all of God's people in every
situation and every place.

The psalmist puts it like this,

> 'Cast your cares upon the Lord
>   and he will sustain you;
> he will never let the righteous fall'
>
> (Psalm 55:22).

The writer of this psalm was being pursued by many
enemies at the time, but he handed over all his anxieties to the
care and keeping of the Lord his God. And in return he
received the gift of peace.

Col. E. H. Joy of the Salvation Army wrote,

> All your anxiety, all your care,
> Bring to the Mercy Seat, leave it there.
> Never a burden he cannot bear,
> Never a friend like Jesus.[5]

So the message for us all is that we should not be too proud
to submit to the Lord. We should hand over our life and all its
concerns to him who is the great burden bearer.

26.
Faith matters

Please read 1 Peter 5:8-11

Some people say that it does not matter what you believe so long as you are sincere in your beliefs. The problem with that statement is that it is possible to be sincerely wrong. We can believe that a number 9 bus will come past where we are standing. We might be completely sincere in our belief but it will be quite useless if that particular bus route comes nowhere near the road where we are waiting.

Beliefs are important, but we can have wrong beliefs, or our beliefs can be directed towards the wrong objects. The only kind of faith that true Christians find eternally valuable is faith in God. The only way to have faith in God is to approach him through belief in the Lord Jesus Christ, believing that he is the Son of God and, therefore, the only way to God.

Several times in these closing verses of Peter's first letter he tells his readers to 'stand firm'. He uses this concept in different forms but the sense is always similar. He wants God's people to be steadfast. He urges them to lean hard upon the Lord — trusting everything to his care and keeping. However, there is one big problem facing each of God's people — the devil.

The devil is real

He has many names. Sometimes he is called Satan. This literally means, 'the adversary'. He is one who accuses God's people. In Zechariah 3 we find a picture of him standing at the right hand of Joshua the high priest. He is in that position so that he can accuse Joshua.

Sometimes this most evil of beings is called the devil. The devil tempted Jesus in the wilderness. He quoted Scripture to try to make Jesus follow his evil insinuations (see Matthew 4:1-11; Luke 4:1-13; Mark 1:13).

In other places he is called Beelzebub. This is the name given to the prince of evil — the one who leads all his evil forces in the fight against God. We read of Beelzebub in Mark 3:22.

He is also described in other ways. In John 14:30 he is called 'the prince of this world'. Paul describes him as 'the ruler of the kingdom of the air' (Ephesians 2:2), and in 2 Corinthians 11:14 we are told that he sometimes appears as 'an angel of light'. 'He slanders God and man, pits one person against another, and undermines the believer's faith in God.'[1]

The devil has one main objective: to thwart God's purposes. He is the enemy of God and of everything that is good, true and right. He is very active everywhere and he has his agents all over the world. They have been well trained by their master and they entice many people into all kinds of evil ways. The devil is behind the power of pornography which shouts at us all from street advertising hoardings, magazine articles, television programmes and books. It may be true that very few of God's people actually yield to the temptation of immoral sexual acts, but many of them gain illicit pleasure from reading about the downfall of those who do indulge in such things.

Another aim of Satan is to tempt people to steal. They may not take money or property, but they may be guilty of stealing time from the boss or undisclosed earnings from 'the taxman'. The devil and his hosts are always busy trying to lead God's people astray and seeking to bring the Lord's honour into disrepute. He is the enemy of all men and women.

Peter writes about the devil's activities. He says that **'The devil prowls around like a roaring lion looking for someone to devour'** (5:8). Perhaps Peter had in mind the hungry lions caged up underneath Rome's arenas and waiting to be released into the midst of helpless Christians. It is in the nature of hungry lions to be always on the look-out for food.

Satan is pictured standing, drooling at the mouth, watching for Christians whom he can lure away from the Lord. His roaring would strike terror into the hearts of God's people were it not for the fact of God's declaration that believers are under the protection of the Lord. Satan may sound threatening but he can never devour (i.e., swallow up) born-again believers for they are safe in the hands of God.

But the devil's greatest ploy is to persuade people that he does not exist. On the island of Jersey there is an area called 'the Devil's Hole'. This is a great black vault in the ground. Fixed into this hole is a statue. It is an artist's idea of what the devil looks like. The figure has a forked tail and horns coming out of his head. He is black, and he has a rather foolish-looking grin around his mouth. When most people see it a smile comes over their faces. This is what Satan likes more than anything. He wants everyone to think of him as a harmless figure of fun — as someone who doesn't really exist and therefore who is nothing to be afraid of!

Christians must combat the devil

God's people need to avoid all wrong things. One of the ways to keep ourselves pure from evil thoughts is to make sure we do not do anything which will stimulate wrong thoughts in our minds. For example if we know we are likely to be tempted to read 'smutty' literature, then we ought to make sure that we never go anywhere near the places where this kind of material is sold. If we really want to follow the Lord, then we must keep away from every evil influence on our lives. We must even 'abstain from all *appearance* of evil' (1 Thessalonians 5:22 AV).

Paul lists various things we are to avoid. He says, 'Flee from sexual immorality' (1 Corinthians 6:18); 'Flee from idolatry' (1 Corinthians 10:14) and 'Flee the evil desires of youth' (2 Timothy 2:22).

However, when we read about the devil we are *not* told to run away. We are urged to stand our ground and resist him. James tells us that if we resist the devil then he will flee from us (James 4:7). But that is easier said than done. He is frightening. His roaring keeps reminding us of his strength and his desire to destroy us. How are we going to obey God's Word in the face of this frightening situation? The Word of God never just says, 'Do this,' or 'Don't do that,' leaving us to work it out for ourselves. Peter gives us very good advice which we must heed if we are going to escape the clutches of the evil one.

He says, **'Be self-controlled.'** He has already said the same thing in 1:13 and 4:7. 'Self-control is man's ability to look at reality with a clear mind.'[2] This refers to an inward attitude to those things which are outside ourselves. It is so easy to depart from what we know to be right. A Christian man is well aware that it is wrong to get over-fond of someone else's wife, but sometimes, alas, he lets go of his self-control. A wife can be guilty of the same sin, too. This is an example of playing with fire and thus falling into the devil's hands. The consequences of this kind of behaviour can only be disastrous (even if the popular Sunday newspapers do not get to hear of it). Another example we could think of would be an over-indulgence of alcohol. Drinking too much of this can disinhibit people and encourage them to let go of their self-control. This is why so many people say that they like a drink; they say, 'It helps you to stop being shy and enables you to let go of yourself.'

Another piece of advice that Peter gives us is to be alert. If there was a dangerous wild animal prowling around on the loose then any sensible person would keep watch for it. Perhaps Peter had in his mind that time in the Garden of Gethsemane when Jesus said to him, 'Stay here and keep watch with me' (Matthew 26:38). But instead of being alert, Peter and the others went to sleep and did not notice the approach of the betrayer and his henchmen.

A third thing that Peter says is that we must stand firm in the faith. When we read of faith in the Bible, it often refers to our belief in God, our trust in Christ. But it can also mean '*the* faith', i.e., the teaching of the gospel. That is what it means here. We do not have to be learned theologians to stand firm in the faith. Indeed many so-called religious experts seem to have departed from the faith. They even deny the fundamentals of God's Word. Some Anglican ministers recite the Thirty-Nine Articles of their church each year and yet openly admit that they do not believe in all of them.

Even on the question of the devil, many theologians say that there is no such being; he is only an influence for evil. Those who read God's Word, believe it and put its teaching into practice are 'standing firm in the faith'. So often people ask those of us who have gone through very trying times in our lives, 'What did that experience do to your faith?' We can only reply very humbly, 'It only strengthened it,' because our faith is not based on our feelings, or our ability to grasp complicated theological arguments. It is based on the clear, straightforward teaching of God's Word. So we need to stand firm on the doctrines taught in the Bible. It, like the Lord himself, is as strong as a rock. It will never let us down.

A word of encouragement

Peter then offers us a word of great encouragement. He says, **'[Stand] firm in the faith, because you know that your brothers throughout the world are undergoing the same kind of suffering'** (5:9). When people are passing through trying circumstances the devil invariably tempts them to get so distressed that they concentrate solely on their own sufferings. Peter says, 'Remember others. You are not the only ones suffering. If you are suffering for righteousness' sake then praise God in it. But you know that other Christians (your brothers) throughout the world are undergoing the same kind of sufferings.' Paul wrote to the Philippians, 'For it has been granted to you on behalf of Christ not only to believe on him, but also to suffer for him, since you are going through the same struggle you saw I had, and now hear that I still have' (Philippians 1:29-30).

When we are suffering, and hear of other believers who are similarly being tested in their faith, then this should encourage us to persevere in our efforts to resist the devil.

Not only is it encouraging to realize that we do not suffer alone, but we need to remember always that our God is **'the God of all grace'** and he has **'called [us] to his eternal glory in Christ'** (5:10). Peter often refers to *grace*. He tells us that God's grace is rich and varied (4:10) and it is given to those who are humble (5:5). It is, therefore, in God that all grace originates and it is from God that all grace proceeds.

Then Peter says that God has called his suffering saints to his eternal glory in Christ. 'The term *call* is not merely an invitation which a person can accept or reject as he pleases. It is a divine summons. It is a royal command which the recipient must obey and cannot ignore.'[3] The apostle also speaks about God's calling in 1:15; 2:9, 21; 3:9 and 5:10. It is in Christ that God has called his people; he has chosen them in Christ 'before the creation of the world' (Ephesians 1:4).

When we suffer for Christ, because of our faith, the pain seems to go on for a long time, but we should encourage ourselves by remembering that Paul said, 'Our light and momentary troubles are achieving for us an eternal glory that far outweighs them all' (2 Corinthians 4:17). Even though we may emerge from a lifetime of suffering feeling very battered and bruised, it is a great comfort to know that God himself will definitely restore us and make us strong, firm and steadfast. It was to Peter himself that Jesus gave this charge: 'Strengthen your brothers' (Luke 22:32). God will restore his people to full strength again after the battle of life has passed.

In the doxology that ends this section (see also 4:11) Peter uses the term 'power', which denotes an attribute or title of great rulers. Unlike the fading authority and strength of earthly rulers, Peter declares, **'To him** [the God of all grace] **be the power for ever and ever. Amen'** (5:11).

27.
Postscript

Please read 1 Peter 5:12-14

In these three verses Peter tells us something about the reasons why he wrote this letter and adds a few details about his personal circumstances. This postscript is not just an after-thought; it is put at the end of this powerful letter for some very specific purposes.

Peter says that he wrote his letter **'with the help of Silas'** (5:12). Silas spent much time with Paul; for example, we read of them both being in prison together at Philippi (Acts 16). This would probably be one of the reasons why 1 Peter reflects some of Paul's letters. Probably Silas was a well-educated Greek-speaker and he would have acted as Peter's amanuensis, not just copying text, but clothing Peter's teaching with the Greek language. Some scholars believe that it was also Silas's task to deliver the letter and explain its teaching.

In this final paragraph Peter explains that he wrote what he modestly calls 'this brief letter' to encourage these Christians. These dear saints certainly needed encouragement. When we consider the many Christian resources that are available to us, and then compare them with the little that they had, we can understand their need. When we think about the terrible persecution that Christians were undergoing in those days, and the likelihood that these same believers were about to have to go through similar experiences, then it was vital that they were given all the help that was at Peter's disposal.

Barnabas was a great encourager of the early Christians. He sets us all an example to follow. Believers today seem to spend a great deal of their time running one another down, instead of trying to build each other up in the truth. Encouragement is a Christian virtue which is in very short supply.[1]

Peter also wanted to testify that **'This is the true grace of God.'** The truth which Peter has been outlining in this letter would not find acceptance by many who call themselves Christians today. These people find it necessary to explain away many of the doctrines stated or alluded to in these chapters. There is so much error being propounded in these days that the Christian church needs more than ever to stand firm in the truth of God and make it the foundation of all of its beliefs and practices.

When Peter writes, **'She who is in Babylon ... sends you her greetings,'** it is clear that he is writing about the company of Christian believers in the place where he wrote this epistle. He has no qualms about mentioning Mark by name, so why should he fear to give the name of a lady if he was referring to his mother or someone else?

Some commentators say that in mentioning Babylon Peter means the city to which the Jews had been exiled many years before. Calvin holds that Peter had gone to Mesopotamia to minister to the Jews in that place.[2] Others believe that 'Babylon' is a fortress in Egypt; but there are strong arguments to support the view that this is a code word for Rome. John called Rome 'Babylon' in Revelation 14:8; 16:19; 17:5; 18:2, 10, 21, and it seems very likely that Peter did the same. Tradition certainly says that Peter was executed near Rome.

In 5:14 the believers are instructed to **'Greet one another with a kiss of love.'** Different countries have varying ways of showing affection. In the Far East it is the custom to give a slight bow towards one another while in the West we tend to show affection by giving a warm handshake.[3] Even today in the Middle East a friend will show affection by giving a warm hug. So how are Christians who live in Britain to obey Peter's injunction written in this verse? Does our traditional reserve really express the warm love which we ought to have towards our fellow believers? I confess that on a few occasions I have felt such a genuine warmth to a fellow believer that I have wanted to show that love in a much richer way than a polite handshake can express. Wayne Grudem says, 'It is much harder to get mad at someone you have just hugged or kissed, and it is much easier to feel accepted in a fellowship which has such a warm welcome.'[4]

The letter ends with the beautiful greeting: **'Peace to all of you who are in Christ.'** How wonderful it is to know that 'peace of God, which transcends all understanding' (Philippians 4:7). Only those who, by grace, are 'in Christ' can experience this peace. Outside of Christ there is no hope and, naturally, no genuine peace which will last for all eternity.

2 Peter

28.
Introducing 2 Peter

Please read 2 Peter 1:1-2

This second letter of Peter is one of the most neglected in all New Testament literature. The early fathers had little to say about it and even Calvin wondered whether the apostle Peter wrote it; but despite his reservations about authorship this great Reformer had no doubt about the rightness of its inclusion in the canon of sacred Scripture.[1]

However, it should not surprise us that liberal scholars have attacked the authenticity of the epistle, because in it Peter 'takes a strong stand against those who would depart from the faith'.[2] Although the style of writing differs from that of 1 Peter, I accept that each of the objections raised by liberal scholars has been answered satisfactorily by other writers.

The letter itself declares that it was written by Simon Peter so that should settle the matter for all those who accept the Bible as the inerrant Word of God. However, for those who wish to delve into the various arguments against Peter's being the author there are numerous commentaries available. Those who have the inclination and the time will find a study of Michael Green's very lengthy (but highly readable) introduction to the 1987 edition of his commentary on 2 Peter and Jude very rewarding.[3]

The writer

He calls himself **'Simon Peter, a servant and apostle of Jesus Christ'**. This is slightly different from his first epistle where he calls himself 'Peter, an apostle of Jesus Christ'.

Peter is often called by this double name, 'Simon Peter'. John's Gospel almost always refers to him in this way. Michael Green suggests that he uses this 'to draw the reader's attention from the Jewish fisherman to the Christian apostle, from the old life to the new, from Simon, the name given him at his entry into the Old Covenant, to Peter, his distinctively Christian name'.[4]

In using the description 'servant', Peter is showing his loyalty to the Lord and also his humility. A bond-servant was a slave. Peter feels that he is honoured to be a slave of Jesus; this means that he acknowledges that he has no 'rights' of his own because he gladly subjects his own desires to the will of his Lord. Peter, the one who was possibly the leader of the apostles, is not ashamed to call himself a servant. Servants of Jesus Christ are not different from other believers; in fact Peter calls all believers servants of God in 1 Peter 2:16. In reading this second letter of Peter we find that the great apostle is proud to stand shoulder to shoulder with the humblest of God's people.

Peter also calls himself an apostle — one who has been sent by his Master to do an important task. He does not say that he is 'the' apostle. He claims to have no higher standing than any of the other apostles. As he gladly stands as a servant with other servants, so he is willing to be numbered with the other apostles of Jesus Christ.

The people to whom he wrote

In his first letter Peter listed the places where his readers lived — they were all in northern Turkey. On this occasion he makes no mention of their homes. However, if, the earlier letter referred to in 3:1 was in fact 1 Peter, then his readers lived in the same geographical region of northern Turkey. However, he seems not to be too worried about where they live. He is more concerned to point out the spiritual possessions which he shares with them. He says that he is writing **'to those who through the righteousness of our God and Saviour Jesus Christ have received a faith as precious as ours'** (1:1).

These believers have *received* faith. They have not earned it. Neither have they won it, as people win 'draws' and raffles in these days. They have been given it freely by God's grace. They have received grace 'through the righteousness of our God and Saviour Jesus Christ' (1:1). Christ, the righteous one, has granted that faith. He is able to do this because he is totally righteous. He is the one who is eternally just (Isaiah 51:4-6), and he has 'revealed his righteousness to the nations' (Psalm 98:1-2).

The faith spoken of here is not the objective body of doctrine of which we read in the Word of God, but it is that ability to believe in Jesus Christ as Lord and Saviour which is granted to all true Christians. Through the righteous death of the Lord Jesus Christ on the cross they have been saved.

Right at the very beginning of this epistle Peter emphasizes the divinity of Christ. Jehovah's Witnesses, and others who deny the doctrine of the Trinity, must find this verse hard to explain away. Yet we find similar descriptions of Christ elsewhere in the New Testament. A few days after the resurrection of our Lord, Thomas addressed Jesus as, 'My Lord and my God!' (John 20:28), and Paul writes, 'For in Christ all the fulness of the Deity lives in bodily form' (Colossians 2:9).

Also notice that Peter said of his readers that they 'have received a faith as precious as ours'. Again he stresses the unity of believers in the Lord Jesus Christ. Whatever position they may hold in the church, every one of them is as important as anyone else. There may be distinctions in the work undertaken by each one, but in regard to their standing before Christ they are all equal.

The greeting he gives

Peter greets his readers with the usual Greek and Hebrew greeting, but he adds that grace and peace can *only* come **'through the knowledge of God and of Jesus our Lord'**. This is the first of some ten places in this letter where the word 'knowledge', or one of its derivatives, is used. The people to whom Peter was writing were being deceived by those who claimed to have true knowledge of God and of Christ, but who denied it by their immoral behaviour. It seems that the gnosticism of the second century was already beginning to be noticed in the late 60s. The knowledge of God is not found through some philosophy or mystical practices, but it is discovered in Christ Jesus alone.

Throughout this letter Peter urges his readers to increase their knowledge of the Lord Jesus Christ (1:8; 2:20; 3:18). This is Peter's main concern in writing this epistle. He urges his readers to increase their personal knowledge of Jesus Christ, their Lord and Saviour. He begins his epistle with a powerful wish for grace and peace through knowledge of God and of Jesus Christ. He concludes his letter with an exhortation to 'grow in the grace and knowledge of our Lord and Saviour Jesus Christ' (3:18).

29.
Spiritual growth

Please read 2 Peter 1:3-7

Peter wrote his first epistle to warn believers in various churches that persecution would be coming upon them. He wrote his second letter to warn that there were also dangers inside the church.

During the last war everyone in this country was well aware of the danger arising from the gathering of Hitler's invasion fleets just across the channel; and the RAF did everything they could to make sure that Goering's aircraft did not achieve mastery in the air. Goering failed to drive Britain from the skies and, as a consequence, England was not invaded. But there was another danger: the enemy within. There were constant streams of slogans in magazines, newspapers and advertising hoardings with warnings such as, 'Be like dad — keep mum', and also the series of amusing Fougasse cartoons headed 'Careless Talk Costs Lives.' Everyone was aware that there might be spies around and each person had to be on guard against the possible danger of a fifth column (the name given to the Norwegians who betrayed their country to Hitler's armies).

The church today needs to be watchful. It has to be on its guard against trouble from within. There is an enemy who is trying to undermine the faith of God's people, and he is very active in attempting to pervert the gospel and lead people astray from the truth as it is in Jesus.

Peter was concerned about false teachers who were spreading error and at the same time he sought to warn true Christians about those who were scoffing at God's Word. Today

the Lord is saying that we must all see how we can defend ourselves against the subtle attacks of the evil one.

Our privileges as Christians

We have God's divine power available to us. Peter says that
the Lord Jesus Christ **'has given us everything we need'** (1:2-
3). When Christmas time comes around our friends start asking us, 'What do you want for Christmas?' As we grow older
and our needs become fewer we find it very difficult to give an
answer to that question. Some people would say, 'I'd give
anything to have my husband back. I miss him so much.'
Some say, 'I'd love to have my health and strength back
again,' and others reply, 'Oh to be young again and have all
my life stretching out before me!'

But nothing of this kind is promised to us. In effect Peter is
saying, 'Never mind about what you would like. Think about
what you already have.' 'He has given us everything we need
for life and godliness.' That is ours **'through the knowledge of
him who called us by his own glory and goodness'**.

To know Christ is to have God's power within us. This
knowledge is personal. If we are true Christians then we have
been called by the Lord. We have been 'called ... out of darkness into his wonderful light' (1 Peter 2:9). He has called us
all, individually, by our own names. Indeed no one can be a
true Christian unless he or she has been called by God's grace
and brought to the foot of the cross to confess his sin. It is then
that he is granted this wonderful gift of faith, which enables
him to believe on the Lord Jesus Christ for salvation.

The ancient philosophers spoke a great deal about knowledge. This is probably why Peter mentions the word so often
in his second letter (1:2, 3, 5, 8; 3:18). The gnostics (of whom
John wrote in his first epistle) were very proud of their knowledge. They said, 'You have to be a special kind of person to
have this knowledge. You need to be let into the secret before
you can be saved.'

However, Peter says, 'Grace and peace [are] ours in abundance through the knowledge of God and of Jesus our Lord'
(1:2). He goes on to say that it is knowing Christ personally
that makes all the difference (1:8). It is knowing more about

our precious Lord that enables us to make progress as believers (3:18). Paul also had the desire to know more about Jesus. He said, 'I want to know Christ and the power of his resurrection and the fellowship of sharing in his sufferings' (Philippians 3:10). Burnham sums up this sentiment very beautifully in the hymn:

> To know my Jesus crucified,
> By far excels all things beside;
> All earthly good I count but loss,
> And triumph in my Saviour's cross.
>
> Knowledge of all terrestrial things
> Ne'er to my soul true pleasure brings;
> No peace, but in the Son of God;
> No joy, but through his pardoning blood.
>
> O could I know and love him more,
> And all his wondrous grace explore,
> Ne'er would I covet man's esteem,
> But part with all, and follow him.[1]

When we have a personal knowledge of Jesus Christ, through faith, then everything is different. Firstly, we know that *we have been called by his own glory and goodness.* It is the pure virtues of Christ that have drawn us to himself and we become vividly conscious of his beauty. Peter himself became aware, for the first time, of the grandeur of the Lord when he caught a great many fish. 'When Simon Peter saw this, he fell at Jesus' knees and said, "Go away from me, Lord; I am a sinful man!"' (Luke 5:8). When we too see something of the glory and goodness of the Lord we realize how impoverished we really are. When we see Jesus with the eyes of faith the first thing that happens to us is that we become aware of ourselves and our sinfulness.[2]

Secondly, we know that *he has given us his very great and precious promises.* Peter loves to use the word 'precious' in regard to the Lord Jesus Christ. He had said in 1 Peter 2:4 that those who come to the Lord Jesus are 'precious to him' because they are part of the spiritual building of his people — i. e. the church. He said that the Lord Jesus Christ is 'a chosen and precious cornerstone' of the church (1 Peter 2:6); and in his second letter he wrote that all believers who have experienced the righteousness of God through believing on Jesus Christ as Saviour have received a faith as precious as his own (1:1). So where do we find such great and precious promises? We discover them in the Word of God — the Bible. We should, therefore, read and meditate upon the promises of God's Word and apply them to ourselves and our own situations.

Thirdly, we know that *we can partake of the divine nature.* This was a very daring phrase for Peter to use because this is what the worldly philosophers were saying in those days. They were claiming that some people could become so holy that they could be absorbed into the actual nature of God. This is similar to the Hindu teaching that pious people can, in the end, become so holy that they can attain Nirvana — i. e. become part of the god himself. However, Peter does not mean this. He is saying that when a person is truly converted God dwells in him or her by the Holy Spirit (John 14:16-17). Because of this wonderful fact, when we desire spiritual holiness we seek to live a Christ-like life.

Fourthly, we know that *the world is no longer our home.* When we see how people behave we realize that the standards of worldly society are very corrupt — and they, in their turn, corrupt people too. This is why Satan tempts us to love the world. He says, 'You will find freedom there. You will be able to indulge in all the naughty behaviour of modern society — and you will find it nice and exciting!' Do not listen when the devil says to you, 'As a Christian you are not under law any more, you are under grace. This means that you can do as you like because you are safe, God will never cast you off. You can sin as much as you like so that you can receive more grace.' If the evil one says that kind of thing to you just refer him to Romans 6 and see what he makes of it. Read it carefully yourself as well because Satan knows it already!

But the believer who is seeking to follow the Lord closely will be relieved that he has escaped the corruption which is in the world, which is caused by evil desires. He will no longer find his pleasures in the atmosphere of the world. The fellowship of God's people will be where he feels most at home. I cannot understand those Christians who say that they like going to a certain 'pub' because 'there is a nice atmosphere there'.

The standards of the Christian life

It requires effort to live as a Christian in this world. The attraction of the worldly system is very great. That is why there is a fall-out of people from the true church of Jesus Christ. The going becomes too tough for some people and they eventually succumb to the cry of the world and, in the end, stop mixing with God's people at all.

This is why Peter says, **'For this reason, make every effort ...'** (1:5). We need to be determined to live as Christians should, otherwise we will fall away. We may not stop attending church, but in our hearts we will cease to find Christ precious. When the time comes that the Lord stops captivating our minds and hearts there will not be much point in keeping up the pretence of being Christians. Peter is warning of the great danger there is of departing from the faith. None of us should say, 'Oh, that will never happen to me!' We all need to be on our guard. The devil is very subtle in the way he tries to draw us away from our precious Lord. So we should always seek to live as holy people and put Christ first in all our thoughts and actions.

Peter gives a list of things which we should **'add to'** our faith. This does not mean that in order to be saved we need something in addition to faith in Christ. We must never forget that we are saved by grace through faith alone. We are not saved by faith plus good works. We are not saved by faith plus taking communion. We are not saved by faith plus church-going and religious ceremonial. We are saved by faith in the Lord Jesus Christ alone for salvation.

However, we do need to grow as Christians. There is a progression of Christian virtues seen here in 1:5-7. I do not believe Peter is saying that we must all come to these eight virtues and tackle them in order. He is not saying, 'When you have mastered faith, then you need to move on to goodness; and when you have reached a certain measure of goodness then you should graduate on to knowledge.' I believe the apostle is saying that we should aim to achieve a measure of maturity in each of these things; and all Christians are to aim at every one of them all of their lives.

Peter says, **'Make every effort to add to your faith.'** Michael Green tells us that this word 'add' is a special word. He says it is the word used to describe the chorus master who put on an ancient Greek play. Such a theatrical performance could be a very expensive business. The idea was that the chorus master put up his own money to help to pay for the chorus, and then added it to what the state paid towards the cost of the play. Green says, 'The word [add] came to mean generous and costly co-operation.' He comments, 'The Christian must engage in this sort of co-operation with God in the production of the Christian life which is a credit to him.'[3]

It is important to notice that this list of virtues starts with faith and ends with love. Faith is the root of everything in the truly Christian life. To faith we should seek to add **'goodness'** — that is the plain, pure quality of wholeness which should shine out from the lives of all true believers. A friend of mine once reprimanded his daughter for wearing a tee-shirt which advertised milk. The slogan implied that *she* was 'full of natural goodness'. Her father was cross because, as he said, 'The Bible makes it clear that no one is *naturally* good.' True goodness can only be seen as the perfection of the Lord Jesus Christ shines out of a person's life.

To goodness we should add **'knowledge'**. There is an old hymn by Eliza Hewitt which expresses this desire:

> More about Jesus would I know,
> More of his grace to others show;
> More of his saving fulness see,
> More of his love who died for me.

To have spiritual knowledge requires us to use our minds correctly and to bring sanctified common sense to bear on our circumstances.

Next there follows **'self-control'**, which Peter mentioned several times in his first letter. What is the difference between self-control and perseverance? Self-control has to do with handling the pleasures of life, while perseverance relates primarily to the pressure of life. James 1:2-8 outlines how we can seek to develop perseverance in our everyday lives.

'**Godliness**' is that quality which speaks of a person being right in his relationship both with God and with his fellow man. A believer who seeks to live a godly life is not someone who 'lives with his head in the clouds', experiencing none of the trials and temptations with which ordinary men and women are plagued. 'He does not take an easy path simply to avoid either pain or trial. He does what is right because it is the will of God.'[4]

'**Brotherly kindness**' is love shown to all people. Even the unlovely are included in this. How much of this brotherly kindness do we display in our lives? So many people feel unloved. It is, therefore, the duty of Christian people to show love to all, regardless of how they are treated.

Finally Peter mentions this most blessed of all Christian virtues, '**Love**'. This is 'the kind of outgoing, selfless attitude that leads some to sacrifice for the good of others'.[5] In 1 Peter 4:8 the apostle wrote, 'Above all, love each other deeply, because love covers over a multitude of sins.'[6]

As we read what Peter says in these verses we need to ask ourselves these questions, 'How well am I growing spiritually? Have I ever been given spiritual life in the first place? (No one has even begun life as a Christian until the Holy Spirit comes upon him or her in converting power.) And, if I do have spiritual life, how much progress have I made in the faith?'

30.
Continuing spiritual growth

Please read 2 Peter 1:8-11

It is important that we carry on making progress in the Christian life. The believer who fails to grow in his spiritual life is not just standing still; he is going backwards.

Peter wrote his second letter to warn his readers of dangers that were about to come upon them — and these were largely going to attack them from within. This is why he urges them to be strong Christians. He says, 'Make every effort to add to your faith ...' (1:5). It is important for all God's people to keep on making progress, to keep moving forward.

Many people believe in Jesus. They make a profession of faith in Christ as Lord. They repent of their sins, and may even be baptized; yet they proceed no further. They think that if they read their Bibles occasionally, pray sometimes, do good deeds and attend church, then that is all that is required of them.

But God expects more. He asks that his people grow in their Christian lives. Peter lists eight virtues in verses 5-7, which he says every believer should try to cultivate in his own life. They are like the floors of a building, with faith as its foundation and love as its capstone. But a building which is just a shell is not of much use. The floors and walls need to be filled in and furnished.[1] In other words, Christians should have something good to show for their lives. This is what the Scriptures mean by saying we should produce fruit.

Fruitfulness

We should desire to produce fruit in our lives — for God's glory. That ought to be our aim in living. The non-Christian only wants to be able to do good. He desires that others see that he is living a productive life. He certainly wants to benefit other people — but his hope often is that the glory of his actions will rub off on himself and he will be praised as a great and good man or woman.

The Hindu wants to attain a higher life-form in his next reincarnation, because of his good works. The Muslim wants Allah to think well of him and reward him because of his obedience to the teaching of the Qur'an. The humanist wants to leave a good name behind him because of his devotion to the welfare of his fellow men and women. But the desire of a spiritually-minded Christian is to produce fruit so that his heavenly Father will be glorified.

It should always be our concern to live our lives with care, displaying more of these eight graces: faith, goodness, knowledge, self-control, perseverance, godliness, brotherly kindness and love. It is salutary for us to ask ourselves, 'How much of each of these qualities do I show in my life?'

The practice of these virtues helps us to know our Lord Jesus Christ better. He demonstrated each of them as he lived his earthly life. We can never achieve sinless perfection in this life, as Jesus did, but every day we should seek to live a Christ-like life. The result of this is that we will be kept from being ineffective and unproductive in our knowledge of the Lord.

We need to ask ourselves questions like, 'Do I want to be more successful in my witness to the gospel?' If we do crave success in this respect, then we should make every effort to live out these blessed qualities as we go about our daily lives. We should make greater efforts to drive out Satan from our thoughts, because he will tell us that it is not worth bothering to try to live like Jesus. He will say, 'It's a waste of time. No one can live like that. You might as well not bother. You'll never attain it.' And when he speaks like that he is right — but even so we must still try to live a Christ-like life. We should make greater efforts to fight the good fight of faith and we should press onward in these blessed graces.

Do we really want to produce more fruit for God's glory?

Then we must give greater diligence to prayer and the study of God's Word. In the parable of the sower Jesus spoke about the things that choke growth in spiritual life. He says that stunted growth is caused by the worries of this life and the deceitfulness of wealth (Matthew 13:22).

Are we consumed by worry about the things going on around us? If that is a problem that we have then we must hand over those worries to the Lord. We must confess that he has met every one of our real needs up until now. And because that is true, is it not inconceivable that he will fail to uphold us in the future?

Do we want to know our Lord Jesus Christ better? Then we should live our lives with faith on one hand and love on the other — and all of these other qualities in between. As a consequence, our lives, in part at any rate, will stop being ineffective and unproductive.

Open eyes

One of the dangers of failing to increase in spirituality is that we become short-sighted and blind. Peter is writing about spiritual blindness here. Paul wrote about unconverted people in 2 Corinthians 4:4. He said that, 'The god of this age has blinded the minds of unbelievers, so that they cannot see the light of the gospel of the glory of Christ.' It is a sad thing for anyone to be spiritually blind because such people cannot see any beauty in the Lord Jesus Christ. To them he is merely a good man who lived 2,000 years ago and who has no relevance to their lives today.

However, Peter is writing to Christian believers. He has been saying, '*you*' and '*us*', and now he says, **'If anyone does not have [these spiritual virtues] he is short-sighted.'** His hope is that his readers are not spiritually blind. However, even though God's people may not be spiritually blind, it is possible for them to close their eyes deliberately to spiritual truth. Some Christians live only for this world. They cannot see into the future. They are not like the faithful people written about in Hebrews 11. Those people of faith 'were longing for a better country — a heavenly one' (Hebrews 11:16).

How ineffective and unproductive the lives of carnal Christians are, who only live for the pleasures of the present! Their aim is to achieve honour and blessing here in this life. They think only of what they can get out of this world. They like teaching which says, 'Being a Christian means being rich in this world's goods.' They say, 'Because I am a Christian I can enjoy the pleasures of this life to the full.' They go further and say, 'Because I follow Jesus I can do what I like. All my sin has been washed away and I can carry on sinning because Christ has cleansed me and I can never go to hell.' They conveniently forget the teaching of Paul in Romans 6 which refutes such arguments.

But this kind of thinking is dangerous and wicked. If we are Christians we should be those who continually look to God and seek to bring glory to him. We should never be seen as selfish and ungrateful people. Such short-sighted Christians fail to look forward to what is in store for them. But that is not all that Peter says about them. He tells us that they have also forgotten to look backwards.

Blind Christians forget what they have been saved from. They have forgotten that before they were converted they were great sinners. They have forgotten that there was a time when they were bound for hell. They have forgotten that they were convicted of the awfulness of their sin by the Holy Spirit's intervention in their lives. They have forgotten that they have been brought to confess their sin and have received the Lord's forgiveness. They have forgotten that they have been given the gift of faith and been enabled to testify of their conversion to Christ. And they have forgotten that they were able to declare their faith in Christ by being baptized, so signifying that their sins had been cleansed through the precious shed blood of the Lord Jesus Christ.

Short-sighted and blind Christians have forgotten all that God has done for them and have slid back into their old ways — the ways of the world. Their lives are so bound up in themselves, and what they want, that no one is able any longer to detect that their declared intention had been to follow Christ until the end. But God wants his people to open their eyes and their memories, and be restored to living a holy life for his glory.

Security

Firstly, every true believer has been *called by grace.* No one
has become a Christian just because he or she made a decision
to follow Jesus. Looked at from the human standpoint, it
seemed that our salvation came to us because we made up our
minds to repent of our sins; we acted by stretching out the
hand of faith and we believed on the Lord Jesus Christ. That
is how it seems from our perspective. However, God was in
our salvation from beginning to end. Paul says, 'We know
that in all things God works for the good of those who love
him, *who have been called* according to his purpose' (Romans
8:28). God has called us to himself, by his Holy Spirit, and we
responded to that call, followed him and were gloriously
saved.

Secondly, every believer has been *elected to salvation.* This
is a hard doctrine for some to accept. But the fact is that God
'saw [us] ruined in the Fall'[2] and he set his love upon us and
chose us for himself. Then he called us to follow him.

One of the titles of God's people is 'God's elect'. That was
how Peter addressed the readers of his first letter (1 Peter
1:1), and that is how we should see ourselves. It is a cause of
great rejoicing that God saw us and chose us for himself. So it
does not matter when others ignore us and walk past us in the
street with their noses in the air. We should remember that
God has elected us to salvation. That fact should bring us joy
and security indeed.

Peter states calling and election as facts. His concern is that
we should 'make them sure'. How can we verify our election
to salvation? We can do it by living out the eight virtues written about in verses 5-7. They will not save us, but they will be
the proof that we are saved. James wrote a similar thing about
faith: 'But someone will say, "You have faith; I have deeds."
Show me your faith without deeds, and I will show you my
faith by what I do' (James 2:18).

When we are assured of our election to salvation we shall
be aware of two wonderful things. Firstly, *we shall never fall.*
Eternal security in Christ is ours. We will stumble every time
we sin, but we will never fall completely out of God's loving
arms. In writing about God's sheep, Jesus said, 'No one can
snatch them out of my Father's hand' (John 10:29).

Secondly, Peter says, **'You will receive a rich welcome into the eternal kingdom of our Lord and Saviour Jesus Christ'** (1:11). When heroes returned from the Olympic games in ancient Greece, they were brought into their home town, not through the ordinary city gate, but through specially constructed gateways; and they were also given a tumultuous welcome. So it will be for each of God's own blood-bought people. When we reach our heavenly home it will be for us just as it was for Bunyan's pilgrim: when we have crossed the river of death all the trumpets will sound for us on the other side.

31.
The importance of a personal testimony

Please read 2 Peter 1:12-18

When I used to work for the BBC as a freelance religious news reporter, I often said to my producer, 'Why are the Corporation so reluctant to have evangelicals on their programmes?' He replied by saying that the problem was that so often evangelical Christians persisted in using phrases like, 'I believe so and so,' or 'I think this ought to happen.' He said that those who were in control at Broadcasting House were not too impressed by people who propounded vague statements of belief. However, he said, 'If anyone gives a personal testimony, saying, "This happened to me ...," then I have no trouble in getting them on the air, whatever their beliefs about the Bible might be.'

It is my strong contention that if we had more people relating what God had done for them personally, then we would see much more blessing in the churches and throughout the land.

However, there is a danger with personal testimonies. They can be flippant, and sometimes they can tell us more about the speaker than about the God whom the person professes to serve. Peter does not fall into that trap.

The importance of truth

Peter wants his readers to keep the truth of God in their minds all of the time. What truth is he writing about? He is telling his readers about Jesus, and he gives him his full title in verses 14 and 16. He calls him **'our Lord Jesus Christ'**. Jesus is the chosen one of God; he is the Christ, the Anointed One. He is the Saviour of sinners; the angel said to Joseph, 'You are to give him the name Jesus, because he will save his people from their sins' (Matthew 1:21). Jesus Christ is the one who is in control of all things; he is the Lord. He also belongs to each of his own people personally; he is *'our* Lord Jesus Christ'.

Peter is concerned that his readers should have a personal knowledge of Jesus because he knows that they will come to know him better by being reminded of **'these things'** (1:12, 15). 'These things' mentioned in verse 12 are faith, goodness, knowledge, self-control, perseverance, godliness, brotherly kindness and love (1:5-7). 'These things' in verse 15 are the facts concerning who Jesus really is.

Peter is writing about the divine power of Jesus (1:3, 16). He is the Saviour. He is the one who died to bring the tremendous power of salvation to lost men, women and children. He is the one who will keep us from falling (1:10; Jude 24), and he is also the one who will eventually take us safely to our heavenly home (1:11).

Peter knows that it is important to keep on reminding these believers of the truth. He says, **'I will *always* remind you of these things.'** He sees it as his duty and his vital concern that the truth of Jesus should be held continually before God's people. He does this, even though he knows that his readers are established in the truth. He realizes how easy it is for Christians to grow cold in their zeal for the Lord. So he believes **'it is right to refresh [their] memory'** of Jesus, all the while that he has breath in his body.

The same obligation is placed today on all those who preach God's Word. 'One of the prime functions of a Christian minister must be to keep the basic facts of Christian truth and conduct always before the minds of his congregation.'[1] George Gallup, of the Gallup Poll international organization, speaking about Christians in the U.S.A. at the end of 1989, said, 'The central problem today is that people are not solidly grounded in their faith, and are therefore vulnerable.'[2]

We all need to be reminded that even the keenest Christian can stumble into sin. We should never think that we are so strong in the faith that we will never slip into sinful ways. We should remember all the time that Jesus died for us. This seems such an obvious thing to remind believers about, but there is something wrong if a Christian becomes tired of hearing the basic facts about the good news of salvation.

In speaking of the bread and the wine at the Lord's Supper, Jesus said, 'Do this in remembrance of me' (1 Corinthians 11:24-25). Jesus knew that we are forgetful, so he instituted this constant reminder for us. A great theologian has put it like this: 'The preaching of the Word represents the gospel to ear-gate; the administration of the sacraments [or ordinances] presents the same gospel to eye-gate.'[3]

It was important for Peter to remind these scattered believers of the truth because God's truth makes his people strong. Lying prophets were about and God's people need to be firm in the faith. 'Their defence and their safety will be in the truth which they possess.'[4]

Peter also realized that it was important to keep on reminding his readers of the truth because his time on earth was shortly (**'soon'** 1:14) coming to an end. Peter had referred to believers as pilgrims in his first epistle (1:1; 2:11) and, using the same figure, he now talks about his own body as a tent. Abraham and the patriarchs had lived in tents because they were nomads; they had no permanent home here on this earth. Both Peter and Paul (2 Corinthians 5:1) viewed their own death in this picturesque form, as the taking down of their tents and moving on to another location.[5]

Tent dwellers do not stay for too long in one location. When we are face to face with the shortness of life we are forced to see things in perspective. Matthew Henry says, 'The nearness of death makes the apostle diligent in the business of life.'[6] What is the business of life? It is to honour God and to seek to win others for Christ.

Jesus had already told Peter that he would die a martyr's death. We can read about that in John 21:18-19. When Peter, who was quite elderly by the time he wrote this second letter, realized that his death was approaching he said, 'I will soon put aside this tent of my earthly body.'

But there is something else that Peter wanted to do before he was taken from this earth. He had been telling them to 'make every effort' to live fruitful lives (1:5) and now he, in turn, would **'make every effort'** to see that after his departure from this life they would be able to remember the truths of the gospel (1:15). No one is absolutely sure what he meant by this but many scholars believe that Peter was referring to the Gospel according to Mark. It is thought that Peter supplied much of the material for Mark's Gospel. Why do people think that? In 1 Peter 5:13 we learn of Peter's friendship with Mark, and in Mark's Gospel many of Peter's faults are put most clearly. It was as if Peter had said to Mark, 'Make sure that you show how badly I behaved.' It is in this same Gospel that we find the central truths concerning Jesus put most concisely. Perhaps this is what Peter meant. He would make every effort to encourage Mark to write his Gospel so that Christians would have the truth about Jesus preserved in written form.

A foretaste of Christ's coming

Peter wants his readers to be certain of who Jesus is. Peter wants to reiterate the details concerning the coming of our Lord Jesus Christ. In the season of Advent the Christian world remembers the coming of Jesus; but Peter is not here speaking of the incarnation. He is not referring to the baby at Bethlehem. He uses a word which is normally used to speak about the second coming of Christ. Jesus came once as a baby (to live and to die) but he is coming again, in the last times, to judge this world and the Scriptures say that his coming will be in great power. In the last book in the Bible we read,

> 'Look, he is coming with the clouds,
>   and every eye will see him,
> even those who pierced him;
>   and all the peoples of the earth will
>   mourn because of him.
>   So shall it be! Amen'

(Rev. 1:7).

Jesus is coming again to establish his eternal kingdom.
And Peter says, 'This is true.' **'We did not follow cleverly invented stories.'** The apostle is going on, in chapter 2, to warn these believers about false teachers who will tell exciting

stories which none the less are full of lies. 'Don't listen to them,' he says, 'Listen to us (the apostles) who tell you the truth concerning Jesus.'

Peter says we know about the coming of the Lord. We have received a foretaste of what his coming will be like. We saw it in Christ's transfiguration.[7] We can read about this event in Matthew 17:1-8; Mark 9:2-8 and Luke 9:28-36. He says, **'We were eye-witnesses of his majesty'** (1:16). Peter, James and John all saw Jesus transfigured into a glorious King on that **'sacred mountain'**. We do not know which mountain it was, but because the Lord was there it was made holy and glorious.

Wherever the Lord is, there glory is displayed. God's people are holy because they have been set apart for his use. Whenever anyone sees the holiness of God, he or she cannot help being drastically affected by his splendour and glory.

An eye-witness is the most effective witness to any situation. Peter tells his readers, 'Don't listen to made-up stories about Jesus. Listen to the truth from those of us who have seen, with our own eyes, his glory.' Perhaps even at that time there were many false 'gospels' going the rounds telling all kinds of outrageous stories about Jesus. We should take very great care that we only base our beliefs on the writings which we find in the Bible, which is the only Word of God.

Not only did Peter see Jesus, but he heard the voice of God declaring his deity. Twice he mentions the voice of God (1:17, 18). These are the words which were spoken by the voice of God: 'This is my Son, whom I love; with him I am well pleased.' The same message was given from heaven by God at the baptism of Jesus. Peter says, 'We ourselves heard this voice that came from heaven when we were with him on the sacred mountain' (1:18). How can anyone doubt that Jesus is the Son of God — God himself in human form?

And every day God's people should be seeking by every means at their disposal to testify to the truth and love of that same Lord Jesus Christ.

32.
The certainty of God's Word

Please read 2 Peter 1:19-21

If the Bible, or any part of it, was proved not to be authentic, then our faith would be founded on a lie. As evangelicals we stand by the Bible as the inspired Word of God, inerrant (as it was originally given), and true in every way.

We endeavour to base everything we do, say and think upon the teaching of God's Word; yet at the same time it is unfortunately true to say that we do not revere it as we should. We spend a few minutes reading it each day. We quote it sometimes in conversation. We really believe that it forms the basis for the whole of our morality; yet we largely ignore its teaching in our everyday lives.

A group of atheists and agnostics (called 'Freedom from Religion') had been campaigning in the U.S.A. to get all of the Holiday Inns group of hotels to offer Bible-free rooms. The hotel group's management responded to this request by saying, 'We've always had the Bibles, and we'll continue to have them because it's a matter of choice if the guest wants to read it or not.'

We might feel sad that this group of people wanted Bibles banned from certain hotel rooms, but the question we should ask ourselves about this story is, 'Do atheists and agnostics recognize the power of God's Word more than we do?'[1]

Peter had been warning his readers to avoid those who are spreading cleverly invented stories (1:16) about the Lord Jesus Christ. The apostle's message is: 'Listen to us. We were eye-witnesses of his majesty on the mountain. We ourselves heard the voice which came from heaven that said, 'This is my

Son, whom I love; with him I am well pleased' (1:17-18).

Peter knew that Jesus was much more than just a great teacher and healer. He knew that Jesus is God himself, who came down to earth in human form.

Every Jew had been taught from childhood that the Old Testament Scriptures (which they called 'the Prophets') were the Word of God. Now Peter is saying, 'Because God became man at Bethlehem, **We have the word of the prophets made more certain**.' Christ is the centre of the Bible. 'Everything in the Old Testament looked forward to him, everything in the New Testament looks back to him. He is the centre of history ... It is in him, in his person, that you find gathered up together all the promises of God.'[2]

The Bible is trustworthy

The Bible is true. It does not merely *contain* the truth; it *is* the truth of God. It is not just an interesting book full of stories; it is the Word of God for all people. Dr Martyn Lloyd-Jones said, 'Whenever I read the Bible I feel it is true, because it does not hesitate to state the facts. It states them bluntly, it states them openly ... It is a great thing to have a book you can trust.'[3]

Many of the Old Testament prophecies had been fulfilled by the time Peter wrote this letter. It is as though Peter were saying, 'If you won't believe what I have said, [about Jesus] then believe what is written in the Word of God.'[4] The whole of the Old Testament was regarded as prophecy.

If we look at Micah 5:2 we read,

> 'But you, Bethlehem Ephrathah,
>   though you are small among the clans of Judah,
> out of you will come for me
>   one who will be ruler over Israel,
> whose origins are of old,
>   from ancient times.'

Everyone knew that this referred to the coming Messiah. Joseph and Mary had been told by Gabriel that the baby born to them would be 'called the Son of the Most High' (Luke

1:32). But Mary and Joseph lived way up north in Nazareth.
How could the baby whom they were expecting be the Messiah, when prophecy declared that the Deliverer was to be
born in Bethlehem? Everyone knew that the prophets always
spoke the truth and that true prophecy had to be fulfilled
exactly. So how was Jesus going to be born in Bethlehem?
The prophecy was fulfilled because a heathen ruler in faraway
Rome decided to issue 'a decree that a census should be taken
of the entire Roman world' (Luke 2:1).

We could also look at Isaiah. He gave many prophecies
concerning the Messiah. In Isaiah 9:6-7 he said,

> 'For to us a child is born,
>   to us a son is given,
>   and the government will be on his shoulders.
> And he will be called
>   Wonderful Counsellor, Mighty God,
>   Everlasting Father, Prince of Peace.
> Of the increase of his government and peace
>   there will be no end.
> He will reign on David's throne
>   and over his kingdom,
> establishing and upholding it
>   with justice and righteousness
>   from that time on and for ever.
> The zeal of the Lord Almighty
>   will accomplish this.'

He said in his prophecy that the Messiah would live for ever.
A hostile crowd many years later took up this point when ridi-
culing Jesus. They said, 'We have heard from the Law that
Christ will remain for ever, so how can you say, "The Son of
Man must be lifted up?" Who is this "Son of Man"?' (John
12:34).

The crowd said that Jesus could not be the Messiah because
he predicted that he would die, while Isaiah said that he
would live for ever. Looking back into the past we know that
Isaiah and Jesus were both correct. Jesus did die, but he rose
again, and he will live and reign for ever. Daniel tells us that
his kingdom is 'an everlasting kingdom, and all rulers will
worship and obey him' (Daniel 7:27).

Because the Bible is trustworthy, we **'will do well to pay attention to it'** (1:19). But how much notice do we take of the Word of God? Do we respect it as we should? I sometimes think that those who follow false religions put Christians to shame when it comes to the way they treat their holy books. Take the Qur'an for instance. No Muslim would put a copy of that book on the floor, or under his arm. He would make sure that it occupied the highest shelf in the room. When he reads it he will, normally, place it on a stand so that it is fingered as little as possible.

Or think about the *Guru Granth Sahib,* the holy book of the Sikhs. No Sikh will read that book without first having a bath and a complete change of clothing — in fact they tend then to dress themselves completely in white. This book occupies the central position in the Gurdwara, the Sikh place of worship. Every member of the congregation bows before it as he or she enters the temple and they make sure that they sit at a lower level than their holy book.

Christians should treat God's Word with much more respect than they do. It is the truth. These other books, though they contain some good, ethical teachings, are not the Word of God. Only the Bible is God's message to mankind. We should, therefore, read it more often. We should take in what we read and meditate upon it. We should carry its teachings into our everyday lives and we should live out the truth of God's Word. It should be like the very breath that we breathe.

The Bible is a shining light

The world in which we live is a dark place. We do not need to spend very long thinking about that fact. People's minds are full of greed. It is not safe to leave anything valuable unattended because it may well be stolen. People's minds are darkened by sin. The devil is very active in leading many astray into wickedness — so much so that children are growing up today not knowing right from wrong. So often, even at school, moral values do not seem to be taught as once they were. Many teachers themselves are living with people as though they were married to them, when in fact they are not.

This is all regarded as perfectly acceptable behaviour in front of young people. Naturally the evil one plays upon these things and draws many into the darkness of untold wickedness.

Even the moral values of God's people are slipping. Our forefathers would be staggered by some of the things we watch on our televisions. They would be amazed that we can find time to attend worldly amusements, but cannot manage to get to the church prayer meetings and Bible studies. They would find it very worrying to see what kinds of moral behaviour we now find church members and leaders accepting as permissible.

Why is life as it is? It is because we live in a dark place. The Greek word means 'dismal'. These original readers of Peter's letters lived in a murky place. We can read of that in 2:1-3: 'But there were also false prophets among the people, just as there will be false teachers among you. They will secretly introduce destructive heresies, even denying the sovereign Lord who bought them — bringing swift destruction on themselves. Many will follow their shameful ways and will bring the way of truth into disrepute. In their greed these teachers will exploit you with stories they have made up. Their condemnation has long been hanging over them, and their destruction has not been sleeping.' Warren Wiersbe puts it like this: 'Human history began in a lovely garden, but that garden today is a murky swamp.'[5]

Peter says that God's Word is a 'light shining in a dark place'. Psalm 119:105 declares, 'Your word is a lamp to my feet and a light for my path.' It is God's Word which shows up all the dangerous places of this life. When we want to know how to live properly we can turn to the Bible and discover that it is shining with the truth of God. It lights up hidden pitfalls in the path and it directs our feet into the right way. Jesus himself said, 'I am the light of the world' (John 8:12). When he began his ministry the people living in darkness saw a great light (Matthew 4:16). Luke tells us that when Jesus was born his coming into the world was like the dawning of a new day 'to shine on those living in darkness and in the shadow of death' (Luke 1:78). He is the morning star rising in the hearts of his people.

Jesus came the first time to bring light into this world, but he is coming again to cast down all the wicked works of darkness and set up his eternal kingdom. That day of the Lord will be a glorious time for all who know and honour him as their Saviour. But at that time those who do not love the Lord will hear these awful words: 'I never knew you: depart from me, ye that work iniquity' (Matthew 7:23, AV). For ever it will true for them, 'Let him who does wrong continue to do wrong; let him who is vile continue to be vile' (Revelation 22:11). There will be no more opportunity for repentance. At that time the number of God's elect will be complete and Jesus himself will call out, 'I am the root and the offspring of David, and the bright Morning Star' (Revelation 22:16).

The Bible is God's Word

No true prophet ever uttered his own thoughts and said they were the Word of God. He never stood up in a meeting and, speaking his own ideas, said, 'Thus saith the Lord, I am saying unto you ...' The true prophet was always concerned that he gave God's Word and not the wishes of his own heart. No prophet who wrote Scripture gave his own interpretation of what God was saying. Also the words he gave fitted in completely with the rest of Scripture.

However, God did not normally issue his commands with a powerful voice from heaven. He used people to convey his Word. He did not employ robots. He actually took people and prepared them for the message he wanted to give. He used their words and their personalities and they spoke from God as they were carried along by the Holy Spirit. Gordon Clark put it like this: 'Isaiah did not get out of bed one morning and say, "I have decided to write some prophecies today." Revelations are not the result of human volition. On the contrary, God picked Isaiah up and carried him along; so supported Isaiah spoke the words from God.'[6]

When the prophets wrote down the sacred Scriptures they were inspired by God. The picture is of a sailing ship. It has no power of its own. Its captain sets the sails and places the rudder in the most advantageous position, but the ship is blown along by the wind. In a similar manner the writers of Scripture were carried along, when they wrote the text, by the 'wind' of

God, the Holy Spirit. 2 Timothy 3:16 also tells us that 'All Scripture is God-breathed.' Modern critics find it difficult to regard the Bible as anything more than an inspiring book compiled from the philosophies of religious people. They refuse to accept that it is the divinely inspired and inerrant Word of God. God chose to use people to write it, just as I have chosen to write this commentary on my word processor. The machine produces my words, but I place myself within the constraints of this machine and I have to abide by its 'personality'.

How do we regard the Word of God?

Is it just a book where we find lovely stories about a helpless baby in a manger and wonderful teaching of an ethical nature? Or is it a book where we find the living God speaking to his people today? Do we discover, as we read it, that Jesus himself is shining out of its pages into the darkness of this world and, through the Holy Spirit's application of the blood of cleansing, he is bringing many people 'into his wonderful light'? (1 Peter 2:9). If we believe God, then we must believe his Word and abide by its teaching. If we are true followers of the Lord Jesus Christ then we must obey the Bible and uphold it in everything we do, say and think.

33.
The danger of false teachers

Please read 2 Peter 2:1-10

'One of the most terrible and terrifying chapters in the entire Bible' is how Dr Martyn Lloyd-Jones described this chapter of Peter's second epistle.[1] As I write, during the last decade of the twentieth century, I believe that Satan must be thinking that he now has even greater opportunities than usual to wreak havoc in the church of Jesus Christ. Because the authority of Christian leaders is being challenged as never before, the way is open for the evil one to influence the running of churches more than ever, and he is planning to increase his evil work of trying to destroy the faith of God's people. In these opening verses of 2 Peter 2 we can learn something of how he goes about causing trouble among the people of God.

Satan uses people to do his work. He uses men and women who are under his control. They are so much under his power that they probably do not even realize that they are being used by the devil to do his wicked work, and they may think that they are doing God a service.

The description of these false teachers

False teachers are like false prophets. Peter had been writing in chapter 1 about the importance of God's prophets. They spoke God's Word. Their purpose was to bring glory to the Lord, and their desire was to benefit the people of God, both spiritually and materially.

But then, as now, **'there were also false prophets among the people'**. Wherever there are true prophets there are false ones as well. The devil always produces counterfeits of the true. They appear as though they are workers for God, yet all the while they are active on behalf of the evil one.

We read about false prophets throughout the Old Testament. These people claimed to speak for God, but in fact they did not. They prophesied lies (Jeremiah 5:31). The Lord said to Jeremiah, 'The prophets are prophesying lies in my name. I have not sent them or appointed them or spoken to them. They are prophesying to you false visions, divinations, idolatries and the delusions of their own minds' (Jeremiah 14:14). God said that he was against them. '"Therefore," declares the Lord, "I am against the prophets who steal from one another words supposedly from me. Yes," declares the Lord, "I am against the prophets who wag their own tongues and yet declare, 'The Lord declares.' Indeed, I am against those who prophesy false dreams," declares the Lord. "They tell them and lead my people astray with their reckless lies, yet I did not send or appoint them. They do not benefit these people in the least," declares the Lord' (Jeremiah 23:30-32).

False prophets can lead true Christians astray. Many people follow them. We have false prophets today. They go under the names of various cults and they have large numbers of adherents. They use the name of Jesus, but he is not the same Lord whom we worship. They strip him either of his divinity or his humanity. We can recognize false prophets because they preach a false religion. Jesus said, 'Watch out for false prophets ... By their fruit you will recognize them' (Matthew 7:15-16).

However, Peter is not talking here about false prophets. He is warning Christians to beware of **'false teachers'**. Paul warned that these would come among the people of God. When he said 'goodbye' to the Ephesian elders he said, 'Keep watch over yourselves and all the flock of which the Holy Spirit has made you overseers. Be shepherds of the church of God, which *he bought with his own blood.* I know that after I leave, savage wolves will come in among you and will not spare the flock. Even from your own number men will arise and distort the truth in order to draw away disciples after them. So be on your guard!' (Acts 20:28-31). Paul kept up this note of alarm throughout his epistles. So it should not surprise us if we still find false teachers today.

How can we recognize false teachers?

We discover that false teachers enter the church secretly. False religions are blatantly opposed to the church of Jesus Christ. It is obvious, even to weak Christians, that their teaching is wrong. But Peter is not talking about opposition in this second letter; he dealt with that in his first epistle. Eric Lane has said, 'One of the most dangerous weapons is false teaching ... Satan [knows] that false teachers do far more damage than persecutors.'[2]

False teachers also **'introduce destructive heresies'**. A heresy is literally something which forces people to make a choice: a choice between what is right teaching and what is wrong doctrine. Wrong teaching is divisive (Titus 3:10). Peter says that in their heresy they **'even [deny] the sovereign Lord who bought them'** (2:1). In writing about the sovereign Lord he may mean God the Father, or he may be referring to the Lord Jesus Christ. It was God who redeemed (bought) his people from the slavery of Egypt (Exodus 12) and it is the Lord Jesus Christ who purchased the salvation of his people at Calvary (1 Cor. 6:20; Acts 20:28).

Peter says that false teachers even go to such lengths as to deny the Lord. Some deny that Jesus is divine; they only think of him as a good man. Some deny that Jesus is human; they think of him only as a god. But if we deny that Jesus is fully God and fully man at the same time, then we deny our own redemption; because only the Lord God can save us, and only someone who is fully human could have died to take the punishment of our sin.

If Jesus' death on the cross purchased salvation for each of his elect people, how can these false teachers deny **'the sovereign Lord who bought them'**? If they are not true Christians then they have never been redeemed from their sin; Christ has not shed his blood for them. So what does Peter mean by this? Perhaps the statement in 2:20-21 helps us on this point. There the apostle makes it clear that these false teachers once claimed that they knew the Lord and the way of righteousness. 'They made it known that Jesus had bought them [probably to make their message appear to be more credible] but they eventually rejected Christ and left the Christian community. As John writes, 'They went out from us, but *they did not really belong to us*' (1 John 2:19); and see Heb. 6:4-6; 10:26-29). Hence their denial of Christ showed that they were not redeemed.'[3]

We need to beware of those who are bringing false teaching into the church today. Some of these say that the resurrection of Jesus was only a spiritual act; they deny that Jesus was physically raised from the dead. Some say that you need something in addition to repentance and faith in order to be saved: you need to perform some ritualistic work (e.g. baptism) before you can be qualified for acceptance in heaven. Some say that you need to be baptized in the name of Jesus only; baptism in the name of the Trinity is wrong, they argue. Some say that the bread and wine must be consecrated by a 'proper priest', so that they are turned into the body and blood of Christ; this is the only way that communicants can obtain grace, they argue. Some say that hell does not exist. They either teach that everyone will be saved, or that those who die unrepentant will just pass into oblivion and be annihilated. Because false teachers are active none of us dare relax our guard; otherwise we too, could be lured away from the faith of the apostles as outlined in the Bible.

The effect of false teachers

Peter says that many will follow them (2:2). Their teaching is powerful. They are not timid in their assertions. They speak with great power and authority and they gain many followers. Indeed Peter says that **'Many will follow their shameful ways.'** The teaching of false teachers often (but not always) leads to unholy living. Sometimes they gain many followers because their teaching can lead to freedom from moral restraints (2:19). The result of this is that the way of truth is brought into disrepute. Instead of being able to say, 'I have chosen the way of truth; I have set my heart on your laws' (Psalm 119:30), the followers of false teachers enjoy the ways of wickedness.

False teachers will exploit the people of God. They seem to be offering excitement and a richer way of life, but all the while they are lining their own pockets. There have been examples of this particularly among certain television evangelists in the U.S.A. False teachers are like those who were in Corinth who '[peddled] the word of God for profit' (2 Corinthians 2:17). They are people who make up 'cleverly invented' stories (2:3; 1:16) to deceive true believers.

Some Old Testament examples

From verses 4-8 Peter gives three examples of the way God dealt with those who are ungodly. These same people are also mentioned in Jude 5-8. Peter speaks about *fallen angels* (2:4). We do not know whether this passage is referring to the fall of Lucifer (Isaiah 14:12-15), or to the puzzling incident recorded in Genesis 6:1-4. But the angels about whom the apostle is writing became too proud and, as a result, they were cast out of heaven. These angels are being punished right now in hell, but they also await the final, dreadful Day of Judgement.

Next Peter writes about *the ungodly in the time of Noah* (2:5). He says the Lord did not spare the ancient world because the people were so wicked and disobedient to God's Word. They took no notice of Noah, whom he describes as **'a preacher of righteousness'**. In the Old Testament Noah is called one who 'found favour in the eyes of the Lord' (Genesis 6:8). 'Noah was a righteous man, blameless among the people of his time, and he walked with God' (Genesis 6:9). Anyone who lived such a holy life would certainly set a good example to others. He would be sure to explain to his neighbours why he was building an ark (something that, like a flood, no one had ever seen before!) and he would warn them of the danger they were all in. As he was a very long time in building it, he would certainly have been a persistent preacher of righteousness to those around him.

Peter also speaks of the destruction of *the cities in the plain* (Genesis 19). The sin of their inhabitants was that of unspeakable sexual immorality and perversion. The city of Sodom has even given its name to an evil practice which is still rampant today.

God condemned these evil practices, and so should we. We should not treat these things as an acceptable way in which to behave, just because some give the excuse that they have an inclination towards homosexuality. The fact that there is a 'Gay Christian Movement' and there are those who claim to be 'gay' ministers of religion does not make it biblical or right. We should certainly seek to love the people who engage in such practices but we should hate and condemn their behaviour for the sin that it is. Paul speaks strongly about this in Romans 1, and we dare not say that this biblical teaching no longer applies.

How we should live

How should we live in the face of all this evil? We should live being aware that **'The Lord knows how to rescue godly men from trials'** (2:9). He protected Noah and his family (the **'seven others'** in 2:5). He provided the ark as a way of escape from his judgement of water, just as he rescued Lot from the judgement of fire. (Peter also used the flood as an example in 1 Peter 3:20 and he will do so again in 3:6). The Lord delivered Noah when he destroyed the ancient world.

God rescued Lot (2:7). It surprises us to see Lot described as **'a righteous man, who was distressed by the filthy lives of lawless men'** (2 Peter 2:7-8). When we read Genesis 19 we only see him as a greedy and selfish man, who treated two of his daughters abominably (Genesis 19:8). Yet the Lord said in effect, 'Lot trusts in me, and also Abraham has prayed for him.' James tells us that 'The prayer of a righteous man is powerful and effective' (James 5:16). Therefore God rescued Lot by the skin of his teeth (Genesis 19:15-17; 1 Corinthians 3:15). We could say that Lot did not deserve to be rescued, but do any of us? That is what grace is: God's love to undeserving sinners.

When the cities of the plain were destroyed we read that they were burned to ashes (2:6). This word **'ashes'** is exactly the same Greek word which the ancient historians used to describe the lava which covered the Roman cities of Pompeii and Herculanium in A.D. 79. Many were destroyed by being burnt them to ashes, but Lot and two of his daughters were rescued. However, Lot's wife looked back (being reluctant to leave the wicked cities) and, because of her lack of enthusiasm for rescue, she was turned into a pillar of salt (Genesis 19:26).

God knows how to rescue godly men from trials. We may

have many trials. They may seem to us to last for a very long time, yet the Lord will deliver us out of them all in his own good time. Paul wrote to the Corinthians, 'God ... will not let you be tempted beyond what you can bear. But when you are tempted, he will also provide a way out so that you can stand up under it' (1 Corinthians 10:13).

God also knows how to deal with the unrighteous. He says that they will be punished in line with the damage they have inflicted. In verse 1 Peter says that these wicked teachers try to destroy the people of God. Therefore, says the Lord, 'They will bring swift destruction on themselves.' He says, **'Their condemnation has long been hanging over them, and their destruction has not been sleeping'** (2:3). In other words, the Day of Judgement is waiting for them. God's name *will* be vindicated, and one day everything which is evil will be completely destroyed.

The Word of God says, **'This is especially true of those who follow the corrupt desire of the sinful nature and despise authority'** (2:10). Evil practices go hand in hand with disobedience to God's laws. The authority of the Lord is supreme. How wicked it is that anyone (especially someone who claims to be a leader in Christian circles) should deny the Sovereign Lord who purchased redemption at the cost of the blood of Calvary! How evil of anyone to disobey the authority of the Lord and his apostles as it is clearly laid down in the Bible!

Warnings for us all

We should be on our guard against false teachers — especially those who may appear secretly among us. We should be like the Bereans (Acts 17:11) and test everything that we read which purports to be God's word. We should remember that God always has his hand upon his people and know that he will keep his word to protect, rescue and deliver them. We should bear our afflictions patiently, knowing that the Lord cares about us all. And we should leave the punishment and destruction of the wicked in God's hand. 'Vengeance is mine,' says the Lord, 'I will repay' (Romans 12:19, AV).

34.
The desires of false teachers

Please read 2 Peter 2:10-16

There is no doubt that as the church grows throughout this world, so the activity of the devil and his evil hosts also increases. His desire is to destroy all the work of the Lord. In the same way, his concern will grow to undermine the people of God and thwart their efforts to reach lost men and women for Christ. One of the ways the devil goes about his evil work is to introduce false teachers into the church of Jesus Christ.

The arrogance of the false teachers

They even speak against angels. Angels are celestial beings who are messengers of God. They have a great work to do in serving the Lord. The Bible speaks about them throughout its pages. Charles Swindoll describes their work like this: 'Angels provide the Lord with every conceivable service we can imagine. They carry his messages and perform his will among us — warning, protecting, helping, and rescuing us. These supernatural creatures do not provide the type of service rendered from man to man. Rather, their service is from heaven to earth, originating from the very throne of God.'[1]

But these false teachers think so much of themselves that they **'are not afraid to slander celestial beings'** (2:10). They are bold enough to say terrible things against God's heavenly servants. They are arrogant, thinking that they are always in the right. Perhaps they speak abusively about angels because they do not believe in the existence of these celestial beings.

Many years ago there was a man who was like this who belonged to the same church as myself. The first evening he arrived he informed the pastor that God had sent him to 'put the church right on a number of important matters'. He then proceeded to undermine the preaching of the elders and to cause havoc in the church. He unsettled many — particularly those who were new converts and several younger women who had unconverted husbands. The word which most aptly describes this clever fellow is 'arrogant' — for there were few things that he could not mend, speak about with authority, or do. The only things which he seemed to know very little about were humility and grace. In many ways he was a false teacher and he did much harm.

These false teachers about whom Peter wrote were not only bold and arrogant, but they seemed to be oblivious of the presence of the Lord. The angels, although they were much stronger and more powerful than the false teachers, did not bring slanderous accusations against these people or any other arrogant being. 'Unlike the false teachers who are careless of the lordship of Christ and are free with their insults, the angels so revere their Lord as they live all their lives in his presence, that no insulting language is allowed to pass their lips, even though it would be richly deserved.'[2]

Next Peter says that these false teachers are **'like brute beasts'** (2:12). They blaspheme in matters they do not understand. They **'mouth empty boastful words'** (2:18). They are like some so-called intellectuals who speak only in long complicated sentences, using many difficult words and concepts. They try to show off and sound clever; yet all the while they do not really understand what they are talking about.

The dictionary tells us that 'to blaspheme' means 'to speak profanely'. In this country the use of profanities seems to be growing more and more common. Perhaps because we are almost getting used to them, my wife and I were pleasantly surprised to read a notice in the bus waiting room of a little Greek town which said, *'Me Blasfemeite'* — 'No blaspheming'.

Believers should take care that they do not utter blasphemies against the Lord; they should not take his name in vain (i. e., use it in a way in which it is not intended to be used). While Christians should make every effort to refrain from using swear words, it is difficult for people to avoid them if they live in an atmosphere where bad language is the normal mode of speech. I made this discovery within a few hours of being in an army barrack room when I was called up for my National Service in 1953. There was so much swearing going on that I caught myself about to use a word which I knew was unwholesome. How readily it seems that words like 'hell' and 'damn' come to the lips of some Christians! That, says Peter, is the language of the false teacher.

Why does Peter say that these false teachers are like brute beasts? He says it because animals only have instincts. An animal cannot reason things out. He behaves in a certain way because he knows he will be rewarded if he makes the correct response. Those who have studied psychology will know about Pavlov's salivating dogs. 'An animal cannot appreciate the feelings or nature of man, and an unbeliever "does not accept the things of the Spirit of God ... and he cannot understand them" (1 Cor. 2:14).'[3] Beasts are **'born only to be caught and destroyed'**. (Presumably there were no dog and cat lovers in Peter's day!) This is the fate of all false teachers. They themselves have lured many astray into error and sinful ways and, in their turn, they too will perish. **'They will be paid back with harm for the harm they have done'** (2:13).

The pleasures enjoyed by false teachers

'Their idea of pleasure is to carouse in broad daylight' (2:13). They enjoy imbibing large quantities of alcoholic liquor. They get so drunk that they lose all their inhibitions. Paul was stating a fact when he wrote to the Thessalonians about those who were still in the darkness of sin. He was speaking of the standard of the non-Christian when he said, 'Those who get drunk, get drunk at night' (1 Thessalonians 5:7; cf. Acts 2:15). But these people, who claimed to be Christians and teachers of the Word, got drunk in the daytime too! Gordon H. Clark puts it like this: 'It was not enough to get drunk at night — these people [had to] consume their lascivious doings all day.'[4]

Peter says that these people **'[revel] in their pleasures while they feast with you'**. They enjoyed taking their excesses into the church meetings. It seems as if they behaved like those at Corinth who used the Lord's Supper as an excuse for a time of feasting and revelling. Paul wrote to them like this: 'Don't you have homes to eat and drink in? Or do you despise the church of God and humiliate those who have nothing?' (1 Corinthians 11:22). These false teachers in 2 Peter 2 thought that Holy Communion was not so much a serious, solemn service as a time for merriment.

Their drunkenness and their feasting brought the people of God into disrepute. Peter says of them, **'They are blots and blemishes'** on the true church, rather than teachers of the Word. He says they are the very opposite of the character of Christ, whom he described in 1 Peter 1:19 as 'a lamb without blemish or defect'. The church should be like her Lord, 'a radiant church, without stain or any wrinkle or any other blemish' (Ephesians 5:27).

Their idea of pleasure was to drink to the full of the sin of adultery. Peter says these false teachers had **'eyes full of adultery'** (2:14). He means that they were always looking for women with whom they could satisfy their lustful craving. Jesus said that 'Anyone who [even] looks at a woman lustfully has already committed adultery with her in his heart' (Matthew 5:28). When they have done this they have no guilty feelings about their behaviour, despite the fact that they have broken the seventh commandment. Someone said to me once, 'The first time you commit adultery you feel awful, but the more you do it, the less you feel guilty about it.' In fact, Peter says about these people, the more illicit sex they have, the more they want. They never stop sinning. 'Their hearts continually desire that which they have no right to possess.'[5]

This is a trap into which any of us could fall. We may not be tempted to commit physical adultery (although Christians are not immune from this), but spiritual adultery is always a danger. We can get tired of the worship of the Lord, and be tempted to engage in 'more exciting' religious experiences. The Christian life was often referred to as 'the way' in the New Testament. The danger is that, the more we depart from the 'way of truth' (2:2) and **'the straight way'** (2:15), the more we enjoy the excitement of wickedness, and the more difficult it is to get back upon the true way of righteousness.

Peter tells us something further about these false teachers: they **'seduce the unstable'**. The more conquests they make, the more they want. And the strong likelihood is that it is the unstable who are the most easily seduced. All leaders in every church should be constantly active in teaching the truth of God! Everyone should seek to be built up in the truth, so that it becomes increasingly difficult for them to be lured astray into the ways of wickedness. Alexander Nisbet, writing 300 years ago said, 'Those who are not rooted in knowledge by clear information and frequent meditation of the truth and have not their hearts established with grace by the frequent exercise thereof, will readily be a prey to soul-deceivers.'[6]

False teachers are also experts in greed. Greed is one of the most grievous illnesses of the late twentieth century. The more money, power and possessions people have, the more they want. Jerome said, 'Whereas other vices grow old as a man advances in life, avarice alone grows young.'[7] While I was preparing this section one of my friends who is a reporter on a local newspaper rang me up for a quote for an article he was writing about some of our large local shops who had opened for trade on the Sunday before Christmas Day. I said, 'I really wonder why people are so greedy they have got to wring every ounce of money out of the public. It seems that their main concern is profit, rather than the welfare of their staff.'[8] Instead of being 'a chosen people' (1 Peter 2:9), Peter says that these teachers have become **'an accursed brood'**.

Finally, the apostle gives an example from Numbers chapters 22-24. Balaam was a prophet who knew that he ought to bring a message of blessing upon the people of Israel. Yet he listened to the repeated requests of a heathen king, Balak of Moab, and in return for much money, he tried to curse the Israelites; but each time he opened his mouth, blessings came out instead of cursing. Once, when Balaam was riding his donkey in an attempt to go to Balak, his donkey spoke to him to warn him against proceeding any further. Peter said that because Balaam loved the ways of wickedness he was made a fool of by his donkey. We sometimes call someone a 'silly ass', but even donkeys know where they live (Isaiah 1:3).

How sad it is that even those who are supposed to be servants of the Lord are led astray from the truth by the lure of money or power! Eric Lane, who was once a clergyman in the Church of England, reminds us that over the last 100 years many of the clergy (deacons, priests and bishops!) who, each time they are instituted into a new living or office, make a public declaration to uphold the Bible, the creeds and confessions of the church, 'then proceed to tear [them] up'. They are happy to receive payment to be pastors of the flock yet they make a second 'stipend' by writing books and giving lectures which deny these same doctrines.[9]

What about us?

Are we conscious that every thought, every action and every word which we speak is uttered in the presence of the Lord? If we were more aware of that fact we would behave in a way which showed more humility and love towards other people.

Do we take care how we behave? Drinking excessive alcohol leads many to act like brute beasts. They think only of their own pleasure, and care nothing that their music and revelry are at such a high volume that they prevent others from sleeping or resting.

Do we make sure that we keep our lusts in check? Satan knows the weaknesses of each one of us and he will play on those deficiencies and try to lead us astray.

Do we love the ways of wickedness? Money has such a strong drawing power. Every week in my mail I receive envelopes which say, in large letters, 'WIN £30,000' or something similar. The advertisers know how prone we all are to want to have more and more money. Paul said that 'The love of money is a root of all kinds of evil. Some people, eager for money, have wandered from the faith and pierced themselves with many griefs' (1 Timothy 6:10). Perhaps we all know of people who were once strong Christians but the desire for more money has contributed to their spiritual decline.

Do we realize that it is madness to accept the temptations offered us by men or the devil, rather than to obey the clear commands of the Lord? Just as the angel of the Lord stood in 'a narrow place' (Numbers 22:26) to prevent Balaam from going in the wrong way, so Jesus says, 'Small is the gate and narrow the road that leads to life, and only a few find it! (Matthew 7:14).

Let us be those who seek to turn from the broad road that narrows down to destruction and turn to walk in the narrow way that leads out into life eternal.

35.
The emptiness of false teachers

Please read 2 Peter 2:17-22

Peter spent a third of this important letter dealing with false teachers and their destruction. He did this because he was so concerned about the spiritual state of the believers in the northern Turkish churches.

He realized that the spiritual condition of God's people is so important. It is not sufficient merely to make a profession of faith and then just drift along. Many people say, 'Well, I'm a Christian. I've repented of my sins and believed in the Lord Jesus Christ. He has washed away my sins and I'm going to heaven when I die; so I don't have to bother about anything else.'

Peter was concerned about people who spoke and acted like that, and so should we be. Christians who drift through life are missing out on so much. Those who stay on the fringes and don't get involved with the activities of the church are keeping themselves away from true Christian fellowship.

But not only are they depriving themselves of Christian love and companionship; they are placing themselves in great danger because false teachers are everywhere. Their aim is to deceive the people of God. They do this by first of all gaining their confidence and teaching them false doctrine, and then by leading them astray.

Peter says that every one of God's people should avoid these false teachers like the plague. We should not even listen to what they say.

They make false promises

They say things that sound wonderful but their promises are empty. They appear like springs (2:17). How refreshing it must be for a thirsty traveller on a hot journey to come across a spring! We can imagine how eagerly he would run up to it and drink from it. Many true believers are thirsty. They are finding the journey of life to be a very tiring business. They feel like the man in the old American song who said, 'Life gets tedious, don't it?' They have a great thirst, and because they are promised something to quench it by these false teachers, they are drawn to them. What these men say seems to make sense.

But then, when the parched Christian gets near enough to examine their teaching he finds out that **'These men are springs without water.'** They promise much, but they can offer nothing of any lasting value. On the surface what they say looks appetizing, but underneath it proves to be dry, empty and worthless.

Dr John Gill, a predecessor of Charles Haddon Spurgeon, wrote, 'These men looked like angels of light, transformed themselves as ministers of righteousness, had a form of godliness, and boasted of their great knowledge; promised great advantages to their followers, but were like deceitful brooks or dry wells, and so disappointed those who came to them, and attended on them, having nothing but the filth and slime of error and iniquity, being destitute both of the grace of God, comparable to water, and of the truth of heavenly doctrine, which is like the rain that fills the wells, pools and fountains.'[1]

Peter then uses another picture which teaches a similar lesson. He says these false teachers are **'mists driven by a storm'**. Again the scene is of someone who is desperate for moisture. To his great joy he sees on the horizon a thick mist being driven towards him by a storm. The weary traveller says to himself, 'Thank you Lord. Here is the answer to my prayers, the promise of soft refreshing rain.' But when the mist arrives, it immediately evaporates in the heat of the blazing sun.

Peter must have often seen that happen when he was fishing on the Sea of Galilee. Jude tells us that these false teachers are like 'clouds without rain, blown along by the wind' (Jude 12). 'Do not listen to these men,' said Peter. **'Blackest darkness**

is reserved for them.' Because of their evil they will be banished to the darkest recesses of hell itself, and there they will remain for ever (see Jude 13). This is similar to what Peter wrote in verse 1 of this chapter. There he said that, by their deeds these men are 'bringing swift destruction on themselves'.

Jude says that they are like wandering stars. He is speaking about the planets, which appear to roam around the sky against the backdrop of the apparently unchanging pattern of the stars. 'This designation is quite suitable to false prophets, who have wandered from the regular paths of righteousness and are heading towards the blackness of darkness.'[2]

These apostates promise excitement. They sound as though they are saying something interesting and important, but it is all **'empty and boastful'**. False teachers are like that. I wonder why some preachers put on an affected voice when they start their sermons. It must have happened in seventeenth-century Scotland too, because Alexander Nisbet writes, 'An attempted lofty style of language in uttering things divine ordinarily flows from some unmortified lust in the speaker,' and he concludes that these people, 'especially [love] applause'.[3]

The aim of false teachers is to lead God's people away from holy living and into evil behaviour. How many true Christians have been drawn into adulterous relationships? The Sunday papers are often exposing the immoral deeds of church members. Peter dealt with this subject in verse 14, but it is of such frequent occurrence that he takes it up again in verse 18. However, we should remember that it is not only sexual immorality which causes people to go astray.

False teachers appeal **'to the lustful desires of sinful human nature'**. Paul lists a great many deviations. He writes, 'The acts of the sinful nature are obvious: sexual immorality, impurity and debauchery; idolatry and witchcraft; hatred, discord, jealousy, fits of rage, selfish ambition, dissensions, factions and envy; drunkenness, orgies, and the like' (Galatians 5:19-20).

Peter says that false teachers aim especially at leading new converts astray in this respect. These young believers are busy trying to escape from the pagan world, **'those who live in error',** and they make an easy prey for wicked men who desire to lure them away from the truth. It is sad that such people are often found waiting outside the venues of evangelistic campaigns ready to pounce upon those who have just 'made a decision for Christ'.

These false teachers promise freedom to those whom they are seeking to divert from the way of truth (2:19). The notion of freedom is an exciting prospect for anyone. No doubt many of the original readers of this letter were, or had been, slaves, so they would know about the preciousness of freedom. The false teacher would say to them, 'Now you are a Christian you are living under grace. You don't need to keep the Ten Commandments. You are free from such restrictions. You can do as you like.' But that is so wrong. Anyone who is in Christ knows true freedom (John 8:36) and that freedom makes him want to follow Christ and obey him whatever happens. George Matheson wrote, 'Make me a captive, Lord, and then I shall be free.'[4]

But what did these false teachers know about freedom? **'They themselves are slaves of depravity.'** They have been mastered by their evil desires. They are under the firm control of the evil one himself. So what right have they to promise freedom to anyone?

They are not real Christians

They claim to be true believers. That is why they purport to be teachers of God's Word. They have a lot to say and it is characteristic of them to tell you what they *do not* believe in. They do not believe in miracles. They do not believe that there is a division between those who are saved and those who are lost. They deny so many of the fundamentals of the faith. And their books pour off the presses in droves.

Whenever I pick up a book which looks like a Christian publication, I first of all look at the name of the author. If I know nothing about the person who wrote it then I look to see who has published it. Certain publishers only produce sound Christian literature. Other publishers specialize in the kinds of books which do not uphold the Bible as the inerrant Word of God (these I avoid); while others still produce a mixture of books (and great discernment is needed over these books).

False teachers do not give a positive message. When they speak, teach or write, what help do they give to troubled consciences and dying sinners? What have they done to strengthen the church or to reform society? Ultimately they are not interested in these things. They are only concerned about themselves.[5]

False teachers often have the outward marks of true Christians. They say that they know **'our Lord and Saviour Jesus Christ'**, but they are only pretending. They know *about* him, yet they have no personal saving knowledge of him. If they knew the Lord as their Saviour they would not have behaved so wickedly. Peter refers to these false teachers as 'they' and 'them' throughout this section. They do not belong to the people of God, those to whom the apostle is writing.

There were many people, even in the time when Jesus was upon the earth, who claimed to be true followers of Christ. Yet he had to say of them, 'Not everyone who says to me, "Lord, Lord," will enter the kingdom of heaven, but only he who does the will of my Father who is in heaven. Many will say to me on that day, "Lord, Lord, did we not prophesy in your name, and in your name drive out demons and perform many miracles?" Then I will tell them plainly, "I never knew you. Away from me, you evildoers?"' (Matt. 7:21-23). Even Judas was sent out with the disciples, two by two, when they 'drove out many demons and anointed many sick people with oil and healed them' (Mark 6:12-13). 'Obviously, Judas knew Jesus; in the name of Jesus he preached and performed miracles. Yet Judas betrayed his Master.'[6]

These false teachers, even if they appear to have escaped the corruption of the world, 'are again entangled in it and overcome'. Peter uses a fishing term when he speaks of being entangled. He would remember what a mess his nets could get into after a busy night's fishing on the Sea of Galilee.

The final state of these people is going to be worse than it might otherwise have been. Speaking about people like this, Jesus said, 'If anyone causes one of these little ones who believe in me to sin, it would be better for him to have a large millstone hung around his neck and to be drowned in the depths of the sea' (Matthew 18:6). These false teachers not only claimed to have known the way of righteousness (2:21), but they tried to lead others astray from what Peter calls **'the**

sacred command that was passed on to them'. Jude describes this command as 'the faith that was once for all entrusted to the saints (Jude 3).

Two proverbs

Peter ends the chapter with two proverbs. These are both about animals — a dog and a pig (see Proverbs 26:11). Both of these were 'unclean' so far as Jews were concerned. Jesus said, 'Do not give dogs what is sacred; do not throw your pearls to pigs' (Matthew 7:6). Peter has already mentioned 'brute beasts' and a donkey in this chapter; now he adds two more animals.

What Peter says about dogs and pigs is pretty revolting. We do not want to know about it — a dog being sick and then going back to sniff it, and a pig going back to her wallowing in the mud. These are horrible actions for us to think about; but the behaviour of false teachers is likewise utterly disgusting.

Peter is teaching that dogs and pigs will always behave according to their natures. A dog gets rid of something which is uncomfortable in its stomach — and feels much better for it. A pig washes the outside of its body — and smells much sweeter for it. Yet, before much time has elapsed, the dog goes back to its vomit and the pig starts bathing in the mud. Pigs will be pigs and dogs will be dogs, and they will both remain so — unless something unheard of happens and they are completely changed into another kind of animal. But 'Can the Ethiopian change his skin or the leopard its spots?' (Jeremiah 13:23).

False teachers, even if they are purged inside and washed outside, will remain false teachers unless there is a complete transformation in their natures and they are cleansed from all their iniquity by the precious blood of Christ. The danger is that these false teachers 'will try to make such dogs and such sows of [true Christians]'.[7]

How each of us needs to be continually on our guard, lest we be led astray by such plausible-sounding teachers! The only way we can remain true to the faith is to live a life filled with prayer and study of, and meditation upon, God's Word.

We should make sure that we only listen to the pure teaching of the Bible and we should spend as much time as we can with God's people in the fellowship of the church — speaking with true Christians about the things of God (Malachi 3:16).

36.
Christic is coming again!

Please read 2 Peter 3:1-9

False teachers sound very plausible. They base their arguments on logical 'facts'. 'Science has proved ...' is one of their lines of teaching. But how can we know what is true so far as God is concerned? Can anyone prove, by scientific study, that God exists? Of course not; the reality of his existence has to be accepted by faith. The standards laid down by Jesus are not 'See and you will believe.' They are always, 'Believe and then you will see.'

But false teachers do not want to believe, because faith in God demands a complete change of life-style. Those who follow the Lord are required to live holy lives. 'If your life-style contradicts the Word of God, you must either change your life-style or change the Word of God.'[1]

False teachers try to change the Word of God. They do this because it is not acceptable to them. They do not want to believe that God's Word is true and that dire consequences follow those who tamper with it in any way (Revelation 22:18-19).

We should reflect upon God's Word

Peter calls his readers **'dear friends'**. This is a favourite phrase of his. He used it in 1 Peter 2:11 and 4:12 and he is going to use it again in this chapter. In verse 8 he says, 'Do not forget this one thing, dear friends.' In verse 14 he says, 'So then, dear friends ... make every effort to be found spotless,' and in verse 17 he says, 'Therefore, dear friends, since you already know this, be on your guard.'

He has been speaking some very harsh things about false teachers and now, in this third chapter, it almost seems as if he is worried in case he has upset his readers. So he quickly re-assures them of his love for them. He uses this phrase 'dear friends'. It means 'loved ones'. Peter wants his readers to know of his loving concern for their welfare.

He goes on to say, **'I have written both of [these letters] as reminders.'** We do not know whether Peter's first letter was the one that we have in our Bibles called 1 Peter. There are arguments for and against that being the one he refers to here. Certainly we know that some of Paul's letters were lost, so it is not inconceivable that Peter wrote other letters. But what-ever the case, our appreciation of the Bible is not diminished.

Peter wanted to stimulate his readers to wholesome think-ing. There is so much unwholesome thinking today, much of which has been put into our minds by our teachers — either when we were at school (where, for example, Darwin's evolutionary principles were taught as though they were proven facts), or through those whom we think of as more clever than ourselves. Many who write in our newspapers and broadcast on our radios and televisions display much error and wrong thinking. How we need to be on our guard lest we assimilate teaching which is contrary to God's Word!

How can we be stimulated to wholesome thinking? This can only come about when we consciously recall God's Word. However, we can only recall what we already know. It is very salutary to ask ourselves, 'How much of Holy Scripture have I memorized?' It is important to learn key scriptures. There are schemes to help us do this. When I was a schoolboy we learnt Psalms 91, 103 and 23 off by heart. We also memorized the Ten Commandments and the Beatitudes. But modern theories of education have decried the learning of things by rote!

What did Peter want his readers to recall? **'The words spoken in the past by the holy prophets.'** He means by that the Old Testament prophets. These have much to say to us for today. **'... and the command given by our Lord and Saviour through your apostles.'** Peter is referring to the commands of Jesus, especially as they were relayed through the apostles.

He includes himself in these apostles because he implies that 'We are your apostles. You know us and we belong to you (and to all of God's people in every age).'

Peter can speak with authority on behalf of the rest of the apostles. He includes both Old Testament prophets and New Testament apostles in his statement and he treats them as being of equal value. This is to emphasize that there is a wonderful unity in the Bible. Both Testaments are the Word of God.

What is common in the message of the Old Testament prophets and the commands of Jesus? It is the call to repentance and faith. The Old Testament prophets were constantly calling the people of Israel to turn away from their sin and turn towards the living God. After John the Baptist had been put into prison, 'Jesus went into Galilee, proclaiming the good news of God. "The time has come," he said. "The kingdom of God is near. Repent and believe the good news!"' (Mark 1:14-15). Paul also declared the same message: 'God commands all people everywhere to repent' (Acts 17:30).

It is this message that they must leave the ways of sin and selfishness and turn towards righteous ways of living which so many people find totally unacceptable.

Then Peter goes on to talk about **'the last days'** (3:3). He means the period of time which started at Pentecost and which will last until the coming of the Lord. This includes, of course, the days in which we live.

Christ is coming back to this earth

This is teaching which is neglected today. It is neglected because some teach that he has already returned. They say that Jesus came back when he rose from the dead. As proof of this they remind us that Jesus said, 'Surely I am with you always, to the very end of the age' (Matthew 28:20). Other people say that the Lord came back at Pentecost when the Holy Spirit descended upon God's people with mighty power (Acts 2). Yet others say that he did not actually mean that he would return to this earth in bodily form. So we have confusion — especially among those who doubt the truth of God's Word.

The doctrine of the second coming of the Lord is also neglected because there are so many different views about it that many have become confused by these different teachings. Some groups say that Jesus will come and take all believers to himself 'in the air', and this will be followed by seven years of great tribulation on the earth. But others teach that Christ is going to come after seven years of trouble. Then he will set up his earthly kingdom, which will last for a thousand years. Still others say that all this talk about seven years of tribulation and a thousand years of earthly reign is spiritual language for the events which will lead up to the glorious reign of the Lord Jesus Christ as king of the universe.

There are equally godly men in all of these camps, and in the many variations of them. Preachers seem to spend a great deal of their time arguing about these matters, while Satan gloats over our disharmony. What were the disciples told when Jesus was taken from them into heaven? The angels said, *'This same Jesus,* who has been taken from you into heaven, *will come back* in the same way you have seen him go into heaven' (Acts 1:11). Should we not be concentrating on this basic statement rather than wasting our time quarrelling about the details? If the Lord had wanted us to know the whole plan he would have made it abundantly clear and even given us a beautifully illustrated chart describing the exact order of these events. The important question for us all is, 'How should we conduct ourselves in view of the second coming of the Lord?' Peter tells us, 'You ought to live holy and godly lives as you look forward to the day of God and speed its coming' (2 Peter 3:11-12).

This teaching that Christ will return to this earth still causes people to mock God's Word. But Peter says that this teaching is very important. We should not neglect any doctrine in the Bible. Someone has worked out that there are about 300 direct references to the Second Coming in the New Testament alone. H. L. Willmington lists sixteen different 'signs suggesting the return of Christ'. These include, 'extreme materialism' (2 Timothy 3:1-2), 'lawlessness' (2 Timothy 3:2-4) and 'increase of wars and rumours of wars' (Mark 13:7).[2]

In saying, **'first of all,'** Peter means, 'This is of primary importance.' Because false teachers scoff at this doctrine we should be all the more on our guard to maintain the true teaching of God's Word. Just because something is ridiculed by learned men, it does not mean that it is not worth bothering about.

But, in any case, these scoffers had it all wrong. They used false arguments. They said, **'Everything has carried on as it always was since the beginning of creation'** (3:4). It was as though they were saying, 'Don't listen to these prophets and apostles. Christ is not coming back to this earth.' They convinced themselves that God has not intervened in the world's affairs since time began and therefore they assumed that he would not do so in the present or at any time in the future.

However, they were wrong in their assertions. They forgot that it was by God's word that the earth was created. In Genesis 1:6 we read, 'God said, "Let there be an expanse between the waters to separate water from water" ... and it was so.' It was also by the direct intervention of God that the flood came to destroy all the wicked people who were in the world during the days of Noah.

These scoffers, of whom Peter writes, would not be prepared to accept that 'We must all appear before the judgement seat of Christ, that each one may receive what is due to him for the things done while in the body, whether good or bad' (2 Corinthians 5:10). If they pretended that God did not intervene at the time when God destroyed the world by water, would they accept that 'By the same word [of God] the present heavens and earth are reserved for fire, being kept for the day of judgement and destruction of ungodly men?' (3:7). But it is so. The fact that people shut their eyes to the power of God at work does not mean that God is not working or that he will carry on allowing them to continue in their wicked ways. God has this world marked out for divine judgement because of the sinfulness of its inhabitants (just as he did in the day of Noah). This is why people do not want Jesus to return. They do not want to face being judged and found lacking in moral standards.

God is merciful in his judgements

Unlike us, God is not hemmed in by time. Time regulates much of what we do. We often say, 'I haven't got time to do so and so.' Or, 'I'll see to it when I've got time.' Sometimes we ask, in a surprised voice, 'Is that the time?' Isaac Watts wrote,

> Time like an ever-rolling stream,
>   Bears all its sons away;
> They fly forgotten, as a dream
>   Dies at the opening day.[3]

But Peter says, **'With the Lord a day is like a thousand years, and a thousand years are like a day'** (3:8). He is reflecting Psalm 90:4. He means that God can see the end from the beginning, and the beginning from the end. With him everything is one big, eternal *now*.

These scoffers, of whom Peter warned, were persisting in saying things like, 'God is impotent, or he's not interested in this world. If he was going to act, he would have done something long before now.' But Peter replied, 'You've got it all wrong. **The Lord is not slow in keeping his promise.'** It isn't that he has forgotten his promise to judge the world. **'He is patient with you, not wanting anyone to perish, but everyone to come to repentance'** (3:9).

However, there are a number of things we should all remember. Firstly, it is vital to remember *the teaching of the Bible.* God says that we are all sinners and none of us has any excuse for our wickedness. There is no reason why we should be deceived by false teachers if we hold fast to the teaching of the apostles and the prophets.

Secondly, we should remember that *false teachers lie when they scoff at God's Word.* We should be wary of those who say that modern scholarship has discredited certain parts of God's Word. We should reject the teaching of those who teach that Jesus is not the Christ of the Gospels.

Thirdly, we should remember that *Christ is coming back to this earth.* We should be watching and eagerly waiting for his return. We should not be unprepared, like the ten foolish virgins of whom Jesus spoke in a parable about the last times (Matthew 25:1-13).

Fourthly, *there is a great Day of Judgement coming upon us all.* Everyone either belongs to God or does not. People are saved or they are lost. They are destined for heaven or for hell. On the Judgement Day it will be clear who are his and who are not. But anyone who just chooses to wait and see what will happen is a great fool. We all need to make sure where we stand in regard to the Lord Jesus Christ, but it is God's will which determines the eternal destiny of each of us. 'When Paul writes that God "wants all men to be saved and to come to a knowledge of the truth"' (1 Tim. 2:4; also see Ezek. 18:23, 32), he does not mean that all men are indeed saved. Although God desires the redemption of the entire race, he does not decree universal salvation. Therefore, in respect to the verb *want* or *wish* theologians distinguish between God's desire and God's decree.'[4]

Fifthly, *there is a wonderful call to salvation* which goes out to everyone, but which will only be received by those who forsake their sin and turn to Christ in faith. It is God's desire that all should repent and be saved. He sent his own dear Son to the cross of Calvary to accomplish salvation for each one of his dear people and he is delaying his final judgement so that more people might hear and respond to the gospel message and be saved. But he says that one day there will be a great judgement (Hebrews 9:27). When that day arrives the age of grace will have run its course. There will then be no further opportunity for anyone to repent (Daniel 12:10). On that day Jesus said, 'Everything that causes sin and all who do evil … will [be thrown] into the fiery furnace, where there will be weeping and gnashing of teeth' (Matthew 13:41-42). Dare anyone disbelieve what the Lord Jesus Christ so awesomely declares?

37.
The day of the Lord

Please read 2 Peter 3:10-16

Why does God allow so much sickness in this world? Surely it cannot give him pleasure when he sees the dreadful pain and sorrow which come upon so many innocent people. He must be distressed when he sees injustice being meted out upon defenceless individuals. He must want the spread of disease to be halted and even wiped out completely. Why does God not do something to intervene in the affairs of the world? Why is it that all the reforming efforts of good men and women bear no, or so little, fruit?

This world has made so much progress in education during the past few hundred years, resulting in far more people having much greater knowledge than their forefathers ever had. So much progress has been made in the field of scientific discovery; we have gadgets and machinery that save us much time and effort. Medicine has improved so much that some diseases have been eliminated altogether, and others are more easily controlled. So why does the world, despite its beauty, remain a place where there is so much unhappiness and wickedness? Why is it that God does not do something about the wrong which still abounds on every side?

The answer is that God did do something about the evil. He sent the judgement of water upon it in the days of Noah; and everyone except eight people were destroyed. This was so that a fresh start could be made. But even God's judgement did not bring about a lasting improvement. Things were no better because mankind did not change; it remained sinful. Selfishness and greed were not done away with and, as a consequence, evil quickly spread all over the earth once again. That is why we live in a world which is frightening in many ways.

In C. S. Lewis's *The Lion, the Witch and the Wardrobe* Peter, Susan, Edmund and Lucy all found themselves in the mythical land of Narnia during the cruel reign of the White Witch. That period was cold and sad; it was always winter, but never Christmas. The inhabitants of Narnia were very oppressed and often fearful, but one thing kept them going. It was the hope that the great lion, Aslan (who was the rightful king), would one day return.

Mr Beaver told the children this old poem:

> Wrong will be right, when Aslan comes in sight.
> At the sound of his roar, sorrows will be no more,
> When he bares his teeth, winter meets its death.
> And when he shakes his mane, we shall have spring
>   again.[1]

The people to whom Peter addressed this letter must have often wondered how much longer they would have to put up with so many trials and temptations. It was to encourage them that Peter wrote to them about the day of the Lord, which will bring hope and 'a new heaven and a new earth, the home of righteousness' (3:13).

The day of the Lord will come

Peter told his readers that they need not fear that they would have to carry on for ever in their sadness. The scoffers had said that Christ was not coming back but Peter pointed out to them that these false teachers had it all wrong. Jesus is going to return. He promised that he would come back, and he always keeps his promises. Peter used the word 'promise' in verses 4, 9 and 13; and in 1:4 he wrote about God's 'great and precious promises'.

So when will the Lord return? That is what the believers wanted to know. They were getting impatient. They were just like us. We wonder how much longer we will have to put up with all the pain and uncertainty of life. We want to know the answers to our questions, and we want those answers straight away.

Peter says, **'The day of the Lord will come like a thief.'** How does a thief commit a burglary? Does he put an announcement in the local paper saying when and how he will break into a particular person's house? No, of course not. He arrives unexpectedly. Jesus said, 'Keep watch, because you do not know on what day your Lord will come. But understand this: If the owner of the house had known at what time of night the thief was coming, he would have kept watch and would not have let his house be broken into. So you also must be ready, because the Son of Man will come at an hour when you do not expect him' (Matthew 24:42-44).

We must be watching for the return of the Lord. Paul writes in a similar way to the Thessalonians. He says, 'Now, brothers, about times and dates we do not need to write to you, for you know very well that the day of the Lord will come like a thief in the night. While people are saying, "Peace and safety," destruction will come on them suddenly, as labour pains on a pregnant woman, and they will not escape' (2 Thessalonians 5:1-3).

Even Jesus himself said that he did not know the time of his return (Matthew 24:36), so why should we worry about the details of these events? Our task is to be prepared for Christ's glorious coming.

I often wonder what would happen if my house was to burn down. Assuming everyone living in it was safe, and I could only take one material thing out of it, what would I choose? Would it be a valuable book from my library which I have built up over the past thirty-five years? Would it be a photograph of my son who was killed in a car crash? Or would it be the computer disc on which this book is stored?

But every single thing of that kind will have to be left behind on the judgement day (as indeed they will if we die before that time). On the day of the Lord everything will be destroyed. **'The heavens** [the atmosphere] **will disappear with a roar; the elements** [everything that goes to make up our world as we know it] **will be destroyed by fire, and the earth and everything in it will be laid bare'** (3:10).

This is figurative language for the events which will take place on the day of the Lord. Does the thought sometimes

frighten you that some mad person might press a button
which will set off such a nuclear war that everything will be
destroyed by fire, **'and the elements will melt in the heat'** ?
(3:12). If that is so with you, do not fear. Such a complete
obliteration of the world cannot happen by accident. It is
God's prerogative alone to bring about such destruction. It is
only on the day of the Lord that such a thing will happen. That
is all in the hands of the Lord Almighty, and it is safely under
his control.

How, then, should we be living?

Peter says that, first of all, we should live holy and godly lives.
The world says, 'You only live once; enjoy yourself while you
can.' The people of old used to say, 'Eat, drink and be merry,
for tomorrow we die.' When I was young the chorus of a
popular song started, 'Enjoy yourself, it's later than you
think. Enjoy yourself while you're still in the pink.' And
people today still say, 'You're only young once, so have a
good time.'

But God's Word says, **'Since everything will be destroyed in
this way, what kind of people ought you to be? You ought to
live holy and godly lives'** (3:11). Peter had written a great deal
about holiness and godly living in his first letter. Now he
speaks of the same thing again. A life lived for the glory of
God is a most attractive life. This command should cause us
to examine our actions, and our motives for what we do.

Secondly, Peter says that we should **'look forward to** [what
he now calls] **the day of God'** (3:12). He re-emphasizes the
need to look forward. We should be **'looking forward to a new
heaven and a new earth'** (3:13). Also he says that **'Since you
are looking forward to this** [day of God] **make every effort to
be found spotless, blameless and at peace with him'** (3:14).

Why should we want to look forward to this day? Because
it is then that Christ will return. If the people of the world
believed that God meant to keep his word they would be terrified at the thought of everything in this lovely world being
destroyed. They would dread living through such a time of the
burning up of all things.

Those who do not know the Lord as their Saviour will find these final events disastrous. It will be a dreadful time for those who have refused to repent of their sin and turn towards the Lord Jesus Christ for salvation. It will be a calamity for those who have continually rejected the Lord and his offer of mercy. But it will be a glorious day for all those who know and love the Lord, because he will come back and everything will be 'new'. It will be like the wonderful experience that a person has at conversion: 'The old has passed away and all things have become new.' As a result of that day, 'The fire will have burnt out of the cosmos every taint of sin, thorns and briars, diseases, everything that causes pestilences, everything that leads to earthquakes and calamities. All will be removed, the earth will be purged of every such thing — that is the meaning of fire. It will burn out everything evil and the result is that there will be "new heavens and a new earth, wherein dwelleth righteousness" of surpassing beauty, wonder and glory.'[2]

Next Peter says that we should **'speed its coming'**. How can we do that? We can do it through prayer and evangelism. There is an ancient prayer from the early days of the church which says, 'Maranatha — Come, O Lord!' (1 Corinthians 16:22) and when we pray the Lord's Prayer we say, 'Your Kingdom come' (Matthew 6:10). We should pray for the coming of the great day of the Lord for then all things will have been accomplished.

Peter writes that the coming of the day of the Lord is delayed because God wants **'everyone to come to repentance'** (3:9). 'Accordingly, if we wish to speed the coming of God's day, we should evangelize the world. When we bring the last of God's children to faith and repentance so that his house may be full (Luke 14:23) then the end comes.'[3]

Fourthly, Peter says that we should be looking forward to our **'home of righteousness'**. 'I'm going home' is a very comforting saying. Home represents a place of security. It speaks of love and peace. It reminds us of the warmth of a family gathering. If we are true believers we should not be sad at the destruction of this old earth with all its pain and sorrow. We should be glad that we are going to experience all the joys and comfort of home.

He says that it will be a home of righteousness. The

prophets often spoke of this. Isaiah tells us that God said,

> 'You heavens above, rain down righteousness;
>   let the clouds shower it down.
> Let the earth open wide,
>   let salvation spring up,
> Let righteousness grow with it;
>   I, the Lord, have created it'(Isaiah 45:8).

Also Daniel was told by the angel Gabriel that the holy city will 'finish transgression, to put an end to sin, to atone for wickedness, to bring in everlasting righteousness' (Daniel 9:24).

Fifthly, Peter says we should **'make every effort to be found spotless, blameless and at peace with [the Lord]'** (3:14). Jesus is described as 'a lamb without blemish or defect' (1 Peter 1:19). He was God's pure Lamb who died on the cruel cross of Calvary to take away our sin. He is the holy Lamb of God, and we should make every effort to be like Christ. We should seek to live lives which are holy. When we became Christians that did not spell an end to sin for us. On the contrary, it opened up the gates for a full attack by Satan upon us. Christians are tempted to sin far more than non-Christians and we must make every effort to resist the devil (1 Peter 5:8-9) and seek to live lives which are holy and godly. It is only then that we can be at peace with God.

Where can we find help?

Where can we obtain guidance in view of the approaching day of the Lord? The only sure help we can receive is from the Holy Scriptures. The Bible alone is where we find guidance for real living. Paul often wrote about the need to be ready for the coming of the Lord. Peter calls him **'our dear brother Paul'**. Peter, and those to whom Peter was writing, obviously had a collection of Paul's letters. Both Peter and Paul quoted the Old Testament frequently. The Old Testament was regarded by the Jews as the Word of God and Peter is saying here that ignorant and unstable people distort Paul's letters just as they twist other Scriptures. Peter is therefore claiming that Paul's letters are just as much the Word of God as the Old Testament writings are.

Just because some of the teaching of the Bible is difficult to understand, that is no reason to dismiss it. Peter acknowledges that parts of Paul's letters **'contain some things that are hard to understand'**, but Peter's own letters were not always that simple! However, that is no reason to ignore them. No Christian will grow if his diet consists only of well-loved Scriptures like Psalm 23 and the Sermon on the Mount. We need to wrestle with other parts of the Bible also. A very helpful way to do this is to attend a church Bible study. We all need to 'search the Scriptures' and we gain much when we do this in company with other believers; we can all help each other to understand what the Lord is saying to us in the days in which we live.

One day Peter and John were walking to the temple at the time of prayer and they were, by God's power, able to heal a cripple. This caused a great crowd of people to gather around them. Peter immediately used that situation to preach the gospel. He told the people how they (because they were Jews) had sent the Lord Jesus Christ to Calvary's cross. Then he said, 'Now, brothers, I know that you acted in ignorance, as did your leaders. But this is how God fulfilled what he had foretold through all the prophets, saying that his Christ would suffer. Repent, then, and turn to God, so that your sins may be wiped out, that times of refreshing may come from the Lord, and *that he may send the Christ,* who has been appointed for you — even Jesus. He must remain in heaven until the time comes for God to restore everything, as he promised long ago through his holy prophets' (Acts 3:17-21).

That promised day when God will send Christ back to this earth to restore everything is fast approaching. We do not know when it will be, but we should make sure that we are ready to meet our glorious King.

38.
Growth in grace and knowledge

Please read 2 Peter 3:17-18

There are many weak Christians in the world today — there always have been. There are many who do not understand what the Bible teaches on important subjects; and even if they do know what the Bible says they do not always carry it out. Also there are many evil people around who are determined to lead true Christians away from the truth. They try to do this either by introducing them to erroneous teaching, or by leading them into doubt and despair.

How can believers withstand these attacks from those who teach error, and those who feel it is their duty to lure people into a life which has no spiritual values at all?

We should be on our guard

Peter is writing to Christians. That is why he calls them **'dear friends'**. His readers had been truly born again and washed from their sin in the blood of Christ. Their eyes had been opened by the Holy Spirit so that they could see their lost state without Christ. They had been enabled to recognize and acknowledge their sin — and repent of it. And they had turned to the Lord Jesus Christ in faith, believing that he is God's Son — the one who died on the cross to save them from their sin.

Peter reminds these believers of what they already knew. They knew that there were false teachers about. They knew that these should be avoided because they denied the Lord

Jesus Christ. They knew that they should steer clear of those who scoff at the idea that Christ is coming back to this earth; and they also knew that these false teachers were on the lookout for any of God's people whom they could lead astray.

There is great danger because it is not only new and weak Christians who are drawn into wrong ways. Others can be vulnerable too. No one is such a strong Christian that he can allow his defences to be lowered; anyone might be lured away from the Lord.

On the positive side Peter's readers knew also that they were secure in Christ. No one could take their Lord away from them. Nothing could remove their home in heaven. Their security in Christ was certain. Their inheritance in Christ had been reserved for them (1 Peter 1:4) and Jesus himself had said, 'No one can snatch them out of my Father's hand' (John 10:29). It was absolutely true that no one could take their salvation from them, but, nonetheless, they still needed to be on their guard.

Although their salvation was certain, they could **'fall from [their] secure position'**. What does Peter mean by saying this? He is talking about when someone fails to live by the teaching of God's Word. When a person, for no good reason, eases up on his attendance at his church it could well be an indication that he is beginning to slide away from the Lord. One of the members of our church put it like this: 'So often when we get a slight suggestion of a cold we convince ourselves that it would be folly to go out; it's too wet; it's too cold; it's too hot; it looks a bit foggy. Yet none of these excuses will deter us from doing the other things we want to do. Ask the football supporter if these things would stop him or her; ask the concert-goer, or the golfer. These excuses for failing to attend to the welfare of our souls disobey God's Word about the "not forsaking the assembling of yourselves together" (Heb. 10:25 AV).'[1]

When we gradually start missing Sunday services and prayer meetings we begin to backslide. When that happens private devotions become a bit of a bore — we no longer find joy in communing with the Lord through prayer and the study of God's Word. The result of all of this is that, although we remain Christians, we fall from the truth; we can make a wreck of our lives.[2]

Because Peter loved these Christians, he wanted them to be protected. They needed to beware of the evil one and all of his hosts and the only protection that a believer can have is the full armour of Christ. Paul explains about each part of this armour in Ephesians 6:10-18. He says that if this armour is to provide the necessary protection *it must be put on.* Peter is saying something similar in these last two verses. He is saying beware, know and grow.

We must grow in grace

Peter's constant concern for his readers was that they should grow. He started this letter with the call to grow in the faith and he ends it with a call to grow. 'Living a Christian life is something like riding a bicycle; if you don't keep moving, you will quickly lose your balance. There is a measure of safety in momentum.'[3]

But before anyone can grow he or she must be alive. Growth is an evidence of life. My little daughter had an amaryllis bulb one Christmas. It looked dead but she planted it according to the instructions on the box. And then she waited. Before long there was excitement. A little green shoot had started to appear out of the top of the bulb. It was alive! The fact that it was growing was the proof of life.

It is the same with spiritual things. If people are not growing in the grace and knowledge of our Lord and Saviour Jesus Christ there is something wrong. Perhaps there is no spiritual life in them at all; maybe they have never truly been born again. Or perhaps the conditions for growth are unhelpful. Just as a bulb needs the right compost, sufficient water, light and air, so a child of God needs the right spiritual conditions in order to grow. He or she needs to be planted in the right kind of soil. He needs to be able to receive good light and breathe pure air. In other words, he should mix with Christians who are helpful and conducive to growth in his spiritual life. He needs to be well watered and fed with the Word of God and prayer — both through his own study and devotions and through the spiritual concern of others for his Christian welfare.

Growth is a gradual process. It is not good for a person to grow up too quickly. Children need time to develop and mature. They need to absorb information at their own intellectual level. They need to exercise to a standard which is right for them, at the stage they have reached. No one likes a child who is too precocious — one who is a little 'know-all'.

So it is in the spiritual realm. It is true that some plants grow quicker than others, but each one has to go through certain stages. There must be development in the right order, otherwise there will be malformations somewhere.

The signs of growth

A person who is growing well displays a certain stability in his life. A child is sometimes moody. He is often quickly changing from one thing to another. He becomes upset very easily if he cannot have his own way. He might be overjoyed one minute and then miserable the next.

But a Christian who is growing **'in grace and the knowledge of our Lord and Saviour Jesus Christ'** is a reliable person. He does not let others down. He does not promise to do something and then forget about it. Because he is growing up in the ways of Christ, he is dependable.

A person who is growing satisfactorily displays a certain discernment in everything. He is not easily swayed by new teaching. Paul said that we should not be like infants 'tossed back and forth by the waves, and blown here and there by every wind of teaching and by the cunning craftiness of men in their deceitful scheming' (Ephesians 4:14).

A man who is growing spiritually is not easily taken in by the latest fashion in church life. When I was a teenager the important thing then was to be taken up with the doctrine of the second coming of Christ, and to 'prove' that your understanding of these events was the correct interpretation. Now there are other teachings which are captivating thousands of Christians.

But a growing Christian is not easily over-excited. He has his feet on the ground. He does not readily become an avid follower of any one personality; he is not like teenagers who go 'crazy' over the latest 'pop star', only to forsake him or her a few months later in favour of the next stage idol. The Christian who is growing up stands back from all of this kind of behaviour. It is not excitement which grips him, but reality in the things of God; that is where he finds real joy.

A person who is growing well is more interested in obtaining spiritual grace than in receiving gifts. Children enjoy Christmas and birthdays because they can unwrap the presents they have been given. The Corinthian church behaved like children because they seemed to have been only interested in spiritual gifts (1 Corinthians 12). Paul did not say to them that these gifts are no good but he said, 'Now I will show you the most excellent way' (1 Corinthians 12:31). Then he gave his wonderful teaching on the importance of love in 1 Corinthians 13.

A growing Christian wants to know more of the Lord and desires to put him first in his life, rather than constantly having uplifting experiences. We need to ask ourselves, 'Where do I stand in the face of this teaching? Am I still behaving like a child?' The writer to the Hebrews complained that his readers were slow to learn. He said, 'Though by this time you ought to be teachers, you need someone to teach you the elementary truths of God's word all over again' (Hebrews 5:12).

Growing in grace and knowledge

We ought to be keen to learn more about the Lord. How much do we know of Christian doctrine? It is so important to know the basic Bible teaching concerning God, Jesus Christ and man. If we do not understand these things we cannot grow in the Christian faith. However, we do not need to be intellectuals in order to be mature Christians. Not everyone needs to be a university graduate. In fact some people who have received very little schooling have gone on to be giants in the teaching of God's Word.

But it is not just knowledge *about Christ* that matters. It is knowing him personally that is vital. Paul said that all his religious upbringing was of little value. He said, 'I consider everything a loss compared to the surpassing greatness of knowing Christ Jesus my Lord.' He went on to say, 'I want to know Christ and the power of his resurrection and the fellowship of sharing in his death, and so, somehow, to attain to the resurrection from the dead' (Philippians 3:8, 10-11).

This is a command that Peter gives. We should **'grow in the grace and knowledge of our Lord and Saviour Jesus Christ'**. Both growth in grace and increase in knowledge are required for healthy Christians. However, Warren Wiersbe warns us, 'Knowledge without grace is a terrible weapon, and grace without knowledge can be very shallow.'[4]

Finally, we should make sure that all the glory goes to the Lord. Peter ends this letter with a lovely doxology of praise. Everything which we do, which is of any value at all, should redound to God's glory and honour. We should not do things so that people think well of us. We should live our lives for God's glory and then stand in the background. Everything that we do, now and in the future, should be for the glory of God. How important it is for all of us to keep on growing and maturing in grace and knowledge so that we can join in joyfully with Peter's **'Amen'** — 'So be it'!

References

Chapter 1
1. See, e.g., E. P. Clowney, *The Message of 1 Peter,* IVP, 1988, p. 16 footnote. For a much fuller treatment of this subject see the 1959 edition of the *Tyndale New Testament Commentary of 1 Peter,* by A. M. Stibbs, IVP, pp. 15-48.
2. Wayne Grudem, *1 Peter,* Tyndale New Testament Commentaries, 1988 ed., IVP, p. 36.
3. *The NIV Study Bible,* Hodder and Stoughton, 1985, p. 1821.
4. For a discussion on this subject see (among many other books) David Jackman, *Understanding the Church,* Kingsway Publications, 1987, pp. 80-81.

Chapter 2
1. Philip Doddridge's hymn, 'O happy day, that fixed my choice, on thee my Saviour and my God!'
2. Clowney, *Message of 1 Peter,* p. 36.
3. David H. Wheaton in *The New Bible Commentary Revised,* IVP, 1970, p. 1239.
4. Clowney, *Message of 1 Peter,* p. 35.

Chapter 3
1. Henry W. Soltan in *The Apples of Gold Calendar for 1989* for 29 January.
2. Grudem, *1 Peter,* p. 59.
3. John Brown, *1 Peter,* Banner of Truth, 1975, vol. 1, p. 34.
4. Robert Leighton, *Commentary on First Peter,* Kregel Reprint Library, 1972, p. 37.
5. Grudem, *1 Peter,* p. 58.
6. Clowney, *Message of 1 Peter,* p. 46.

Chapter 5
1. Clowney, *Message of 1 Peter,* p. 55.
2. Simon J. Kistemaker, *Peter and Jude,* Evangelical Press, 1987, p. 53.
3. Matthew Henry, *Commentary on the Whole Bible,* Marshall, Morgan and Scott, 1960 ed., p. 739.
4. R. Jamieson, A. R. Fausset and D. Brown, *Commentary on the Bible,* Wm Collins, vol. VI, p. 600.
5. Quoted from *Gadsby's Hymns,* no. 69 (starting 'Sons we are, through God's election') published by Gospel Standard Publications.

Chapter 6
1. Andrew McNabb in *The New Bible Commentary,* IVP, 1953 ed., p. 1132.
2. Wayne Detzler, *Living Words in 1 Peter,* Evangelical Press, 1982, p. 23.
3. Clowney, *Message of 1 Peter,* p. 63.
4. Detzler, *Living Words in 1 Peter,* p. 21.
5. Kistemaker, *Peter and Jude,* p. 61.

Chapter 7
1. Leighton, *First Peter,* pp. 97-8.
2. A hymn by Medley (No. 7 in *Gadsby's Hymns*).
3. Mrs C. F. Alexander's famous hymn which starts, 'There is a green hill far away.'

Chapter 8
1. Larry Crabb, *Inside Out,* Navpress, 1988, pp. 159-60.
2. Boice, J. M., *Foundations of the Christian Faith,* IVP, 1986, p. 407.

Chapter 9
1. Kistemaker, *Peter and Jude,* p. 79.
2. Clowney, *Message of 1 Peter,* p. 78.
3. NIV Study Bible, p. 1850.
4. Kistemaker, *Peter and Jude,* p. 82.

Chapter 11
1. Clowney, *Message of 1 Peter,* pp. 91-2.
2. Grudem, *1 Peter,* p. 111.
3. Roy Irving (ed.) *Adult Teaching Guide,* June-August 1988, Scripture Press.

Chapter 12
1. Detzler, *Living Words in 1 Peter,* p. 45.
2. William Gurnall, *The Christian in Complete Armour,* vol. 1, Banner of Truth simplified edition. p. 117.

Chapter 13
1. Corrie ten Boom, *The Hiding Place,* Hodder and Stoughton, 1971, p. 97.

Chapter 14
1. Louis A. Barbieri, Jr, *First and Second Peter,* Everyman's Bible Commentary, Moody Press, 1957, p. 55.
2. Kistemaker, *Peter and Jude,* p. 107.
3. F. B. Meyer, *Tried by Fire,* Morgan and Scott, p. 101.

Chapter 15
1. Kistemaker, *Peter and Jude,* p. 109.
2. Clowney, *Message of 1 Peter,* p. 121.
3. Detzler, *Living Words in 1 Peter,* p. 57.

Chapter 16
1. Barbieri, *First and Second Peter,* p. 59.
2. As above.
3. Quoted in the *Adult Teaching Guide* for June-August 1988.
4. Grudem, *1 Peter,* p. 140.
5. Albert Orsborn in *CSSM Choruses,* Scripture Union. no. 301.
6. Grudem, *1 Peter,* p. 142.

Chapter 17
1. Grudem, *1 Peter,* p. 144.
2. Leighton, *First Peter,* p. 257.
3. Brown, *1 Peter,* vol. 2, p. 568.
4. William Hendriksen, *Exposition of Ephesians,* Baker Book House, 1967, p. 250.
5. Barbieri, *First and Second Peter,* p. 61.

Chapter 18
1. Detzler, *Living Words in 1 Peter,* p. 67.
2. Kistemaker, *Peter and Jude,* p. 127.
3. As above, p. 127.
4. Alan Stibbs, *1 Peter,* p. 129.
5. Detzler, *Living Words in 1 Peter,* p. 66.
6. Stibbs, *1 Peter,* p. 131.

Chapter 19
1. David Cook, *Thinking about Faith,* IVP, 1986, p. 76.
2. Quoted in Kistemaker, *Peter and Jude,* p. 135.
3. Quoted in *The Independent* on 1 July 1989.
4. Grudem, *1 Peter,* p. 153.

Chapter 20
1. This is just one interpretation of this difficult passage. Wayne Grudem has a very detailed appendix on this theme in his commentary, pages 206-239.

Chapter 21
1. David Cohen in *Christian News World* for August 1989.
2. Kistemaker, *Peter and Jude,* p. 160.
3. J. I. Packer, *Laid-Back Religion,* IVP, 1987, p. 48.
4. T. S. Eliot, *The Complete Poems and Plays of T. S. Eliot,* Faber and Faber Ltd, 1969, Chorus III from 'The Rock', p. 155.
5. *Gadsby's Hymns,* no. 1149.

Chapter 22
1. From James Montgomery's hymn 'Prayer is the soul's sincere desire', *Hymns of Faith,* no. 455 (and many other hymn books).

Chapter 23
1. Quoted by John Blanchard in *Gathered Gold,* Evangelical Press, 1984.
2. Kistemaker, *Peter and Jude,* p. 175.
3. From the hymn, 'Jesus and shall it ever be' by Joseph Grigg, *Hymns of Faith,* no. 521.

Chapter 24
1. Grudem *1 Peter,* p. 187.
2. As above, p. 186.
3. This is part of H. F. Lyte's hymn which starts, 'Praise my soul the King of heaven.'
4. Leighton, *First Peter,* p. 469.
5. Clowney, *Message of 1 Peter,* p. 204.

Chapter 25
1. Quoted in *Church News Service.*
2. Kistemaker, *Peter and Jude,* p. 197.
3. J. Calvin, *Calvin's Commentaries Ephesians – Jude,* Associated Publishers and Authors, p. 2492.

4. Barbieri, *First and Second Peter,* p. 86.
5. *CSSM Choruses,* No. 537. Used by permission of the Salvation Army Publishing and Supplies Ltd.

Chapter 26

1. Kistemaker, *Peter and Jude,* p. 201.
2. As above, p. 201.
3. As above, p. 204.

Chapter 27

1. See Lawrence J. Crabb and Dan Allender, *Encouragement, The Key to Caring,* Navpress, British edition 1986, and Derek Wood, *The Barnabas Factor,* IVP, 1988.
2. Calvin, *Ephesians — Jude,* pp. 2495-6.
3. See J. B. Philip's paraphrase of this verse.
4. Grudem, *1 Peter,* p. 202.

Chapter 28

1. Calvin, *Ephesians — Jude,* p. 2589.
2. Barbieri, *First and Second Peter,* p. 93.
3. Michael Green, *2 Peter and Jude,* Tyndale New Testament Commentaries, revised edition, 1987, IVP, pp. 13-66. See also Kistemaker, *Peter and Jude,* pp. 213-233. Also helpful is *The Illustrated Bible Dictionary,* IVP, 1980, p. 1207, which lists those commentaries favouring non-Petrine authorship and those which accept that Peter did write this letter.
4. Green, *2 Peter and Jude,* p. 67.

Chapter 29

1. Hymn No. 771 in *Gadsby's Hymns.*
2. See D. M. Lloyd-Jones, *Expository Sermons on 2 Peter,* Banner of Truth Trust, 1983, pp. 16-18.
3. Green, *2 Peter & Jude,* p. 76.
4. Warren Wiersbe, *Be Alert, (2 Peter, 2 & 3 John and Jude),* Scripture Press, 1989, p. 22.
5. *NIV Study Bible,* p. 1859.
6. See comment on that passage (p. 149).

Chapter 30

1. I am indebted to Henrietta C. Mears for this picture. She edited *Survey of the Bible,* Gospel Light Publications, 1953. See p. 416.
2. From Samuel Medley's hymn, 'Awake, my soul, in joyful lays.'

The second verse goes:

> He saw me ruined in the Fall,
> Yet loved me, notwithstanding all:
> He saved me from my lost estate:
> His loving-kindness, O how great!

Chapter 31
1. Green, *2 Peter and Jude,* p. 86.
2. T. K. Jones, 'Tracking America's Soul', in *Christianity Today,* 17 November 1989, p. 26.
3. R. B. Kuiper, *The Glorious Body of Christ,* Banner of Truth, 1967, p. 202.
4. R. C. H. Lenski, *The Interpretation of the Epistles of St Peter, St John and St Jude,* Augsburg Publishing House, 1966, p. 281.
5. Barbieri, *First and Second Peter,* p. 103.
6. Henry, *Commentary,* p. 748.
7. *NIV Study Bible,* p. 1860.

Chapter 32
1. Quoted in the December 1989/January 1990 issue of the *International Daily News Bulletin of the Hour of Revival,* from *New Life,* Australia.
2. Lloyd-Jones, *Sermons on 2 Peter,* p. 104.
3. As above, p. 114.
4. Barbieri, *First and Second Peter,* p. 105.
5. Wiersbe, *Be Alert,* p. 39.
6. Gordon H. Clark, *II Peter, A Short Commentary,* Presbyterian and Reformed Publishing Company, 1975, p. 29.

Chapter 33
1. Lloyd-Jones, *Sermons on 2 Peter,* p. 134.
2. Eric Lane in an unpublished Bible Study given at Westhoughton Evangelical Church, Lancs, during the autumn of 1989.
3. Kistemaker, pp. 282-3.

Chapter 34
1. Charles R. Swindoll, *The Pre-eminent Person of Christ, A Study of Hebrews 1-10,* Insight for Living, 1989, p. 17.
2. Green, *2 Peter and Jude,* p. 12.
3. Irving (ed.), *Adult Teaching Guide,* p. 77.
4. Clark, *II Peter,* p. 49.
5. Barbieri, *First and Second Peter,* p. 113.

6. Alexander Nisbet, *1 and 2 Peter,* Banner of Truth Trust, 1982, p. 264.
7. Quoted by John Blanchard, *Gathered Gold,* p. 133.
8. From an article written by Jim Stevens in *The Bracknell Times* dated 4 January 1990.
9. Eric Lane in an unpublished Bible study given on 3 October 1989.

Chapter 35
1. John Gill, *An Exposition of the New Testament,* vol. 2, William Hill, 1853, p. 866.
2. Clark, *II Peter,* p. 55.
3. Nisbet, *1 and 2 Peter,* p. 268.
4. Hymn No. 297 in *Hymns of Faith;* it is also found in many other hymnbooks.
5. I am greatly indebted to Eric Lane for his Bible study of 3 October 1989 which contained these thoughts.
6. Kistemaker, *Peter and Jude,* p. 312.
7. R. C. H. Lenski, *Peter, John & Jude,* p. 334.

Chapter 36
1. Wiersbe, *Be Alert,* p. 92.
2. H. L. Willmington, *Willmington's Book of Bible Lists,* Tynedale House Publishers, Inc., 1987, pp. 170-71.
3. A verse from Watts' hymn which starts, 'O God our help in ages past' (No. 41 in *Hymns of Faith.)*
4. Kistemaker, *Peter and Jude,* p. 335.

Chapter 37
1. C. S. Lewis, *The Lion the Witch and the Wardrobe,* Fontana/Lions, 1950, p. 13.
2. Lloyd-Jones, *Sermons on 2 Peter,* p. 200.
3. Kistemaker, *Peter and Jude,* p. 339.

Chapter 38
1. Eric Clarkson in a sermon preached at Great Hollands Free Church on Sunday morning, 19 November 1989.
2. An idea suggested by Barbieri, *First and Second Peter,* p. 125.
3. Irving, *Adult Teaching Guide,* p. 89.
4. Wiersbe, *Be Alert,* p. 113.